Post-Western World

How Emerging Powers Are Remaking Global Order

Oliver Stuenkel

polity

First published in 2016 by Polity Press

Polity Press
65 Bridge Street
Cambridge CB2 1UR, UK

Polity Press
350 Main Street
Malden, MA 02148, USA

ISBN-13: 978-1-5095-0456-5
ISBN-13: 978-1-5095-0457-2(pb)

A catalogue record for this book is available from the British Library.

Library of Congress Cataloging-in-Publication Data

Names: Stuenkel, Oliver, author.
Title: Post-western world : how emerging powers are remaking global order / Oliver Stuenkel.
Description: Malden, MA : Polity Press, 2016. | Includes bibliographical references and index.
Identifiers: LCCN 2016005450| ISBN 9781509504565 (hardcover : alk. paper) |

Typeset in 11 on 13 pt Sabon by Toppan Best-set Premedia Limited
Printed and bound in the UK by Clays Ltd, St. Ives PLC

For further information on Polity, visit our website: politybooks.com

Contents

Maps, graphs, and tables

Maps

Graphs

Tables

Acknowledgments

I would like to thank my undergraduate, graduate, and executive students at Fundação Getulio Vargas (FGV) in São Paulo and Rio de Janeiro, as well as the many exchange students from all over the world who greatly contributed to this book through their comments and critiques during our discussions.

Special thanks go to Amitav Acharya for his support. This book would not have come to fruition without him. In the same way, the encouragement of Louise Knight and Nekane Tanaka Galdos of Polity Press was crucial throughout the writing process.

Over the past year, I have been able to discuss the ideas here exposed in a variety of settings, and I thank Sumit Ganguly at the University of Indiana in Bloomington for inviting me for a great discussion. Raffaele Marchetti was a wonderful host during my time as a visiting professor at Libera Università Internazionale degli Studi Sociali Guido Carli (LUISS) in Rome, where I had time to write and present my research. Renato Baumann of the Institute of Applied Economic Research (IPEA) in Brasília kindly asked me to be part of the Brazilian delegation to the BRICS Academic Forum in Moscow, where I had the chance to hear useful comments, particularly from Russian policy makers and my friends at the Observer Research Foundation (ORF) in New Delhi. Paula Almeida invited me to discuss my research at FGV Law School in Rio de Janeiro. Robin Niblett invited me to the London Conference at Chatham House, offering a great opportunity to discuss my ideas with policy makers from around the world. Tom Carothers and Richard Youngs, who coordinate the Carnegie Rising Democracies Network, to which I belong, organized three terrific meetings in Bali, São Paulo, and Brussels, allowing me to discuss some of the ideas in this book with former policy makers and academics. Jean-Baptiste Jeangene Vilmer of the French Foreign Ministry invited me to participate in a great discussion at Sciences Po in Paris.

Thorsten Benner at the Global Public Policy Institute (GPPi), where I am a nonresident Fellow, provided great support, useful advice, and a leafy balcony in Berlin to work on this book. Marcos Tourinho, Alan Alexandroff, Alexandre Moreli, João Marcelo Maia, and Elena Lazaro gave very useful comments on several occasions. Matias Spektor, my colleague in São Paulo, provided guidance, moral support, and inspiration, on things both RI and non-RI throughout. Margarita Kostkova and Al Montero kindly read and commented on the manuscript. I am also grateful to the anonymous reviewers at Polity Press. I alone, however, am responsible for any shortcomings of the work.

I owe a special debt of gratitude to Joice Barbaresco, Guísela Pereira, Ana Patrícia Silva, Eun Hye Kim, Leandro Silvestrini, João Teófilo, and Allan Greicon for their research support and for keeping our São Paulo office up and running. I would also like to thank Celso Castro for his support and encouragement over the past five years.

Marita and Hélio Pedreira provided a great place to write (and rest) in Maresias, as did Marielza and Marcelo Della Costa in Nova Friburgo.

Several other people have been immensely important—mostly in dragging me away from my desk—namely Seth

Kugel, Leandro Piquet, Flavia Goulart, Andrew Downie, Hanna Meirelles, Fabio Rubio, Patrick Schlieper, my sisters, and my parents. My wife Beatriz was amazingly supportive, as always, commented on several parts of the book, and her working hours are a comforting reminder that political activism is sometimes even more demanding than academia. This book is dedicated to Anna, Jan, and Carlinha, the three newest members of our family, who will grow up in a post-Western world.

Oliver Della Costa Stuenkel, São Paulo, February 2016

Introduction

The way we understand the world today occurs within an unusual historical context. The West has held a dominant position both economically and militarily for the past century and a half.[1] More important, the main concepts developed by many leading International Relations (IR) scholars to explain global affairs—when making sense of the past, analyzing the present, or predicting the future—are profoundly Western-centric. Rather than producing value-free and universalist accounts of global affairs, the majority of international affairs analysts in the Anglosphere provide provincial analyses that celebrate and defend Western civilization as the subject of, and ideal normative referent in, world politics.[2]

To those thinkers, when it comes to the past, non-Western thought is rarely seen to have had a decisive role in the history of ideas. The so-called "global conversation" is mostly limited to US-based commentators, academics, and foreign-policy makers. Norms are understood to have generally diffused from the Western center to the periphery. Non-Western actors either adopted or resisted such new ideas, but rarely were they the agents of progress. According to this widely accepted model of "Western diffusionism," history is seen as a Western-led process, which creates little awareness of non-Western contributions to ideas on global order. The discipline of international relations has so far failed to embrace the far more nuanced perspectives that scholars of global history, anthropology, and other disciplines have been adopting for decades.[3] Most mainstream analyses of the history of international affairs begin therefore with the rise of the West, while pre-Western or non-Western history receives little if any attention.[4]

That is highly problematic, as key events in the history of global order, such as the transition from empire to multilateral order made up of nation-states, were not Western-led processes but products of intense bargaining between Western and non-Western actors. Even colonial administrators were often unable to create rules through top-down imposition, as is generally thought. The most important example is the rise of self-determination, the bedrock of today's liberal global order, which is not the product of Western thinkers but of anticolonial movements, which, long before Woodrow Wilson, acted in opposition to Western interests—notably succeeding in establishing the global norm at the height of Western dominance in the decades after World War II, when traditional historic accounts depict non-Western agency as entirely absent.[5] Throughout history, the spread of ideas was far more dynamic, pluridirectional, messy, and decentralized than we generally believe.

The United States played a key role in the construction of the post–World War II order, and Henry Kissinger is right when he argues that no other country would have had the idealism and the resources to deal with such a range of challenges or the capacity to succeed in so many of them. US-American idealism and exceptionalism were essential in the building of a new international order.[6] And yet, when explaining the rise of post–World War II order, liberal US-based international relations scholarship in particular often imagines the world to have voluntarily handed the reins of power to the United States. What is often overlooked in that context is that the distinction between legitimacy and coercion is problematic, and that the latter was an important element of consolidating liberal order—just as in any previous system.[7] This order-building involved the stationing of US troops in the defeated Axis powers; threats against and strong-arming of communists in France and Italy; overthrowing recalcitrant governments in Latin America, Africa, and Asia; and systematic efforts to impose US political and economic preferences around the world.[8]

This selective reading of history leads to an overemphasis on Western agency, ownership, and cultural attractiveness, and plays down the decisive role of military power in the creation and maintenance of today's global order. On a broader scale, favorable historical conjunctures, such as the end of the Cold War or the so-called Arab Spring, in which some believed liberal pro-Western forces dominated, are interpreted as supportive evidence for Western claims, while adverse historical conjunctures such as the recent deterioration of civil rights in China or the end of democracy in Egypt, Thailand, or Russia, instead of undermining liberal claims and principles, are simply interpreted as the result of lower levels of historical development, or temporary aberrations.[9]

Harvard University's Graham Allison calls the last one thousand years "a millennium in which Europe had been the political center of the world."[10] Such views dramatically underestimate the contributions non-Western thinkers and cultures have made, and how much the West depended on foreign knowledge, technology, ideas, and norms—such as from China and the Muslim world—to develop economically and politically.[11] They also disregard the fact that non-Western powers have dominated the world economically for much of the last thousand years. Many important events occurred outside of Europe throughout history, such as those creating and sustaining the Chinese, Ottoman, and Mongol Empires. The global evolution of rules and norms was profoundly affected by, for instance, the Mughal Emperor Akbar's promotion of religious tolerance in India in the sixteenth century, or the Haitian anticolonial rebellion in the early nineteenth century, which inspired slaves across the Americas. Those events, however, often do not fit into a Western-centric narrative of history.[12] Indeed, Western-centrism has led us to retroactively co-opt many influential ideas and norms such as democracy, human rights, and diplomacy as Western, extrapolating current Western superiority back into the past, and thus creating a simplistic teleological history, even though such ideas often emerged in many places at the same time, or built on each other, and thus have no sole origin.[13]

The same is true about the present, and most observers regard the West as essential to maintaining global stability. Western-led institutions such as the G7, the OECD, and NATO are generally seen as benign while groupings without Western participation are thought of as either ineffective (the G77), quirky and nonsensical (the BRICS),

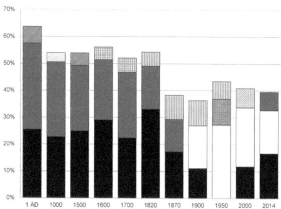

Graph 0.1 World's largest three economies, GDP at PPP as percent of world total; historical output within the boundaries of modern countries. *Sources:* Angus Maddison, World Bank

or threatening and malevolent (the Asian Infrastructure Investment Bank [AIIB] or the Shanghai Cooperation Organization).

Few analysts care to ask about the global public contributions provided by such organizations, and most generally view them with suspicion. Although rarely stated explicitly, this points to a latent sense of Western entitlement and a notion that non-Western leadership initiatives lack legitimacy. In the same way, global agenda setting—the result of initiating, legitimizing, and successfully advocating a specific policy issue in the economic or security realm—is generally seen as something that only Western actors do. Non-Western thought is rarely considered to be a source through which to construct legitimate knowledge of the modern world.[14]

Most important (and this is one of the main arguments of the book) our understanding of the creation of today's order, its contemporary form and predictions about the future, are limited because they seek to imagine a "Post-Western World" from a parochial Western-centric perspective. This view, developed by most contemporary international relations (IR) scholars, embraces a normative division between Western universalism and non-Western particularism, and Western modernity and non-Western tradition. A major Western narrative remains that there is one vanguard modernity, an idealized type of Western modernity, that will dominate the world. Non-Western actors are thought of as relatively passive rule-takers of international society—either they resist or socialize into existing order—yet they are rarely seen as legitimate or constructive rule-makers and institution-builders. It is no coincidence that many leading US-based scholars expect Western global leadership to coincide with the end of the cyclical nature of the rise and decline of great powers in global order.[15]

Non-Western agency is by and large only recognized when actors fail to live up to Western standards, or if it poses a fundamental threat to the West, such as the "yellow peril" emanating from China a century ago, anticolonial movements in Africa, terrorists coming from the Muslim world, or a perceived nuclear threat posed by Iran.[16] Recognition of non-Western ideas is also at times used to conveniently disassociate the West from concepts that from today's perspective are regarded as unsuitable or dangerous. For example, Stalinism and Maoism are often portrayed as versions of oriental despotism. Far from being anti-Western, however, communism is very much a Western idea; indeed, it is the result of a utopian experiment inspired, essentially, by the most radical ideals of the European Enlightenment, and Karl Marx's ideas were profoundly Western-centric and parochial.[17]

Toward post-Western chaos?

As a consequence, the future of global order—possibly no longer under Western rule—is generally seen as chaotic, disorienting, and dangerous. At the Chatham House's 2015 London Conference, for example, the basic assumption made explicit in the first session and the keynote conversation was that the end of unipolarity would inevitably lead to a "leaderless" and dangerous world. "Can we expect…the rise of anarchy?" a discussion point for the opening debate asked.

Such pessimism in the face of the West's relative decline is widespread. John Mearsheimer, a leading realist scholar, sees "considerable potential for war" (a prospect he describes as "depressing"),[18] and Randall Schweller sees the global system breaking down, moving from a US-led era of order to chaos. International affairs, he writes, will be defined by lack of structure, leaders, followers, and states unable to cooperate effectively. He affirms that "power is being dispersed more evenly across the globe…. This will make working together to get things done more difficult." Taking a step further, he warns that "old schools of thought will become obsolete, and time-honored solutions will no longer work.... The new norm is increasingly the lack of a norm." The only alternative to US leadership is "banality and confusion, of anomie and alienation, of instability without a stabilizer, of devolving order without an orderer."[19] He fails to explain just why cooperation in a more multipolar order is more difficult, or why global norms will disappear. Yet one thing, he asserts, seems certain: no country or grouping will be able to maintain global order like the West did. This assessment also profoundly mischaracterizes the past decades as a peaceful period; proxy wars, instability in the Middle East, and bloody conflicts in Afghanistan, Vietnam, and Korea, as well as in many African countries, are a stark reminder that millions of people around the world do not associate US-led liberal order with peace and stability. Granted, no single view is representative of the entire field, and several IR scholars, particularly realists, write about how great power concerts can produce stability.[20] Among (often highly influential) pundits and policy-minded academics, however, alarmism often prevails.

Echoing a broad consensus in the West, *The Economist* in 2014 matter-of-factly stated, "Unfortunately, *Pax Americana* is giving way to a balance of power that is seething with rivalry and insecurity."[21] While chaos and disorder are indeed possible scenarios, Western-centrism profoundly impoverishes our analysis of the dynamics that will shape global order in the coming decades. The newspaper regarded the claim to be so natural that it saw no need to explain it any further, merely reporting that recently "a Chinese fighter-jet and an American surveillance plane passed within 20 feet, just avoiding a mid-air collision." That is hardly a convincing example of post-American chaos; it merely shows the West's role as a self-interested stakeholder in today's unequal distribution of power. And indeed, at first glance, the West stands to lose the most from multipolarization. But while China is commonly compared to Wilhelmine Germany, thus automatically framing it as a threat, it may be useful to step back and ask whether we could also compare contemporary China to the United States in the late nineteenth century. Mastanduno writes of it, "a massive country that viewed itself primarily as a regional power, whose economy grew rapidly to the point of overtaking, peacefully, the previously dominant economies of the prior era, and whose security relationship with the prior dominant power was a cooperative one."[22]

Anders Fogh Rasmussen, NATO's Secretary General from 2009 to 2014, categorically affirms that "when the United States retreats, terrorists and autocrats advance."[23] Yet there is little evidence of any correlation between current instability in some parts of the world such as the Middle East and a more cautious US role. Quite to the contrary, current trouble in the region can be seen, partially, as a consequence of an overactive US policy under President George W. Bush. And still, in 2015 *The Economist* placed a disintegrating US-American flag on its cover, arguing that the country "must not abandon" the Middle East. [24] Despite a highly uneven record in stabilizing other regions, there is still a strong conviction that Western involvement is needed to prevent a complete breakdown of order elsewhere. Non-Western engagement in other regions, such as China's growing presence in Africa and Latin America, Russia's meddling in the Middle East, or Brazil's attempt to negotiate a nuclear deal with Iran, are often seen, on the other hand, by Western observers as destabilizing or strengthening autocrats. This sentiment, however, is not shared in many regions of the world. In fact, it often surprises Western analysts when they hear that many Brazilian, South African, or Indian policy makers, when asked about the greatest threat to international stability, point not to North Korea, Iran, or China but to the United States.

To adequately assess how global order will evolve, it is therefore necessary to go beyond the Western-centric worldview the dominant international relations literature brings with it and offer a more balanced account, one which considers not only US-American and European but also Chinese and other forms of exceptionalism and centrism, which do not place the same importance on Western agency in the past, present, or future. Similarly, it is necessary to import into international relations the many insights that global history, a far less parochial discipline, provides.[25]

In this book, I discuss some of the key questions regarding what multipolarization means for the future of global order, seeking to go beyond a Western-centric perspective. How can a more balanced reading of the history of global order change our discussion about its future?

What does the trend of multipolarization mean for the distribution of military power, the battle for influence, and the capacity to produce new ideas and set the global agenda? How will such changes affect international institutions? Are we headed to a world marked by frequent strife, or will the end of Western dominance, certain to generate temporary disorientation and anxiety in some parts of the world, make the world more peaceful? While it is impossible to fully address all these questions in a satisfying manner, this analysis will discuss how the Western-centrism inherent in many influential thinkers' analyses affects our understanding of these issues.

With these questions in mind, this book is organized into six chapters: chapter 1 briefly analyzes the pre-Western global order and the rise of the West and Western-centrism. Chapter 2 critically assesses the much-touted "rise of the rest" and describes its consequences in the economic and military realm, asking whether a post-unipolar order could be durable and peaceful.[26] Chapter 3 argues that rising powers will be far more capable of converting their growing hard power into actual influence, legitimacy, and soft power than is generally thought. Chapters 4 and 5 analyze the web of global and regional institutions that non-Western powers, especially China, have begun to establish to complement existing institutions and to gain more autonomy. Finally, chapter 6 will assess implications for global rules and norms.

To summarize, the book makes four key arguments, which organize the chapters:

First, our Western-centric worldview leads us to under-appreciate not only the role non-Western actors have played in the past (the history of global order is not as purely Western as we like to believe) and play in contemporary international politics, but also the constructive role they are likely to play in the future. With powers such as China providing ever more global public goods, post-Western order, marked by a "managed rivalry" and what I call "asymmetric bipolarity," will not necessarily be more violent than today's global order (chapter 1 deals with the past, chapters 2 and 6 with the future).

Second, the economic "rise of the rest," particularly China, will allow it to enhance its military capacity and eventually its international influence and soft power. I question the commonly used argument that China will never turn into a truly global power like the United States because "it has no friends,"[27] as I argue that soft power is, to a significant degree, dependent on hard power. As China and other emerging powers rise economically, they are likely to gain more friends and allies, just as the West has done in the past by offering tangible benefits (chapters 2 and 3).

Third, rather than directly confronting existing institutions, rising powers—led by China—are quietly crafting the initial building blocks of a so-called "parallel order" that will initially complement, and one day possibly challenge, today's international institutions. This order is already in the making; it includes, among others, institutions such as the BRICS-led New Development Bank and the Asian Infrastructure Investment Bank (to complement the World Bank), Universal Credit Rating Group (to complement Moody's and S&P), China Union Pay (to complement MasterCard and Visa), CIPS (to complement SWIFT), and the BRICS (to complement the G7), more than twenty initiatives described in detail in chapters 4 and 5.[28]

Fourth and finally, these structures do not emerge because China and others have fundamentally new ideas about how to address global challenges or because they seek to change global rules and norms; rather, they create them to better project their power, just as Western actors have done before them. They also arose because of the limited social mobility of today's order and because of existing institutions' incapacity to adequately integrate rising powers. As part of a hedging strategy, emerging powers will continue to invest in existing institutions, recognizing the strength in today's order. Emerging powers embrace most elements of today's "liberal hierarchical order" but they will seek to change the hierarchy in the system to obtain hegemonic privileges (such as the right to act without asking for a permission slip), so far only enjoyed by the United States. Furthermore, eluding the facile and overly simplistic extremes of either confronting or joining existing order, the creation of several China-centric institutions will allow China to embrace its own type of competitive multilateralism, picking and choosing among flexible frameworks, in accordance with its national interests (chapter 6).

Western-centrism affects the way we see the world, and how we interpret contemporary political developments. The most visible manifestation is the today globally accepted Mercator map (Map 0.1), which distorts the world in the West's favor, making regions closer to the equator look far smaller than they really are. Greenland, for example, appears to be as large as the African continent, and far greater than India or Iran. Even Scandinavia seems larger than India.

Yet while Greenland's size is 2.166 million km^2, Africa's extension is 30.22 million km^2—fourteen times larger. Even India (3.288 million km^2) is significantly larger than Greenland or Scandinavia (0.928 km^2). While no two-dimensional map can adequately project the world, the Hobo Dyer map (Map 0.2) is better at representing each

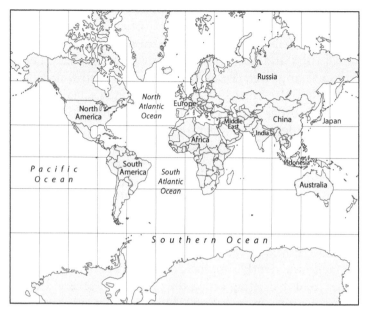

Map 0.1   Mercator map

continent's actual size, depicting Africa's vast extension compared to Europe.

Even more disconcerting for some, in countries such as Argentina or Brazil, it is not entirely uncommon to see maps most Europeans would describe as "upside down"— yet unusual as they seem, they are no less adequate or realistic than maps that place the North on top (Map 0.3).

Paradoxically, Western-centrism is not limited to Western analysts—indeed, anti-Western thinkers are equally— sometimes even more—Western-centric, and marked by broad ignorance about non-Western affairs. For example, while students in Kenya, Indonesia, and Paraguay learn about Napoleon, they are unaware of Empress Cixi, who dominated Chinese affairs for a good part of the nineteenth century, and whose actions are crucial to understanding modern China. Great non-Western leaders who did not engage much with the West, such as Kangxi, China's leader

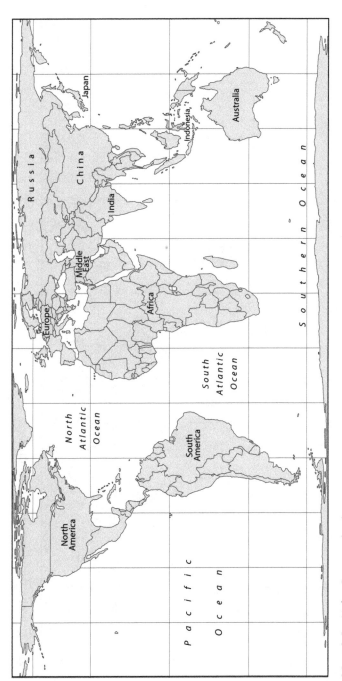

Map 0.2 Hobo Dyer projection

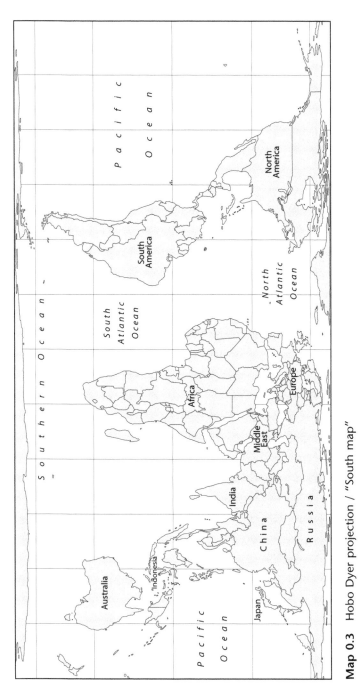

Map 0.3 Hobo Dyer projection / "South map"

during 1654–1722, or Ahuitzotl (Aztec leader from 1486 to 1502), are usually completely ignored; not only in the West, but everywhere else in the world as well. Yet their legacies and impact are crucial to understanding how non-Western powers behave today and in the future.

For instance, while most books about world history written by international relations scholars in the United States analyze the consequences in Europe of Japan's defeat of Russia in 1905, very few will include the fact that Japan's military victory—one of the first times a non-Western army had beaten a modern Western power (others include Ethiopia's victory against Italy a decade earlier)—sent shock waves through Asia and energized leading thinkers across the continent. Rabindranath Tagore, Sun Yat-sen, Mohandas Gandhi, the sixteen-year-old Jawaharlal Nehru, the young soldier Mustafa Kemal (who would later become Ataturk), and a schoolboy called Mao Zedong were all ecstatic, dreaming of Asia's rise. Newborn children were named Togo, in honor of the Japanese admiral victorious in the Battle of Tsushima. Cemil Aydin writes that "the global moment of the Russo-Japanese War influenced international history by shattering the established European discourse on racial hierarchies once and for all, thus delegitimizing the existing world order and encouraging alternative visions."[29] The Japanese example showed that non-Western peoples were able to modernize without losing their own cultural identity. It is precisely this type of information that is necessary to grasp global dynamics, understand contemporary trends, and meaningfully predict future developments.

Paradoxically, thus, a post-Western world is likely to sound odd to scholars in Asia, Africa, and Latin America, since they too have largely Western-centric perspectives (often of the anti-Western type). Both sides—those enamored with the West and the postcolonial thinkers who blame every misfortune in history on the West—suffer from a Western-centric fixation that is unhelpful for making sense of the past, present, or future. Even Russia, the West's most virulent critic, is profoundly Western-centric, as what it strives to recover from beneath the liberal distortions is little more than a mirror image of the West as it is seen through the lens of Russian common sense. The antagonization of the "false" Europe (suffering from what Russians see as "post-Christian" trends such as homosexuality or atheism) translates into a construction of a "true" Europe centered on Russia, not a genuine non-Western alternative.[30]

The dangers of Western-centrism in the contemporary debate

Why does all of this matter? Going beyond Western-centric perspectives allows us to appreciate multiple interpretations of global order as well as key issues ranging from humanitarian intervention, to the BRICS grouping, and rising powers' provision of global public goods. That matters because non-Western views about key international events are generally given little attention.

The intervention in Libya after Resolution 1973 provides a useful example. While observers in the United States described it as a "model intervention,"[31] for the BRICS countries, the West had broken the rules by transforming the responsibility to protect into a mission for regime change.[32] Brazil's and India's criticism of the way NATO conducted the intervention in Libya was met with surprise in Washington because of the deeply ingrained view that since only Western powers are willing and capable of leading "hard" interventions and show a willingness to put their soldiers in harm's way, others had only limited legitimacy to participate in the debate over such matters.[33] Yet for Brasília, Delhi, and Pretoria, the way the P3 had handled the affair—including France's decision to supply weapons to the rebels when an arms embargo was in place, and an unwillingness to share information about the bombing campaign or when it would stop—symbolized a unipolar mindset that cared little about rules and norms when real interests were at stake, underlining the non-inclusive aspect of today's global order.

In the same way, Turkey's and Brazil's initiative to negotiate a nuclear agreement with Iran was rejected by the United States partly since, in the eyes of policy makers in Washington, these two countries lacked the legitimacy to take the lead in such a sensitive matter (or the power to implement such an agreement).[34] Charles Kupchan, a scholar at the Council on Foreign Relations, writes that Brazilian President Lula's decision to meet Iran's Mahmoud Ahmadinejad serves as proof that Brazil would "not accept the Western Global Order."[35] Turkey's quarrels with Israel were supposedly evidence of Turkey's "drift away from the West" and India's voting behavior in the UN shows that "its interests and status as an emerging power are more important determinants of its foreign policy than its democratic institutions," thus implying the United States' democratic institutions were somehow more important to US policy makers than national interest. Yet the history of US foreign policy is littered with instances when strong partnerships with nondemocratic regimes were established to promote US national interest: for example, in the Middle East where Saudi Arabia remains an important US ally. This highly US-centric argument shows how difficult it will be for policy makers in Washington to adapt to a truly multipolar world in which the United States will be one among several large actors.[36] The behavior of Brazil, Turkey, and India was not antisystemic in any way, yet they were accused nonetheless because they did not behave according to US interests. Only those who regard US leadership, rather than the system's rules and functionality, as the decisive element of today's order will call emerging powers revisionist.

In the same way, the concept of the Responsibility to Protect (R2P) and the entire debate about sovereignty is structured around the notion of Western diffusionism. R2P is routinely seen as a Western concept, and Western commentators frequently point to "revisionist" and "irresponsible" non-Western powers unwilling to share the global burden and truly support R2P. Most Western observers see R2P essentially as an expression of Western enlightened liberal thought. For them, the main challenge is to convince emerging powers of the usefulness of the concept. Just as Hedley Bull and Adam Watson argue in the opening sentence of their seminal work, today's rules and norms are essentially seen as "the expansion of the international society of European states across the rest of the globe."[37]

This overlooks R2P's partly African origins and the fact that all governments, including the BRICS, committed to R2P at the UN World Summit in 2005, making it a truly global concept. While it is generally thought that non-Western emerging powers are reluctant to embrace R2P, rising powers' views on the norm in question are far more nuanced. Common accusations depicting the BRICS as irresponsible stakeholders are misguided, as emerging powers have supported R2P in the vast majority of cases.[38] In addition, as Isaac Terwase Sampson writes, "Though heralded as a new paradigm in international response to serious humanitarian catastrophes, elements of what is now known as R2P were already institutionalized in Africa, particularly within the ECOWAS region."[39] While many policy analysts around the world still confuse R2P with humanitarian intervention (R2P is far broader and also involves a state's duty to protect its own population), "ECOWAS has already developed and commenced the operationalization of its mechanisms on conflict prevention; management and resolution with an appreciable success."[40]

This mistaken dichotomy of an all-powerful West against a reactive rest is not limited to supporters of R2P. Critics of the concept are divided into two groups. The first is part of a "politically correct Western left," as Rahul Rao writes, "so ashamed of the crimes of Western imperialism that it finds itself incapable of denouncing the actions of Third

World regimes."[41] The second, often based in the Global South, regards the concept as an imperialist plot by the powerful that is meant to disguise military interventions conducted to defend economic interests. Both groups err by regarding the principle of R2P as a Western concept serving Western interests, forgetting the important contributions non-Western thinkers and leaders have made to develop it.

The argument that non-Western powers are categorically opposed to intervening in other countries' affairs to protect individual rights is not supported by historical evidence. In 1964, India was the first country to formally introduce the issue of apartheid at the UN. Brazil organized the first important UN seminar on apartheid in 1966, an event that contributed to an initiative in the General Assembly to diplomatically isolate South Africa—a highly interventionist stance of which many Western powers were critical. In the same way, India's 1971 intervention in East Pakistan—which helped stop genocide against the local population—was strongly criticized by Western powers and led to India's temporary diplomatic isolation. It was only thanks to the Soviet veto that the UN Security Council did not condemn India. The crude "West vs. rest" dichotomy and the belief that R2P is Western (implying a need to convince non-Western actors of its usefulness) is thus unhelpful from a historical, theoretical, and policy perspective.

In the same way, when speaking about the provision of global public goods in the security realm, contributions by non-Western powers are often overlooked. For example, in the last decade, China has become the largest single military contributor to United Nations peacekeeping operations of the P5. China is setting up a permanent peacekeeping force of 8,000 soldiers, pledged to donate $100 million over the next five years to the African Union for the creation of an emergency response force, and will contribute $1 billion over the next ten years for the establishment of a China–UN "peace and development fund."[42]

In 2015, about one-fifth of all UN peacekeepers came from China. India provides even more troops. In the field of antipiracy in the Indian Ocean, China is making a significant contribution with its naval forces. Unlike the United States, China has not accumulated any debt with the UN over the past years. More recently, the Chinese government has sent a battalion to South Sudan, and there is a presence of Chinese military advisers in Iraq to help stabilize the country. While there is no consensus about exact figures, China has provided significant amounts of development and humanitarian aid for decades, and it has recently launched a series of initiatives to strengthen infrastructure links in its region, such as the "One Belt One Road" strategy, which will be described in detail in chapter 5. In the same way, India is a so-called "emerging donor" with a growing number of aid projects both in their neighborhood and in Africa. Finally, for the first time, China nominated its peaking year—2030—for carbon emissions. This does not mean that China's (or India's) global engagement is flawless or even positive from an overall perspective, yet it serves as a reminder that the world's second-largest economy, along with other emerging powers, can no longer easily be categorized as a "free-rider," "shirker," or "rising spoiler," as so many Western analysts suggest to sustain the specter of post-Western chaos. It is simply no longer possible to say that China assumes no international responsibility, or that its behavior is significantly less in accordance with today's rules and norms than that of the United States.

Instead of objectively assessing emerging powers' contribution of global public goods, Western-centrism often leads analysts to focus on hopes about China's political collapse. From a Western perspective, it is difficult to understand how China's Communist Party has been able to hold on to power for so long because it contradicts the generally accepted expectation that economic growth goes hand in hand with Westernization and democratization—even though there is only very limited historical evidence for this claim.[43] Aaron Friedberg, a professor at Princeton with some policy making experience, writes that "the ultimate aim of the American strategy is to hasten a revolution, albeit a peaceful one, that will sweep away China's one-party authoritarian state and leave behind a liberal democracy in its place."[44] His assertion that when far-reaching political change comes to China "it will doubtless owe something to America's long-standing policy of engagement" vastly exaggerates US influence in Chinese domestic affairs. Believing that a democratic China would embrace US-led order, Friedberg does not recognize that even a liberal and democratic China would seek regional hegemony and work towards limiting US influence in Asia. Rather, there is a broad consensus in China that the country's fall from preeminence is a historical mistake that should be corrected.[45]

The BRICS: No motley crew

The rise of the BRICS grouping provides a final, useful case study of how Western-centrism distorts our capacity to adequately assess political developments. Initially, Western analysts routinely described the BRICS as "a disparate quartet,"[46] a "motley crew,"[47] or as an "odd grouping."[48] The idea of the BRICS as a bloc, according to this narrative, was deeply flawed; the BRICS member countries were deemed too diverse to ever act in unison.[49] As the grouping institutionalizes, some commentators now regard the BRICS grouping as a potential threat to Western dominance and merely analyze the yearly presidential summits, yet it is far more than that. In fact, the history of the BRICS grouping can be divided into three phases. In the first phase (2001–2007), "BRIC" (then still without South Africa) stood for little more than an investment category invented by Goldman Sachs. The second phase (2008–2014) saw the emergence of BRICS as a political platform, though of largely informal nature. The transition to a third phase began in 2015, marked by a process of institutionalization and the launch of the New Development Bank.

Today, the BRICS countries see the grouping as a tool to strengthen South–South relations and a way to adapt to a more multipolar order, underlined by the over twenty intra-BRICS meetings per year in areas as diverse as agriculture, health, and education. Those meetings are often the first instances in which member states engage on such a broad number of issues.[50] However, rather than neutrally analyzing the potential impact of institutions created by emerging powers—such as the BRICS-led New Development Bank (NDB) or the Asian Infrastructure Investment Bank (AIIB)—a question that is often asked first is whether they will undermine or damage existing order.[51] While Western scholars will agree that emerging powers matter individually, to most analysts in Europe or the United States the grouping (as an institutional phenomenon) is little more than an ephemeral oddity bound to disappear soon, and thus requires little attention. Western-centrism thus greatly reduces analysts' capacity to make sense of, contextualize, and predict non-Western powers' behavior or to meaningfully engage them.

The term "alternative order," often used in the context of BRICS-related analyses, has an inherently threatening connotation, yet this approach wrongly assumes non-Western initiatives to have a destabilizing effect. The BRICS countries are not frontally attacking US-American hegemony, but they contest the West's pretensions to permanent stewardship of the existing system largely because it no longer seems legitimate to emerging powers, particularly in the realm of economic governance.

While policy makers from Beijing, Delhi, and elsewhere in the Global South seek a larger role within the existing framework, they do not feel established powers are willing to provide them with adequate power and responsibility; reforms at the World Bank and the IMF have been too slow and not sufficiently far-reaching. The World Bank remains, despite its name, essentially a Western-dominated institution in the eyes of emerging powers, and there is little prospect that this will change any time soon. The institutional reform agenda of the first decade of the twenty-first century has largely failed. It is this resistance to reform of global structures that strongly contributed to the rise of the incipient parallel order described below. Just as the West has used international institutions like the World Bank and the IMF to project its power and draw countries into its sphere of influence, China and other non-Western powers will use their new institutions to cement their newly won centrality, tighten economic ties to other countries, and eventually generate stronger political influence. In addition, they will enhance non-Western powers' capacity to navigate the international system according to their own interests, picking and choosing institutions on a case-by-case basis. Rather than creating their own "distinctive set of rules, institutions, and currencies of power, rejecting key tenets of liberal internationalism and, particularly, any notion of global civil society justifying political or military intervention," as some analysts believe,[52] China and other emerging powers are likely to construct these institutions according to paradigms and interests broadly similar to those of Western powers—with the benefits and incoherences those structures entail.

Today's order: Easy to join—as a follower

All this points to a more fundamental disagreement about the nature of today's global order: for the West, a world order that is "easy to join and hard to overturn" simply does not need new structures. For Ikenberry, today's order is the "most successful order in world history ... power and rules are not enemies, they can be friends, and they are both necessary in the production of liberal order."[53] There is no question that today's global order has produced remarkable benefits for humanity. China's achievement of bringing more human beings out of poverty than at any other moment in history would not have been possible without a global context in which relatively underdeveloped states could take advantage of an open market.[54] In the same way, the post–World War II order has been remarkably successful in avoiding wars between great powers. Ikenberry calls the post–World War II order a "distinctive blend of command and reciprocity, coercion and consent" in which the United States acts as a "liberal hegemon." Rather than being a flat liberal order (akin to what President Woodrow Wilson had in mind after World War I), today's order is built around institutionalized hierarchies, but the system also has "consent-based logics" embedded in it.

And yet, the ambiguous mix of hierarchy and rules makes Ikenberry's hopes that China and other rising powers will join today's order sound somewhat disingenuous, for he does not spell out where in the pecking order China is supposed to fit in, and implies that the US would somehow retain its stewardship. It is precisely this issue that irks policy makers in Brasília, Delhi, and Beijing, when they hear Western calls for emerging powers to become "responsible stakeholders." Indeed, several emerging powers articulate their grievances concerning what they consider a hierarchical order where the strong often enjoy special rights, and where existing institutions do not offer sufficient space for newcomers—thus automatically generating contestation.

This reflects historic concerns by non-Western powers about the two faces of liberal nationalism: internationalist when turned toward the West, and imperial at the expense of the non-West, a contradiction that would still be highly influential in 1919, when Woodrow Wilson's liberal edicts did not apply to non-European peoples seeking freedom, and in 1945, when the UN's liberal rhetoric did not apply to French and British colonies. Wilson, a symbol of liberal thought in the twentieth century and today embraced as a visionary foreign-policy maker, notoriously proclaimed that he would "teach the South American republics to elect good men."[55] It is this ambiguity and moral incoherence that has been liberalism's main Achilles' heel, particularly in the Global South, where the rhetoric of liberal internationalism is still seen as a fig leaf for great powers promoting their national interest: inside Europe, civilization meant peace, outside of it, violence.[56] Not only did Wilson, who aspired to build an "open and fair" international order, reject Japan's proposal to include racial equality in the Covenant of the League of Nations, he also failed to criticize unequal treaties that gave Western powers extraterritorial privileges, for example in China. Global law and global governance often serve to institutionalize new hierarchies and gradations of sovereignty, to legitimate depredations of political autonomy and self-determination in ways that are at times reminiscent of nineteenth-century imperialism.[57]

Indeed, there is a legitimate argument that contemporary praxis of cosmopolitanism, convinced that the international space is safe and must overcome boundaries to enlighten the few remaining backward societies in the world, relies on the unequal distribution of power in the international system. Historically, enlightenment cosmopolitans often developed moral justifications for later exercises in imperialism. In the same way, liberal cosmopolitan discourse flourished in the unipolar moment afforded by the end of the Cold War.[58]

In that sense, the end of unipolarity may be seen as an existential threat to the cosmopolitan project and universalist Western rhetoric, as the West will lack the material (and possibly one day military) superiority to get away with openly seeking to remake the world in its image. Many thinkers, in the West and elsewhere, express concern about humanity's capacity to avoid war and engage in joint problem solving in such a new environment. And indeed, there are legitimate fears about what such a development will mean for the future of democracy and human rights. Autocrats across the world may be increasingly disinclined to tolerate mostly European and US-American-financed organizations openly promoting democracy abroad in the context of a global shift of power away from established powers towards emerging actors.[59]

The goal of this book is not to take sides between the West and non-West (thorny concepts to begin with, as I seek to show), or to denounce the West for past or present misdeeds or hubris. Such routes tend to draw a dangerously one-dimensional picture of the West. In addition, actors other than the West, such as China, have just as often fallen victim to hubris. [60] After all, the postmodern fascination with difference, especially in this context between the West and the non-West, can lead to an exaggerated focus on otherness which is impractical.[61] Rather, I seek to show that most observers (both Western and anti-Western) exaggerate the role the West has played in the past. I would like this book to contribute to the discussion on how to adapt to a more multipolar order in which key decisions can no longer be taken by a group of Western liberal democracies that largely think alike. This necessity, it must be noted here, does not depend on the fulfillment of forecasters' often-unrealistic expectations about China's or India's future growth trajectory. Today's post-unipolar order already obliges us to adapt our views as well as the institutions that help us deal with global challenges. In a global economy led by Asia, the conceptions of center and periphery, key to many economic and political analyses of the global order, will need to be adjusted in fundamental ways.

This book argues that, with power spread more evenly, the world faces an opportunity to strengthen cooperation and engage far more voices than ever before in human history, despite the fact that managing such a system will be far more complex. One additional advantage is often overlooked: The post-Western world will be—largely thanks to the economic catch-up in the developing world—more prosperous, with far lower levels of poverty on a global scale, than any other previous order. What is most needed is a broad debate that provides space for differing points of view, which may challenge some broadly accepted notions. At the same time, we must avoid a one-dimensional view of Western vs. non-Western contributions and understand how ideas that appear from different historical and cultural contexts can have a wider relevance.[62]

All peoples develop and sustain their own myth about the founding history of their tribe, nation, or civilization. A key element of this myth concerns why the grouping is unique and why it deserves a special place in global history. Just like any other civilization, the West has developed a strong sense of exceptionalism and a belief that it has a unique contribution to make in the world.[63] While such narratives are normal and, to some degree, even to be welcomed, believing that the end of Western dominance will inevitably lead to chaos will limit our capacity to identify and exploit future opportunities for cooperation.

Beyond alarmism

Looking into the post-Western world, Moisés Naím predicts that in the twenty-first century "power is becoming easier to disrupt and harder to consolidate," predicting a troubling trend toward a far less resilient global system with weaker national and international institutions. If "the future of power lies in disruption and interference, not management and consolidation," Naím writes, "can we expect ever to know stability again?"[64] "The world," Kupchan foresees, "is headed toward a global dissensus."[65] In the same way, Schweller seems to resign himself to throwing his hands up in despair and then turning philosophical: "Disorder is not necessarily something to fear or loathe. We may, instead, embrace the unknowable, embrace our unintelligible world, our futile struggle to come to terms with its incomprehensibility."[66] Such a statement is proof of both Western parochialism and a global order in which the West never really had to engage others on a level playing field and build a genuine dialogue. Western hegemony is so deeply rooted and ubiquitous that we think of it as somehow natural, reducing our capacity to objectively assess the consequences of its decline.[67]

Developing constructive ideas about how to strengthen future cooperation is crucial, for despite some success stories the international community has utterly failed to address a broad range of issues we can no longer afford to ignore, ranging from climate change and migration to organized crime and protection of civilians in conflict. Identifying opportunities for better cooperation will require an open mind not only with regard to differing interpretations of the present, but also of both past and future.

In a sense, fears about a post-Western order are misguided in part because the past and present systems are far less Western than is generally assumed (the world order already contains many rules and norms that emerged as a product of clashing Western and non-Western ideas). Transition to genuine multipolarity will be bewildering to many. And yet it is likely to be far more democratic than any previous order in global history, allowing greater levels of genuine dialogue, broader spread of knowledge, and more innovative and effective ways to address the many global challenges we will face in the coming decades.

– 1 –

The Birth of Western-Centrism

For most international relations scholars, it was the rise of the West that led to the creation of the first global order in history. The dominant accounts of world order in global history begin with the dawn of the modern ages, when Christopher Columbus "discovered" the Americas in 1492, a moment that marked the beginning of Western expansion across the globe; and 1648, when the Peace of Westphalia established the nation-state as the key building block of international order. Echoing a broad consensus, Hedley Bull and Adam Watson write that prior to the rise of the West, "There was no single, agreed body of rules and institutions operating across the boundaries of any two regional international systems, let alone throughout the world as a whole."[68] As Charles Kupchan writes, in the nineteenth century Europe's major powers

> exported European conceptions of sovereignty, administration, law, diplomacy and commerce. In this sense, Europe not only eclipsed and dominated the rest of the world, it also established a global order based on uniquely European values and institutions. Europeans effectively replicated at the global level the founding principles of their own regional order.[69]

In *The Rise of Christian Europe*, the historian Hugh Trevor-Roper predicts,

> The new rulers of the world, whoever they may be, will inherit a position that has been built up by Europe, and by Europe alone. It is European techniques, European examples, European ideas which have shaken the non-European world out of its past—out of barbarism in Africa, out of a far older, slower, more majestic civilisation in Asia; and the history of the world, for the last five centuries, in so far as it has significance, has been European history.[70]

For thinkers of the so-called English School, a prominent international relations theory, the "expansion of international society," refers to the process by which European rules and norms, inspired by Latin Christendom, gradually spread and included the rest of the world in one universal normative space. This matters greatly for the contemporary debate about global order because this perspective shapes contemporary thinkers, and concepts such as democracy and civil liberty are implicitly still at times believed to be somehow alien to the non-Western world. Writing about the United States' relationship to non-Western powers, G. J. Ikenberry and Daniel Deudney predict that "civilizational differences" will overshadow ties and that "human rights and political democracy are not just Western in origin but Western in character, and their realization is incompatible with the core values of non-Western civilizations"[71]—a notion also articulated by Robert Kagan, who embraced the dichotomy of Western democracy and non-Western autocracy.[72]

These typical Western-centric views unconsciously adopt a common, though highly distorted interpretation of history, based on a questionable meta-narrative: Western people were agents of progress, carriers of new and usually enlightened ideas, that helped generate progress elsewhere. Indeed, our conviction of the West's decisive role in global history is so overwhelming that, when Henry Kissinger published *Diplomacy* in 1994, he did not bother to mention in the introduction that his book was in fact about *Western* diplomacy, ignoring the rest of world and its history unless it temporarily became the object of Western interest. Kissinger's book was barely different from the many world histories written by international affairs scholars over the past decades and centuries, which assume that there was very little worth recording prior to the beginning of Europe's discoveries and the Peace of Westphalia (with the exception of ancient Greece).[73]

Seeking to explain why such a worldview is so problematic for the discussion of contemporary global order, this chapter takes up three points. First, I briefly describe the nature of global order prior to the rise of the West. This analysis demonstrates that, though usually overlooked by international affairs scholars, there was an international order in place already. Furthermore, concepts such as religious freedom, human rights, and sovereignty were already widely discussed outside of Europe.[74] Including this into a broader historical analysis is necessary to understand the West's role not as a creator of global order per se but as one arguably important actor of many. Surely, Kupchan's argument that the West's contributions were unique is true—yet in the same way, so are Chinese, Muslim, Jewish, and African contributions and none of them developed without being strongly influenced by others.

Thus, for peoples in the Middle East, Africa, and Asia, international order and globalization did not begin with the rise of the West. Rather, Western dominance is merely one chapter in a far longer historical process. While Western thinkers often call China a "rising power" or "emerging power," this description is often seen as inadequate in China, which thinks of itself as a world power with a far longer tradition than any Western actor. After all, of China's fourteen dynasties, ten had longer tenures—each—than the entire history of the United States. As a consequence, Western global rule is at times seen as a

historical aberration—symbolized, in China's interpretation of history, by the "century of humiliation" that is now
in the process of being corrected (and, critics say, utilized
by the Chinese government as a rallying cry to boost
nationalism).

A second section of this chapter will briefly analyze why
Europe, historically a weak and disunited area of little
economic importance, began to advance dramatically
around 1500, four centuries later dominating the globe
like no other civilization had ever done before. Most historians point to natural or cultural advantages Europe
benefited from at the time, facilitating the emergence of
new ideas and technologies. This analysis, however, questions mainstream accounts that assume that Europeans
have pioneered their own development independently, and
that the East has been a passive bystander. For example,
Abd al-Rahman I, the founder of the Muslim dynasty that
ruled most of the Iberian Peninsula for centuries, implemented policies that contributed to planting the seeds for
Europe's intellectual flowering in the High Middle Ages
and the Renaissance. This analysis is important to the
discussion, as it shows the inaccuracy of common notions
in the West about its supposedly pure origin. Like any
other culture, Western civilization's origins are the result
of a complex interplay of many different actors, many of
whom are non-Western. This interplay, not a clear-cut
imposition or elimination of Western ideas, will be the
dominant dynamic in the future.

Finally, this chapter will shows that although the West
saw itself beleaguered and adopted foreign norms until
recently, its role as the first globally dominant civilization
beginning in the mid-nineteenth century strengthened a
self-image as the embodiment of modernity, a tendency
that made Western countries extremely self-confident and,
at the same time, dogmatic and parochial. So resounding
seemed the West's military and economic success over the
past two centuries that European and US–American thinkers and policy makers found it difficult to distinguish

between modernization and Westernization.[75] Along the same lines, the end of the Cold War contributed to the emergence of a remarkable sense of hubris, which essentially understood all alternatives to Western modernity as dead ends. It was thought to be merely a question of time until other societies around the world would grasp that reality. Providing this background is of great importance for the contemporary debate; key elements of this intellectual approach survive today and affect the way international relations scholars think about the rise of non-Western powers. The result is an outsized sense of Western ownership of the rules and norms that make up contemporary global order. Put differently, a Western-centric version of history directs contemporary theory development in international relations.

Western-centrism assumes the West to be fundamentally different from anything else and produced the intellectual premise of dividing the world between the West and the rest (or center and periphery). That downgraded the "rest" to one grouping, whose primary characteristic is their otherness, that is, the fact that they are not Western. This leads us to neglect the differences among developing countries as well as the rich interactions that took place between regions such as Asia and Africa. The spread of ideas was far more pluridirectional and difficult to categorize than the usually used simple center-periphery axes can show. Gandhi's ideas about civil disobedience, for example, had a profound impact on the African-American civil rights movement, a historical phenomenon that today is seen as a central element of the United States' self-perception. Some of Gandhi's ideas, in turn, were partly influenced by Tolstoy's vision of an autarkic rural utopia.[76] More recently, researchers found that the design of the Statue of Liberty was influenced by Egyptian architecture, which left a strong impression on Frederic Auguste Bartholdi when he traveled to Egypt in 1855 (the Statue was originally designed to become a lighthouse for the Suez Canal).[77]

Finally, by extrapolating Western strength to the past, based on contemporary dominance, scholars and policy makers began to believe that the West's rise was a purely endogenous phenomenon, which did not depend on other civilizations' contributions. Such a radical distortion of history was necessary to develop the intellectual framework to align the many liberal ideas that emerged in Europe at the time with the most illiberal practice of all: imperialism.

Pre-Western Global Order

It is notable how little the general observer knows about the global economy or global order prior to the rise of the West, and how little scholars use events that occurred prior to 1492 or 1648 to develop theories. The notable exception is ancient Greece, stylized into a type of precursor to the West. Contrary to most scholars who believe that there was no global economic system prior to the West, the only element that kept pre-Western order from being completely globalized is that it did not include the Western Hemisphere. The European economy had no leading role in creating a global economic system, but joined a preexisting one. Europe, Abu-Lughod writes, was "an upstart peripheral to an ongoing operation."[78] Most symbolic, perhaps, was the Mongol leader Genghis Khan who, after arriving in present-day Hungary in 1225, decided not to conquer Europe, but to attack China, which he regarded as more important. The Chinese general Cheng-ho's fleet of 20,000 men traveled to the Red Sea and the East African Coast in the early fifteenth century, before European seafarers had gained the navigational know-how to travel to the Americas or into the South Atlantic.

Europeans often engaged with non-European political and economic actors long before 1492. In the early centuries AD, Roman ships frequently came to Southern India to purchase spices and silk, usually paid for in silver. At one point, a South Indian king sent an emissary to Rome to find ways to deal with the Roman Empire's balance of payment problems. Indian Ocean trade gained momentum in the third century BC, allowing for broad exchanges not only of goods but also of culture and religious ideas, which led to the spread of Indian Sanskritic religion in the region. Intercontinental trade, centered on the highly cosmopolitan Indian Ocean, was thus far more regulated and institutionalized than trade in the West—not marked by plundering but largely by supply and demand. Recently, Roman coins minted in Cologne were excavated in Thailand, underlining how widespread trade networks were at the time.[79] The broad dissemination of Islam's legal traditions also helped create a set of rules and norms to sustain a near-global economy, including the legal instruments required for mercantile credit, an important element of international order at the time.[80]

For centuries, European traders were obliged to operate within local structures of political authority in Africa and Asia and the rules and norms that undergirded them. Such was the case with the Chinese, Japanese, and Mughal Empires. As the last was established, in the mid-sixteenth century, European traders accepted subordinate positions, just like other local Indian rulers—which involved local rulers playing Europeans off against each other during negotiations for trading concessions (though the East India Company later learned to do the same). In doing so, they accepted the sovereignty and legitimacy of the Mughal rulers, representing, thus, the existence of an international system with accepted rules and norms prior to Western dominance. Britain signed treaties between 1750 and 1850 with several extra-European political entities across Asia and Africa, which suggest the existence of a fairly coherent system of mutually recognized sovereignty: that is, the existence of a global order.[81]

Even after 1492, Europeans' dealings with Asians or Africans were often dictated and negotiated on the basis of European weaknesses and limitations. Contrary to what is commonly believed, even at the height of imperialism in the mid-nineteenth century, much of the world remained outside of direct European control. Western powers rarely controlled African territories in their entirety, and often depended on negotiated local partnerships. That also means that institutions such as the slave trade were far from an autonomous European enterprise. Rather, the practice had a long tradition in Africa prior to the arrival of Europeans, and strongly depended on partnerships with local African leaders who collaborated with the West, often on equal terms. For example, in Ouidah, in modern-day Benin, the French, English, and Portuguese all built quarters, yet, as Law writes,

> There was never any question that the European establishments were in the final analysis subject to local control, rather than representing independent centres of European Power. This was explicitly addressed in the policy of the Hueda kings of forbidding fighting amongst Europeans in the kingdom, even when their nations were at war in Europe.[82]

Western-led world order, since its inception, was not always about forcible imposition of European preferences and agendas, but also about complex negotiations and compromise, affecting norms on both sides. Similar things can be said about Great Britain's colonization of India, which was much more the product of the pursuit of personal gain (on both sides) than a long-term strategy devised in London. The idea that Great Britain was morally obliged to bring Western norms to India was invented much later. In the same way, the British East India Company did not build India's administration from scratch: Rather, it was the Mughals' revenue system that gave it the financial means to build a subcontinental *raj* in the century after the Battle of Plassey (1757).[83] Even at the height of their power, European colonial powers failed to establish serious territorial dominance and did not fundamentally transform Asia.

In many ways, non-Western regions were more developed than Europe throughout the centuries. By the seventh century, Asia possessed a modern university (Nalanda, in India) with around ten thousand students, offering courses in Buddhist philosophy, language, literature, architecture, medicine, and public health, among others. After more than seven centuries of teaching, Nalanda and other institutions of higher education around Pataliputra were demolished in the 1190s by invading Turkic armies. The entire faculty and the monks were killed, and all its symbols—Buddhist statues and a nine-story library—completely destroyed. At the time, Europe had nothing comparable: Nalanda ceased to exist between the founding of Oxford in 1167 and the establishment of Cambridge in 1209.[84]

In 1650, Istanbul, at 700,000 inhabitants, was the largest city in the world, and Beijing the second largest. Muslim North Africa was also more urbanized than Europe: Paris had 125,000 inhabitants around 1500, while Cairo had almost half a million inhabitants, with Fez having already declined from 250,000. Calicut in India had half a million, and Pegu in Burma and Angkor in Cambodia were large cities.[85] It was not until 1850 that London displaced Beijing as the world's largest city.[86] In 1800, China's GDP per capita was still above that of Western Europe, and living standards and life expectancy in the Yangzi Delta were comparable to those in Great Britain.[87]

East Asia was a key center of global economic development throughout the sixteenth, seventeenth, and eighteenth centuries.[88] According to economic historian Angus Maddison, China's GDP in 1820 was $228.6 billion—almost four times greater than in 1600.[89] Historical data shows that China held the position of the world's leading economy as late as 1870.

Considering that global order prior to the nineteenth century was truly multipolar, there is little reason to believe that the West was the sole producer of ideas and norms

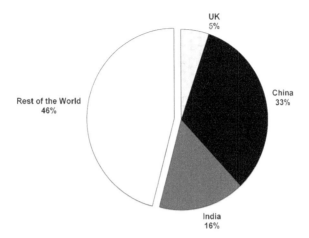

UK
5%

China
33%

Rest of the World
46%

India
16%

Graph 1.1 The world's three largest economies in 1820, in PPP. *Source:* Angus Maddison[90]

that shape our contemporary international system. Indeed, there is a lot of sound historic evidence that key elements such as a territorially established monopoly of political authority, the social regulation of warfare and modern diplomacy—that is, the establishment of permanent channels of communication between representatives of independent political communities—emerged in many places around the world, not just in Europe. As Marcos Tourinho writes, "even fairly mainstream histories of international law (which are centered in Europe and follow the overall logic of expansion) point to several earlier examples of normative constructs analogous to what would later happen in Europe."[91] This is particularly relevant when considering that the period of actual Western dominance was far shorter than generally assumed. As Frank points out, "during the period 1400–1800, sometimes regarded as one of 'European expansion' and 'primitive accumulation' leading to full capitalism, the world economy was still very predominantly under Asian influences."[92] Without previous developments in Asia, the Middle East, and North

Africa, Europe's rise would not have been possible. In the same way, China's return to the top in the twenty-first century occurs partly due to the many advances generated in the West in the past two centuries. In both cases, not endogenous, supposedly "pure" factors led to each region's rise, but sustained a complex interaction.

The Rise of the West

After its role as an economic and cultural backwater, the West rose to prominence in a remarkable way. Europe was no more advanced or more progressive than all other regions prior to the beginning of colonialism (1492), and it was thus not Europe's cultural and technological superiority that allowed it to spread its modernizing influence across the planet. If Europe was so similar to the rest, why did it pull ahead?

According to a dominant Western worldview, since specific European characteristics, such as empowering Protestantism, rationality, institutions, entrepreneurship, technology, separation of political and religious power—in short, civilizational exceptionalism—were absent elsewhere, the rest of the world was destined to remain stagnant. Eurocentrism thus ended up imputing to the East a permanent "iron law of non-development." Ideas by many key European thinkers, such as Karl Marx, followed this Western-centric logic.

The dominant view remains that Europe's development can be explained by endogenous factors alone, and that Europe rose in a vacuum. However, explanations based on long-standing primordial factors, either racial or cultural, are not satisfactory, not only theoretically but also empirically, since divergence took place very late. Furthermore, they tend to be part of a larger argument interpreting history in a teleological fashion, which implies interpreting the past from the standpoint of the present, projecting current advantage back on to the past, and often in almost spiritual or mythological terms.[93] The result is often per-plexing, as when contemporary ideas are extrapolated backwards even against historic evidence: Samuel Hun-tington, for example, argued that the rule of law has been decisive throughout Western history, even though during long periods of time, "the rule of law was observed more in the breach than in practice."[94]

There are many examples that show that Europe was less exceptional than generally assumed. For example, Ashoka's promotion of religious rights in the third century is among the earliest political defenses of religious toler-ance anywhere, and when a later Indian emperor, Akbar, was articulating similar pronouncements in Agra in the 1590s, the Inquisitions were extensive in Europe, and her-etics were being burned at the stake.[95] This does not mean that India is the "true" origin of human rights; rather, the entire debate about where such ideas come from points to a lack of understanding of how constant and pluridirec-tional interaction shaped global history, and how ideas such as human rights should not be classed only as "Western" in current debates.

Rather than a set of unique civilizational factors as highlighted in these Western-centric accounts, it seems more likely that a particular combination of factors, producing a window of opportunity, allowed Europe to succeed: slower growth in Asia, unique access to a massive amount of resources from the Americas and slaves from Africa, higher military capability due to constant rivalry in Europe and over the colonies, and a state system more capable of embracing innovation and industrialization.

A slowdown in Asia

Like Europe after the disintegration of the Roman Empire, parts of Asia entered a period of disarray around the time Europe rose. This was partly due to their internal destruc-tion, as was the case with Arab-held parts of Asia, which was laid to waste by Tamerlane, the Turko-Mongol conqueror, around 1400.[96] The economic difficulties faced by Asia—partly as a result of the closure of Chinese seaports due to the continued threat from the north—led to the breakup of a previously sophisticated system. While growth continued, the region was weakened by the time Portugal, a new player, entered the Indian Ocean soon after 1500. The Portuguese would have hardly been able to project power in the Indian Ocean had they arrived there a century or two earlier. And still, Western explorers did not encounter spaces free of rules and norms. Quite to the contrary, there is ample evidence of sophisticated trade routes on both land and sea. Western conquerors greatly benefited from local knowledge.

Another crucial explanation for a weakened Asia was an economic slowdown in China. After centuries of dynamism, the latter part of the Qing dynasty (1644–1912) was marked by stagnation. The government was facing too many internal challenges to think about imperial projects. Expansion was usually understood as a continental enterprise, not one involving fleets, which were the major carriers of new ideas. Struggling with the modernization of its economy, the empire barely grew in the nineteenth century. Particularly in the latter half of that century, this stagnation can be explained by political instability and foreign domination. In addition, China's economic heartland was beginning to suffer from overpopulation and a lack of arable land. Coal was available that, in theory, could have strengthened economic development, but its deposits were located too far away from the economic centers along the coast.

Easily accessible resources for European powers

Europe, by comparison, was luckier. Large quantities of easily accessible coal were found in Britain. This decreased the need for wood to support the Industrial Revolution there. More important still, the unique combination of cheap land and natural resources in the Western

Hemisphere and cheap labor in the form of slaves (paid for with sugar from the Americas) was crucial to boost Europe's economy. Europe's appropriation of American and African resources also helped it to catch up, allowing it to reduce Europe's trade deficit with Asia. Between 1500 and 1800, 85 percent of the world's silver production and 70 percent of the world's gold output came from the Western Hemisphere. While Western IR scholars often affirm that Great Britain embraced free trade in its empire, colonies were not modernized, but rather were kept poor in order to provide commodities to finance Europe's modernization.[97] Under two centuries of British rule, India's per-capita GDP grew by 5.5 percent—essentially a complete standstill—whereas growth set in once it became independent. To get a sense of how vast the impact of the slave trade was, it is estimated that the export of slaves, combined with Europe's occupation, reduced Africa's population by up to 50 percent.[98] Notably, neither China nor Indian states had access to anything comparable. If the Americas had been more accessible to South Indian centers than to European centers, Blaut writes, then India could have "become the home of capitalism, the site of the bourgeois revolution, and the ruler of the world."[99] In that sense, contingency was a decisive factor.

Military superiority and openness to technological change

Increasing military superiority of the European armies vis-à-vis those in Asia began at the start of the eighteenth century. Frequent warfare on the Continent and rivalry over colonies led to the need to invest in military power, so governments developed sophisticated tax systems, increased the efficiency of their bureaucracies, and developed their arsenals—and all this, of course, was made easier by the highly lucrative slave trade and the natural resources coming from the Western Hemisphere.[100] As a consequence, European armies soon were far superior to

Asian armies. As John Darwin says, "Maybe it was not Europe's modernity that triumphed, but its superior capacity for organized violence."[101]

China did occupy new territories as well, but they were located in the interior, less productive and too far away from the coastline to have a meaningful impact on economic growth. China also did not engage in a slave trade at a scale comparable to Europe. Paradoxically, the Chinese government would have had a good excuse to project its military power, since a large number of Chinese migrated to other regions. Yet largely because China saw itself as a continental power and not a maritime one, it failed to emulate Great Britain's expansion. In addition, leaders in Beijing were traditionally more concerned about internal cohesion and stability, whereas European governments were more prone to risk-taking, promoting commercial capitalism, making them, in the end, far more responsive to the opportunities technological innovation offered.[102] Europe's advantage over China and the rest of Asia was thus far more the result of a fortuitous combination of factors than the sudden manifestation of a superior civilization. With just one of the above factors missing, the West would hardly have been able to rise the way it did. Still, our understanding of history is dominated by what Hobson calls "the myth of the pristine West":

> That the Europeans had, through their own superior ingenuity, rationality and social-democratic properties, pioneered their own development in the complete absence of Eastern help, so that their triumphant breakthrough to modern capitalism was inevitable.[103]

The Eastern Sources of Western Civilization

Major developmental steps in the West thus could not have occurred without the East. The importance of Islam for Europe's socioeconomic development provides a powerful example of how much the West's rise benefited from contributions by other civilizations. Worried about how close the Arabs had come to defeating the Franks around Poitiers in 732, Edward Gibbon wrote in *The Decline and Fall of the Roman Empire* that had the Muslims won the famed battle,

> the Arabian fleet might have sailed without a naval combat into the mouth of the Thames. Perhaps the interpretation of the Koran would now be taught in the schools of Oxford, and her pulpits might demonstrate to a circumcised people the sanctity and truth of the revelation of Mahomet.[104]

However, it is unclear whether the famous 732 victory of Poitiers of the Franks (led by Duke Odo and Charles Martel, Charlemagne's grandfather) over the Arab–Berber coalition (led by Adb al-Rahman), hailed by many historians as decisive in defending the West against Islam, was really that beneficial for Europe. After all, a Muslim triumph would have spread knowledge across the continent, including astronomy, algebra (the term comes from al-Khwarizmi's book *Al-Jabr wa al-Muqabalah*), trigonometry, the decimal system (which evolved in India in the early centuries of the first millennium), Greek philosophy, and medicine. Much of what was known in the Latin West about the classical world was transmitted to Europe by Muslim scholars in Spain. Levering Lewis writes that the Franks' victory "must be seen as greatly contributing to the creation of an economically retarded, balkanized, fratricidal Europe that, in defining itself in opposition to Islam, made virtues out of religious persecution, cultural particularism, and hereditary aristocracy."[105]

Indeed, medieval Muslim culture was, in many ways, more advanced than its contemporary European counterpart, and it was partly thanks to the Arab occupation of the Iberian peninsula and continued attempts to occupy what is today France that the idea of Europe emerged in the first place. A scribe in a Latin chronicle written in 754 called the victors at Poitiers *Europenses*, the first recorded use of a Latin word for the people of Europe. Not surprisingly, it was written in al-Andalus.

The rulers of al-Andalus pursued a policy of civil pluralism that permitted a diversity of mores, beliefs, and institutions unmatched in the West since Augustan Rome. While Arabic was slowly imposed as the language of law and commerce, no pressure was exerted on the Catholic majority to convert to Islam. Perhaps most symbolic of this tolerance, at the time of the Conquest of 711 Cordoba's Visigothic church building had been divided by treaty to serve Muslims and Christians equally, allowing both groups to worship under the same roof. Jews and Christians occupied notable positions in the administration: Cordoba's ambassador to Constantinople, for example, was a Catholic bishop. Admittedly, despite the liberal elements, al-Andalus was no democracy: nonbelievers had to wear badges to identify themselves, and they were only allowed to ride horses with prior permission. In some aspects, such as women's rights, al-Andalus was less liberal than the rest of Europe, particularly after Charlemagne began prohibiting polygamy.

Still, it was the Muslim invasion of the "Great Land" beyond the Pyrenees that contributed to the establishment of a European identity. And it was not the battle of Poitiers but an internal power struggle among factions within Islam that kept Muslims from advancing beyond the Iberian Peninsula, giving Charlemagne the time he needed to consolidate his empire and thus lay the foundation for European civilization. Indeed, the Carolingian ruler could hardly have fought the Saxons (famously resistant to Christianity) and the Lombards in Italy had the expansive jihad continued.

An important aspect of al-Andalus under Adb al-Rahman was its money economy; Charlemagne's empire, by contrast, was based on barter-and-services arrangements, dramatically reducing tax revenues. Abd al-Rahman made al-Andalus the channel through which the science and philosophy of classical antiquity, preserved and augmented in the Dar al-Islam, would flow steadily into the Occidental void. Henri Pirenne stressed Europe's external dependence when he pointed out in 1935 that there could have been "no Charlemagne without Mohammed."[106]

However, just as it is wrong to see the West as the cradle of democracy and liberty, it is equally misguided to argue that their origin is non-Western. Rather, the debate around the origin of supposedly Western ideas that led to the creation of today's liberal order can be best described by Peter Katzenstein's parable of the "history of the fortune cookie," pointing to the futility of assigning specific historical origins to broad ideas such as democracy or human rights:

> In the nineteenth century, fortune cookies were a Japanese invention. Nobody then thought about marketing them: In the 1920s and 1930s, American-Chinese would go to Japanese confectionery stores in California to buy Japanese fortune cookies. Japanese cookies became fully Chinese in the 1940s, most likely because of the internment of American-Japanese after Pearl Harbor. Japanese-run shops were closed or relocated, and the little scraps of wisdom were now written in English rather than Japanese. By the 1940s, fortune cookies were common in San Francisco and modern California, enjoyed especially by G.I.s on leave who soon demanded them nationwide. By 1946, "Chinese fortune tea cakes" as they were then called, were removed from the Office of Price Administration control list. Fortune cookies found their way into American restaurants and later to restaurants in Europe and all over the world—except for China.... Full of unintended consequences and historical twists and turns, it reflects diverse practices spanning East and West.[107]

Rather than one civilization dominating another and imposing its views, it is, as Katzenstein points out, "always a give and take," even if there is an extreme power asymmetry. Muslims adopted habits of the local population from the Iberian peninsula in the same way that European imperialists adopted plenty of new cultural aspects as they dominated Asia and Africa.

When the West, in turn, became stronger and began to dominate other regions, a similar pluridirectional process took place. Western influence created strong resistance in Asia, initially thwarting industrialization by swamping markets with cheap European manufactured goods. The arrival of European medicine led to a swelling of Asian populations, which, without corresponding economic growth, led to increased poverty. At the same time, Western influence led to hybrid innovation in Asia, in ways similar to those by which Islam helped Europe modernize. Jamal al-Din al-Afghani (1838–1897), a pan-Asian intellectual, thinker, wanderer, and activist intrigued by the economic rise of the West, founded several newspapers across the Arab world and sought to modernize Islam and create a common identity so that populations in India, Egypt, and Turkey could compete with Europe. Liang Qichao (1873–1929), a Chinese thinker, struggled with absorbing some of the virtues of the West while maintaining Confucianism, which provided the political and social basis of Chinese society. Could a modern Chinese nation come into being without destroying China's proud cultural identity? Was nationalism or cosmopolitan pan-Asianism the answer? Rabindranath Tagore dealt with very similar challenges. He had doubts about whether other Asian nations should follow modernizing Japan, which was seen by many Asians as a model. "The New Japan," Tagore argued during a reception in Tokyo with the Japanese prime minister, "is only an imitation of the West." He saw many advantages in eastern civilization over a demoralized and inhumanely utilitarian West, yet in the end he was shocked by Japanese expansionist tendencies, reducing his enthusiasm for pan-Asian ideas.[108]

The Hubris of Power and the Rise of Western-Centrism

When European intellectuals first engaged with China, they did so in a context of relative economic inferiority. The majority of Enlightenment thinkers positively associated with China and its ideas, including Montaigne, Malebranche, Leibniz, Quesnay, Wolff, and Hume. Voltaire famously argued, "If as a philosopher one wishes to instruct oneself about what has taken place on the globe, one must first of all turn one's eyes towards the East, the cradle of all arts, to which the West owes everything."[109] He was not alone in his notion that China was the world's leading civilization. German intellectual elites had long before come to learn about and admire China. In the same way, they eagerly studied Indian religion, literature, and art. In 1789 Kālidāsa's Sanskrit play *The Recognition of Sakuntala* was translated into English and German. Johann Wolfgang von Goethe expressed his fascination with Indian culture—in the same way he popularized Hafiz's Persian ghazals and Chinese literature among Europe's intellectual elites.

Leibniz wrote, "In fact, everything exquisite and admirable comes from the East Indies.... Learned people have remarked that in the whole world there is no commerce comparable to that of China."[110] Artifacts brought back by officials of the East India Company were of great interest to Johann Gottfried von Herder and Friedrich Schlegel. Both dedicated time to studying Sanskrit, an empirical linguistic and religious touchstone for future romanticism in German thought.[111] Adam Smith regarded China as an exemplar of market-based development, and observed in 1776 that China was a much richer country and had a more developed economy than any part of Europe.

In the middle of the nineteenth century, however, Europe's dominance reached extraordinary levels. At the time, the inception of European industrialization and colonialism, which then profoundly altered Europe's view of its own role in global affairs, led to a considerable deterioration of Asia's and the Middle East's reputation.

While there were many Indophiles in the British imperial hierarchy in the eighteenth century, London's stance toward India became far more negative in the nineteenth century. James Mill, whose book on India shaped the British understanding of the subcontinent (though he never visited India), wrote that while Europe had previously seen India as a "people of high civilization,...they have in reality made but a few of the earliest steps in the progress to civilization."[112] T. B. Macaulay explained he had "never found [a person]...who could deny that a single shelf of a good European library was worth the whole native literature of India and Arabia."[113]

In the case of China, the point of inflection was the First Opium War from 1839 to 1842, seen in China today as the beginning of the "Century of Humiliation," which would only end when Mao Tse Tung declared the Republic after defeating Japan in World War II. By the end of the nineteenth century, China was regarded as "colonialism's last frontier," a hotly contested, economically promising yet politically chaotic actor increasingly unable to shake off foreign domination. Political intrigue in Beijing and corruption in the provinces allowed social problems to fester. The construction of the railway, modern and efficient, put millions of young men working in more traditional sectors of transport out of their jobs, leading to social unrest. A severe drought, plus rising crime and economic disruption in response to the growth of foreign spheres of influence then led to the rise of the anti-foreign, proto-nationalist movement by the Righteous Harmony Society (or Boxers) between 1899 and 1901, opposing foreign imperialism and Christianity.

Soon, Boxers were attacking foreigners and railway workers across the country, spreading fear and chaos that the Empress Cixi proved first unwilling but later unable to suppress. The murder of Baron August Freiherr von

Ketteler, a German minister, and the Empress's ultimatum for all foreign legations to leave Beijing, ultimately led to war, and China's imperial troops joined the Boxers. In an attempt to humiliate China, units of foreign armies marched through the Forbidden City. The Boxer Protocol, as the peace treaty was called, was harsh, as was to be expected. Europe's leaders ridiculed Chinese civilization, and Western forces had easily vanquished what intellectuals a century earlier still regarded as the world's most advanced civilization. The state of affairs in China would deteriorate further for another fifty years. By 1913, the Middle Kingdom's GDP stood at $241.3 billion; it fell to $239.9 billion in 1950.[114]

World domination carries considerable danger for intellectual work, particularly for historians and social scientists, dramatically increasing the risk of triumphalism. Technological advancements in Europe and the United States radically transformed their societies, making them look very different from their Asian counterparts. That increased the self-perception of being a people apart from the rest of the world; from this perspective the roots of success appeared to have dated back rather longer than they actually did. It was this aspect more than anything else that changed the nature of global order. In this context, Europe's economic and military success made intellectuals far more self-absorbed than had been the case at the beginning of the nineteenth century. Europeans expected nothing less than permanent mastery of the world. A similar phenomenon could be observed a century later: the end of the Cold War led thinkers in the United States to wonder whether the end of history had arrived—conveniently, precisely at the moment of unrivalled US hegemony.

As Goody observes,

> this idea of difference, of divergence, was produced largely by Europeans...in the eighteenth and nineteenth centuries when the economy of the Industrial Revolution in Europe gave that continent a distinct economic advantage over the

rest of the world....In other words, there was a strong element of teleology behind the European claim that its tradition distinguished itself in earlier times when its subsequent superiority was seen as having its origin.[115]

Europe's economic rise, it seems, led European thinkers to adopt an increasingly distorted view of the rest of the world. Europeans changed from regarding China as an example and model to calling the Chinese a people of eternal standstill. Indeed, the coming of the Industrial Revolution and the beginnings of European colonialism in Asia seemed to create a narrative so irresistible that most intellectuals fell for the notion that the West had found a universal truth and a moral obligation to guide the rest of the world. An exaggerated sense of uniqueness developed (even though several important intellectuals had commercial interests in the colonial enterprise).

It was this sense of superiority that led liberal and progressive thinkers such as Bentham, Mills, and Macaulay to defend the undemocratic and nonrepresentative structures Great Britain created around the world. Liberalism and empire do not contradict each other but are strongly related: in the context of the British Empire, Singh Mehta describes liberalism as doctrinaire in its certainties, universalist, aloof, unconcerned with grasping the unfamiliar, inattentive to what is, and concerned, instead, with projecting what will and should be.[116]

Following 1818, when the British suppressed the Marathas, the last serious threat they faced in India, and when the Whigs ascended in the 1830s, liberal thought assumed a paternal posture: an odd mix of maturity, familial concern, and an underlying awareness of the capacity to direct, and if need be, coerce. Liberal writers at the time frequently used the metaphor of childhood and viewed Indian religiosity in terms of superstition. India, John Stuart Mill often argued, was a "backward society" in need of tutelage. Liberal thought was fundamentally shaped by the unequal relationship between Europe and the rest of the world. It is particularly here that the contrast to traditional liberalism's benign indifference towards the private and collective identities of peoples was most striking.

In the same way, the universality of freedom associated with liberalism did not correspond to the sustained political exclusion of various groups and "types" of people. Such contradictions, of course, did not escape observers. Sir Henry Maine, for example, wrote at the time, "the paradoxical position must be accepted in the extraordinary experiment, the British Government of India, the virtually despotic government of a dependency by a free people." Liberalism thus exposed its exclusionary basis (as Locke wrote, "political inclusion is contingent upon a qualified capacity to reason")[117]: given the constitutive nature of the impulse to better the world, there was a constant tension with other liberal notions such as tolerance.

The Western-centric perspective that emerged in the nineteenth century, and that remains present to this day, is not only limited to Western thinkers but is also found in postcolonial or anti-Western writers, who tend to vastly overestimate the importance of the West in global history, and who contribute to an attitudinal climate that is fixated on the West.[118] Hobson identifies two subdivisions: one imperialist, the other anti-imperialist:

> The former I call "paternalist Eurocentrism," which awards Western societies a pioneering agency such that they can auto-generate or auto-develop into modernity while conversely, Eastern societies are granted conditional agency and are unable to auto-generate or self-develop.... By contrast, the anti-imperialist variant takes the form of anti-paternalist Eurocentrism.[119]

Anti-paternalist Western-centrism, indeed, is obsessed with the extraneous relation with the former colonial powers, which often helps those in non-Western countries who seek to demonize an idea by erroneously calling it

Western, ignoring important parts of their own history: this treatment has been leveled at concepts such as democracy, science, or human rights. This has been a powerful tool among conservative religious and political elites in developing countries, reducing the support for democracy around the world (a dynamic that Amartya Sen calls "the dialectics of the colonized mind."[120]

Karl Marx's work is perhaps the most interesting example showing that Eurocentrism was by no means limited to those who supported capitalism or imperialism. Rather, Marx believed foreign intervention in what he called backward societies such as China and India was necessary for them to change. He asserted,

> Indian society has no history at all, at least no known history. What we call its history is but the history of the successive intruders who founded their empires on the passive basis of that unresisting and unchanging society. The question, therefore, is not whether the English had a right to conquer India, but whether we are to prefer India conquered by the backward Turk, by the backward Persian, by the Russian, to India conquered by the Briton.... England has to fulfill a double mission in India: one destructive, the other one regenerating—the annihilation of old Asiatic society, and the laying of the foundations of Western society in Asia.[121]

Like Marx, Hegel called China a "rotting semicivilization," and he said India and China were damned to remain in "perpetuate and natural vegetative existence" unless the West would bring progress to them.[122] These views constituted a remarkable similarity between Marx, Lenin, Rosa Luxemburg, and liberal imperial capitalists at the time. Lenin awarded the West hyper-imperial agency, while the rest's agency is essentially eliminated altogether, and its role is reduced to passive victim. The desire for constructive dialogue between civilizations and mutual learning, so cherished by earlier thinkers, was eclipsed by hubris.

Marx may have been critical of capitalism and colonialism, but he regarded them as necessary steps to lay the foundation for a new form of society, which non-Western societies would never achieve on their own. Immanuel Wallerstein, the father of world-systems theory, despite often being seen as anti-Western, was just as Eurocentric, seeing the West's rise as an endogenous phenomenon rather than a complex process that made use of many ideas developed elsewhere. Notably, the early twentieth century saw not only the apex of Western-centrism, but also the birth of international relations as a discipline.

Western-centrism then spread around the world. Hindu nationalists who rejected Western influence and who promoted traditional values could not escape the contradiction that Hinduism as it figures in Indian politics today is a byproduct of an encounter with the West. In fact, anticolonial movements reinvented Hinduism as a religion so that it could serve as a valid defense against the West, thus unwittingly creating a simplified belief system molded on the Western concept of religion.[123]

Indeed, Western-centrism in the academy since then is by no means limited to Western thinkers. As Ayse Zarakol describes, elites in the non-West all over the world—even those critical of the West—embraced the dichotomy of backwardness and modernity: "They believed, along with their European contemporaries, that there really was a developmental lag between civilizations." Western superiority was no longer framed as mere material advantage, but as cultural, moral, and social.[124] According to Blaut, Western-centrism contributed to a very particular understanding of global history, a phenomenon he called "tunnel history":

History and historical geography as it is taught, written, and thought by Europeans today, lies, as it were, in a tunnel of time. The walls of this tunnel are, figuratively, the spatial boundaries of Greater Europe. History is a matter of looking back or down in this European tunnel of time and trying to decide what happened where, when, and why. "Why" of course calls for connections among historical events, but only among the events that lie in the European tunnel. Outside its walls everything seems to be rockbound, timeless, changeless tradition....Non-Europe (Africa, Asia east of the Bible Lands, Latin America, Oceania) receives significant notice only as the venue of European colonial activities, and most of what was said about this region was essentially the history of empire.[125]

This becomes particularly obvious when we analyze the history of Asia under European dominance. While Western-centric history emphasizes either how important Western influence was in bringing democracy to the region (paternalistic Western-centrism) or how it permanently crippled Asian societies (anti-paternalistic Western-centrism), the most important story is generally overlooked. "The real story in Asia in the long nineteenth century," Darwin writes, "was one of Asian persistence, and not of Asian defeat."[126] China is the best example: Despite a century of partial occupation, foreign meddling, decline, and chaos, the idea of China survived, and China today still has largely the same frontiers as in the 1830s, when Western powers began to attack it. The same applies to countries such as Turkey, Iran, Egypt, and Japan, which did not cease to exist in the face of Western dominance (even though some of them were highly diverse and could have, in theory, disintegrated). The reasons for such resilience remain misunderstood or unexplained in our Western-centric history.

Western-centrism is common today in Latin America, Africa, and many parts of Asia, where European history is seen as far more important than that of other parts of the Global South. It is precisely this global pattern that has led to today's remarkable situation in which countries in the Global South know virtually nothing about each other—and if they do, the knowledge they possess comes from Western sources: Brazilians and South Africans who want to learn more about China buy Kissinger's *On China*, and Africans eager to learn about India read books like Edward Luce's *In Spite of the Gods*. These books invariably contain Western-centric views that analyze the world according to US or European interests, complicating efforts by those in developing countries to articulate their own views regarding the world's most pressing questions, such as the rise of China. China's rise, for example, is often seen in the context of two competing Western narratives—that China will rise and seek to undermine and ultimately destroy Western order; or that it will socialize, democratize, and seal the "End of History," the latter implying that Western-style democracy and capitalism have successfully completed their universal diffusion. The overriding sentiment regarding the rise of China in both Europe and the US is fear, and Western analysts often warn that China's rise will "eclipse" the sun of the Western Enlightenment, which will be blotted out by China's economic dominance and a shadow that will cover the Western world. It is far from clear whether that should be other regions' initial sentiment as well, but countries such as Brazil, South Africa, and Russia have yet to develop their own narratives regarding ongoing developments, even though initiatives such as the BRICS grouping are signs that a more profound engagement is underway.

It is remarkable how broadly Western-centrism has informed mainstream thinking in international affairs. Popular books that seek to explain the rise of the West, such as Larry Diamond's *Guns, Germs, and Steel*[127] or Ian Lewis's *Why the West Rules—For Now*,[128] are strongly influenced by geographic and cultural determinism. The concept of Western-centrism itself remained limited to a relatively small group of academics. Academics who wonder why we call Europe a continent, India a subcontinent, and China a mere country, are not influential and are seen as quixotic and driven by anti-Western anger (which is no doubt true in some cases), even though these are pertinent questions.

The Origins of "Western Order"

The Western-centric distortion is perhaps most visible when looking at the rise of today's order, often called "Western order." One key example is the Second Hague Conference in 1907, where Western ideals of great-power primacy clashed with non-Western proposals for treaty-based multilateral cooperation, producing two diametrically opposed concepts about how to organize the international order. Marcos Tourinho writes concerning this conference,

> On one side, great powers sought to establish, in the classic European form, a system of differentiated prerogatives on the basis of their size and power. On the other, a group of Latin American states led by Ruy Barbosa insisted that international governance arrangements had to be necessarily founded on a regime strictly based on the sovereign equality of all states. Largely because of this dissent, the compulsory international court of justice failed to materialize—but at that point it became clear that international society was not exactly playing by European rules.[129]

In the following decades, individuals such as Lloyd George, Woodrow Wilson, and Winston Churchill, generally seen as key figures in the construction of global order after the World Wars, were in practice opponents of self-determination, either based on their convictions of white racial superiority, or pragmatic considerations that led them to maintain their imperial structures. Mark Mazower describes Churchill's reluctance to accept the legitimacy of anticolonial movements: "Churchill...urged not merely aerial bombing but the use of mustard gas against 'uncivilised tribes' in India and Mesopotamia....Meanwhile, what was euphemistically known as 'air control' remained the chief operational means of holding down large areas of the Middle East."[130]

Great Britain's decision to allow Iraq to become an independent country in 1932 was by no means based on noble principles of self-determination; rather, policy makers in London believed a weak and newly independent kingdom would be easier to control than a restive mandate. Elsewhere, colonial rule broke down because it became politically and economically unsustainable, not because of a teleological process or a predetermined benevolent scheme. Britain's retreat from India was a strategic choice, enabling focus on reestablishing its empire in Southeast Asia. For London and Paris, colonies were seen as crucial in helping finance the reconstruction of their infrastructure destroyed by World War II, after troops from those very colonies had helped them avoid defeat by the Axis Powers. Making fundamentally the same point, Shashi Tharoor challenges a Western-centric notion of history:

> It's a bit rich to oppress, enslave, kill, torture, maim people for 200 years and then celebrate the fact that they are democratic at the end of it. We were denied democracy.... We had to snatch it, seize it from [Britain]. With the greatest of reluctance it was considered, in India's case after 150 years of British rule.[131]

It was, in short, non-Western activists and policy makers from around the world, not Western thinkers, that transformed self-determination from a principle into a right. Since the anticolonial struggle preceded Wilson's ideas of self-determination, it is thus wrong to argue that non-Western thinkers activists merely appropriated an idea originally born in the West that they had not thought of before. The success of anticolonial leaders created one global normative system, overcoming the obstacles created by Western-centric international law, and reinterpreting the UN Charter, which was designed to maintain the colonial system and white rule. When the anticolonial movements used the UN as their major platform, Europe's imperial leaders criticized the institution. Charles de Gaulle called UN meetings "no more than riotous and scandalous sessions where there is no way to organise an objective debate and which are filled with invectives and insults."[132]

Non-Western powers have also influenced issues of sovereignty and equality of all nations. While the United States considered proposing weighted voting during the creation of the UN, it was due to resistance of smaller states that each state today has one vote at the UN General Assembly. Countries such as Brazil and Mexico were also crucial in promoting universal membership of the UN when the process of decolonization began, while India led the campaign to place the issue of racial discrimination and inequality on the UN's agenda.

After the creation of the UN, US-led order was not, as is often thought in the United States and Europe, a unidirectional and welcome expansion of Western ideas to the rest of the world, but a complex bargaining process. Smaller powers were often coerced to accept US political and economic leadership. In many countries around the world, democratically elected leaders were overthrown if they were thought to pose a threat to US hegemony. For example, for today's Latin American political leadership, the coup against Salvador Allende in Chile marked one of the most formative events. It was this violent element that marked the first contact of several of today's political leaders in the Global South with US-led liberal global order.[133]

Western powers thus never had a universal normative system of equal states in mind (the key element of today's order), and until the 1960s actively sought to avoid such an outcome. Kupchan and others are right to point out that anticolonial movements embraced the European-style nation-state and self-determination to rid themselves of their colonial masters. Yet agency, in this case, was not with the West, but largely with the former colonies, as mentioned above. It would be wrong, then, to claim that today's global order is a product purely of Western enlightened thought. The expansion of Western ideas was never the dominant logic—rather, it was a far less structured process of contestation, appropriation, and adaptation, which created something entirely different.[134] That suggests that the terms "Western World" (and, to some extent "Post-Western World"), are guilty of Western-centrism, even though the term "Post-Western World" may be justified to denote the end of Western dominance, that is, "Western-led order."

This shows that, even if non-Western actors were ever to concentrate power in a way the West once did, policy makers in Beijing would not be able to impose their views or project their interpretations of global rules and norms on the rest. Instead, it shows that the powerful tend to struggle enormously to have it their way. Rather than imposing or being imposed on, future global rules will continue to be the product of intensive contestation and negotiation, always building on preceding systems of rules. New orders rarely emerge from scratch or destroy existing structures completely. The old parts live on and become the materials out of which restructuring develops when formerly peripheral players become central actors in the new system. A glance at the creation of post–World War II order confirms this: rather than being a completely novel organization that broke with the past, the UN can very much be seen as an adaptation of existing structures, such as the League of Nations. In the same way, China—a country that seems set to occupy a more prominent role in a more multipolar post-Western global order—is unlikely to undo the rules, norms, and structures that exist today. Rather, it will modify them according to its interests, yet building on the past, like any great power with system-shaping capacity, such as the United States, has done before.

Conclusion

Our decision to ignore pre-Western global order generates an underlying impression that it took the West's global activism to create order on a global scale, and that the West essentially invented globalization. The realization that today's global order is not purely Western in origin helps us develop better theories of why emerging powers are unlikely to overthrow it: it is not as foreign to them as our Western-centric perspective suggests. They have a considerable stake in the rules and norms that undergird order. It is Western leadership, not the essence of our system, that rising powers will challenge once they are in a material position to do so. Only those who regard Western hegemony, rather than a functioning order, as essential, will regard future developments as a threat.

It may be common knowledge among Western historians that the East was a leading source of scientific creativity; however, Eastern entities are not seen as comparable in importance to the vanguardist West, the ultimate embodiment of modernity.[135] This notion is so sweeping in both the West and elsewhere that norm leadership by non-Western powers is still seen as unusual. Cooperation between non-Western powers is seen as either negligible or threatening, as all important relations and discussions in international affairs are expected to be mediated by the center.

Throughout history, the West was not the only center of power to interpret history selectively. China very much fell victim to the same hubris and egocentrism, and for a long time, its leaders considered themselves to be the Middle Kingdom (as its very name—中国/ Zhōngguó—implies). This is symbolized by a now famous letter written in 1793 by China's Qianlong Emperor to King George III, in which he framed relations between the Qing Dynasty and Great Britain into a sinocentric diplomatic framework.[136] In the same way, the above analysis does not mean to diminish the West's crucial role in the construction of global order. And yet, as the above analysis shows, the so-called "rise of the rest" generates a false impression of a transition of power to those who never actively participated in the creation of global rules and norms. Many

Western thinkers' theoretical considerations are based, implicitly or explicitly, on the assumption that the West has been solely responsible for the creation of today's order, and that it has a singular sense of ownership in it. This could not be further from the truth. In fact, a careful analysis reveals that even the most basic elements of today's global order—such as the nation-state—emerged not thanks to European ideas and subsequent diffusion, but *in spite* of the influence of highly hierarchical models of order developed in Europe.[137] Even anti-Western or postcolonial thinkers operate within a limited worldview that regards the West as its key dimension, and they also usually overestimate the role the West has played in the past. This broader historical view helps us realize that the current process of multipolarization is far less extraordinary, or threatening, than is generally believed.

– 2 –

Power Shifts and the Rise of the Rest

Ideas such as the "The rise of the rest," as shown in the previous chapter, are Western-centric, as they exaggerate the degree to which contemporary global order is Western in origin. In addition, as Amartya Sen observes, in dividing up the world along civilizational lines, "the divisive power of classificatory priority is implicitly used to place people firmly inside a unique set of boxes, underestimating the vast mutual influence between them."[138]

And yet, provided that its Western-centric bias is recognized as an important caveat, the usage of the phrase can be justified. After all, "Western world" may not necessarily refer to the origin of global order, but to the West's historic concentration of economic and military power after the end of the Cold War and at the turn of the twenty-first century; this may be better described as "Western-led order." The book's title refers to the coming end of this unusual concentration, and not to a world in which today's rules and norms no longer matter. In the same way, then, "rise of the rest," though crude and imprecise, may be used as shorthand for the ongoing decentralization of economic power, as long as its users make clear that this idea fails to reflect the vast diversity between regions outside of Europe and North America, wrongly suggesting the existence of a unified, cohesive "rest." "Economic multipolarization" or "economic deconcentration" may be more adequate descriptions.

How will this trend toward multipolarization and eroding unipolarity affect global order? Before answering this question, it is worth noting that there is no consensus in the academic literature about whether today's global order still constitutes unipolarity. The United States never had complete control, not even at the end of World War II, when US GDP temporarily represented almost half of the world's economy. Instances such as the US inability to prevent Soviet repression of a revolt in Hungary, the French loss of Vietnam, the revolutions in Cuba and Iran, the acquisition of nuclear weapons by Israel, Pakistan, and India, or the Suez invasion by US allies Britain, France, and Israel showcase that the US did not always get its way in the second half of the twentieth century.

Throughout the Cold War, the so-called liberal Western order did not look particularly benign or worth embracing to nonmembers of the club, such as India, China, Indonesia, Congo, Iran, and Guatemala—home to a considerable part of humanity at the time. Furthermore, as shown above, many of the rules and norms that are today often thought to be Western-inspired, such as national sovereignty and self-determination, are in fact the product of negotiations between Western and non-Western actors and are not Western impositions. In fact, the global application of international law can thus be seen not as a sign of Western strength but of its weakness, as the West was no longer able to maintain colonialism, the far more hierarchical form of order that preceded multilateralism. Western policy makers often embraced international rules and norms because exerting control through them was rightly believed to be more cost-effective than brute force, relieving Western powers of great burdens.

Despite the fact that no previous country concentrated as much military and economic power as the United States in the second half of the twentieth century, US hegemony was thus never truly global. Still, it is quite common for mainstream analysts to describe post-World War II order as the "American century."[139] In the same way, Nuno Monteiro emphasizes the unipolar nature of today's global order, and even predicts that there is no end in sight to US dominance.[140] Contradicting these common views, Simon Reich and Richard Lebow argue that the debate on what comes after US hegemony is misguided. Hegemony, they argue, ended decades ago, and today it is nothing more than a "fiction propagated to support a large defense establishment, justify American claims to world leadership, and buttress the self-esteem of voters."[141] Rejecting claims of US leadership after the end of the Cold War, the authors argue that while the United States has hard power, it is no longer capable of converting it into actual influence over others. Contradicting authors such as Ruggie and Keohane, the authors suggest that policy makers in Washington are no longer effectively managing the economic system, nor are they able to maintain and enforce global rules.

Predictions about the future thus depend on how we define unipolarity. When it comes to military power, the United States is overwhelmingly dominant, still nearly outspending the rest of the world combined, even though China has been advancing considerably over the past decade. When it comes to the distribution of economic power, today's order can no longer be described as unipolar, as the United States' share of the global economy stands at a mere 14 percent and can be expected to decline further at a relatively slow rate. In climate negotiations, the system is completely multipolar. The global financial system, however, remains relatively unipolar, with New York (and London) as the world's global financial center(s), and the US dollar the dominant global reserve currency. Some important features of current order are unipolar. Still, we are witnessing a process of multipolarization, which will be discussed below.

Building on the historical background provided in the first chapter, this section of the book will critically analyze this process, looking at the shifts of power in the economic and military realms. Will China overtake the United States? What are the dynamics that are likely to shape global order? Will it be peaceful? Will it be durable?[142]

Toward Economic Multipolarity

It is remarkable how often economic forecasters fail to get it right. History shows that straight-line extrapolations are almost always wrong. Yet specialists cannot seem to resist them, lured on by wishful thinking and a desire for certainty. When we think back to the most momentous events during the past decades, many, including Japan's attack on Pearl Harbor, decolonization in Africa, the Iranian Revolution, the collapse of the Soviet Union, or the terrorist attacks on September 11, 2001, were fairly unpredictable.[143] The following discussion is thus not supposed to predict actual events, but rather point to important issues and dynamics that may shape them.

In the past decades, we have witnessed a broad process of economic multipolarization, a multifaceted phenomenon that included higher growth rates primarily in Asia and Africa. In their book *Emerging Markets*, Ayhan Kose and Eswar Prasad show that a group of emerging economies (including China and India) have grown by about 600 percent since 1960, compared with 300 percent for the West. Over the past two decades, they write, emerging markets' share of world GDP, private consumption, investment, and trade nearly doubled.[144]

Still, the key element of ongoing multipolarization is the rise of China. Its economy has grown almost 10 percent per year on average in the thirty-five years since its transition to a market economy began. Even taking the abrupt slowdown in 2016 and beyond into consideration, China is the only country capable of seriously challenging

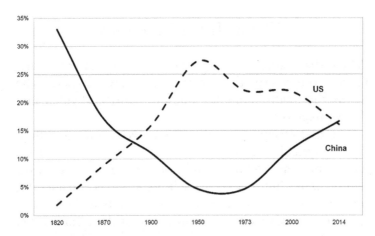

Graph 2.1 The Western blip: US and Chinese share of global GDP (PPP)

the Western-led order at this point. This is not meant to diminish the importance of other actors such as India, Brazil, Indonesia, and Russia; but they are very unlikely to have, individually, a broad systemic impact in the coming years. That is why the analysis below will focus on China alone.

Critics of this approach will argue that Gross Domestic Product (GDP) is an incomplete indicator of a nation's growth. After all, China had the largest GDP in the early nineteenth century but was certainly not at that time a global power of the same standing as the imperial powers of Western Europe. This comparison overlooks that the global economy was far less interconnected back then. Today, by comparison, being the world's largest economy inevitably generates a far more profound global power projection than at any previous point in history. GDP is by no means an ideal or complete measurement of a country's power, yet it is still the best single proxy when discussing shifts of power. I will discuss other types of power in the course of this chapter and in the next.

China: Three Scenarios

When discussing the ongoing multipolarization trend, China's future growth trajectory is decisive. Experts who assess this highly complex question can be divided into three categories.

The first grouping expects China's economic growth to recover quickly and remain above that of the rest of the world for years to come, and not only catch up with the United States but quickly leave it behind by a considerable margin. This group tends to have strong faith in the Chinese government's capacity to avoid many of the pitfalls other emerging powers have faced, such as the middle-income trap.[145] Since China has been able to defy doubters for the past three decades, their thinking goes, why should it not continue to defy them in the future? Notably, thinkers of this category do not regard China's autocratic form of governance as an obstacle to constant high-level growth. Some even consider it to be an advantage, and point to the political gridlock democratic developing countries such as India and Brazil face. As a consequence, they generally doubt those who expect that as Chinese citizens become wealthier they are more likely to ask for political power, questioning the legitimacy of the Communist Party and destabilizing the country politically. Eric Li, a Shanghai-based venture capitalist, argues that China needs a different development framework, based on a different idea of modernity. According to him, the Chinese system is meritocratic, highly adaptable despite one-party rule, oriented to the long term, pragmatic, and not individualistic. "The Chinese political system", he says, " ... comes close to the best formula for governing a large country: meritocracy at the top, democracy at the bottom, with room for experimentation in between."[146] Several analysts predict that current economic reforms undertaken by President Xi Jinping will actually improve China's outlook. For example, Yukon Huang, a China specialist at the Carnegie Endowment and a former

World Bank director for China, writes that "rigorous implementation of these reforms will alter market incentives so that annual gross domestic product growth in the coming years could rise to 8-plus percent."[147] He predicts that the government will successfully correct the policies that had driven up debt levels and strengthen drivers of productivity so that growth will be more sustainable. Crucially, they will also reduce the rural–urban divide, often seen as a potential source of political tension. Continued Chinese growth around 6 percent per year or more over the next twenty years would inevitably bring about dramatic changes in global order, increasing China's material interests around the world and allowing it to invest heavily in its military, increase foreign aid, and globalize its currency.

Arvind Subramanian, currently the Chief Economic Adviser to the Government of India, is equally optimistic, predicting that

> by 2030, relative U.S. decline will have yielded not a multipolar world but a near-unipolar one dominated by China. China will account for close to 20 percent of global GDP (measured half in dollars and half in terms of real purchasing power), compared with just under 15 percent for the United States. At that point, China's per capita GDP will be about $33,000, or about half of U.S. GDP. In other words, China will not be dirt poor, as is commonly believed. Moreover, it will generate 15 percent of world trade— twice as much as will the United States. By 2030, China will be dominant whether one thinks GDP is more important than trade or the other way around; it will be ahead on both counts.[148]

The second group is more agnostic about the long-term viability of China's political system and recognizes the need for China's government to transform the economy, which will lead to lower growth rates, but believes China is still likely to continue to grow faster than Europe and the United States. This group takes challenges like the middle-income trap, an unfavorable demography, environmental degradation, domestic political instability, corruption, and the possibility of war between China and neighboring countries seriously, but does not expect them to reduce growth to below 3 to 4 percent over the coming decade.

The third group believes that China will be unable to sustain even moderate growth. Part of this group also believes that China's political regime is already in terminal decline, and that an unpredictable political transition will negatively affect economic growth. David Shambaugh, a leading China scholar at George Washington University, for example, wrote in an op-ed in the *Wall Street Journal* in 2015, "We cannot predict when Chinese communism will collapse, but it is hard not to conclude that we are witnessing its final phase."[149]

These three groups most profoundly diverge on a series of challenges China is facing: environmental degradation, unfavorable demographics, low innovative capacity, the lack of political freedom and risk of regime change, the risk of war in the region, and, most important, its unsustainable economic model. While this list is by no means exhaustive, it provides a good general sense of the major debates. I will briefly discuss each issue here.

Environmental damage

Partly as a result of rapid and largely coal-fueled industrialization over the past three decades, China faces a public health crisis due to large-scale environmental damage. Responsible for a third of the world's carbon-dioxide emissions, China's domestic environmental conditions are appalling: a third of the country's surface and more than half of its underground water are unfit for human contact, and air pollution is thought to kill 1.6 million Chinese per year.[150] In addition to the economic cost, China's toxic environment negatively affects Chinese citizens' perceptions of their government, and the issue frequently leads to public protests. In response, the government has begun to adapt and there has been a considerable increase, in both relative and absolute terms, of energy generated from nonfossil fuels. China today produces more solar power than nuclear power. Wind, water, and solar power together already account for roughly one-third of China's total electricity-generation capacity.[151] Furthermore, China's Central Bank and the United Nations Environment Programme (UNEP) have launched a "green finance task force" to promote the issue, still incipient in China. In 2014, as part of a landmark climate agreement with the United States, China promised that emissions would peak in 2030, and it is now spending far more on renewable energy than any other country, including the United States. In 2015, it announced the creation of the biggest national market for greenhouse gas quotas in the world. Beijing is also a world leader in wind power, and is second in solar power only to Germany, a remarkable achievement considering that the country began to invest in green energy at a much later stage.[152] Despite these efforts, concerns about the environment are likely to strengthen those calling for more sustainable growth, making high growth in the future less likely.

Unfavorable demographics

China faces a massive demographic challenge: its working-age population is now shrinking, and it will take more than a decade before the easing of its one-child policy will reverse the trend—not only regarding the low number of children, but also the severe gender imbalance. China's dependency ratio (the proportion of children and retirees relative to working-age citizens) will inevitably rise, reducing economic growth, while also increasing the costs of elder care. The number of fifteen- to thirty-year-olds will fall 25 percent from 2015 to 2025.[153] That also has positive implications, as it will lower the risk of unemployment and social tensions. This is particularly relevant, as a strong increase in workers' productivity over the past decades has limited the number of new jobs. Provided that the government can raise the retirement age along with increasing life expectancy, the economic effect of overall aging can be limited. Finally, the rural workforce is still above 300 million, and large numbers could still migrate to urban areas to replace people retiring.[154] Still, there is little doubt that China's unfavorable demographics will negatively affect its growth potential in the coming two decades.

Low innovative capacity

A frequently discussed topic when discussing China's growth prospects is its innovative capacity. Beijing's authoritarian regime, some argue, makes China's economy less likely to innovate, which is crucial for an economy that is trying to focus on high-value-added industries and to compete with other industrialized economies. Lack of freedom of speech does not seem to create an environment conducive to innovation. And yet there is very little conclusive evidence that China's innovative capacity is lower than countries with a comparable GDP per capita. Indeed, Chinese innovative capacity seems to be growing in many areas, including renewable energy, consumer electronics, instant messaging, and mobile gaming, both regarding domestic players and at multinationals with significant research and product-development presences.[155] China's authoritarian regime is likely to negatively affect the country's standing in several areas—such as international higher education—but it is unlikely to significantly reduce Chinese GDP growth projections over the coming years.

The threat of regime change

Many scholars believe that as societies grow richer, they inevitably demand political rights. In the case of China, that would increase calls for regime change, political transition, and possibly a period of instability and lower economic growth. Indeed, while democracies such as Brazil,

Indonesia, and India have elections to channel public discontent, the Chinese government has fewer options, repression being the usual response. As governments are frequently voted out of office in democracies, a transition of power would most likely generate profound instability in China.

China's authoritarian system also has its fair share of admirers, however. In his book *The China Model: Political Meritocracy and the Limits of Democracy*, Daniel Bell argues that Chinese-style political meritocracy can help to remedy the key flaws of electoral democracy: "The political model in China ... is not simply democracy at the bottom and meritocracy at the top: it is also based on extensive and systematic experimentation in between the lowest and highest levels of government."[156] He argues that there is a much more sophisticated understanding of multiparty democracy in China than of Chinese-style meritocracy in the West, implying that most Western analyses projecting China's political decline are uninformed and Western-centric.[157] Francis Fukuyama says what matters most is a government's capacity to adjust to new circumstances: "All societies, authoritarian and democratic, are subject to decay over time. The real issue is their ability to adapt and eventually fix themselves."[158]

China scholars have been predicting the demise of China for years. Gordon Chang published *The Coming Collapse of China* in 2001, arguing that "the People's Republic has five years, perhaps ten, before it falls."[159] In the same year, Li Fan wrote that the question was no longer "if but when" China democratized.[160] In 2015, David Shambaugh said he believed the "endgame of Chinese communist rule has now begun,"[161] after having for years argued that China's political system was more stable than most Western observers thought.[162] Due to authoritarian regimes' lack of transparency, it is extremely difficult to predict when or whether they will collapse. Yet considering that the Communist Party has survived other profound crises, its imminent demise and ensuing economic chaos seem unlikely at this point. That does not mean that democracy in China is impossible or alien to Chinese culture: in the 1980s, China's leaders seriously discussed experimenting with democracy. If democratization were to take place, it is not assured that it would negatively affect economic growth.

Risk of war in the region

In 2014, remarks made during the World Economic Forum in Davos by Japanese Prime Minister Shinzo Abe about China and Japan being in a "similar situation" to that of Germany and Great Britain ahead of World War I (and arguing that China's growing investment in military spending led to instability in the region) led to heated debates among Asia analysts. Recent developments in the region are indeed worrisome. China has unresolved border disputes with several countries in its neighborhood, both in the South China Sea and with India. China's land reclamation projects in the South China Sea, building islands with enough space for military facilities, is likely to maintain high levels of geopolitical tension for years to come. The United States has a mutual self-defense treaty with Japan and in 2012 it confirmed that this covered the Senkaku Islands (known to the Chinese as the Diaoyu Islands). In November 2013, China set up an "air defense zone of identification" in the area and a few days later two US-American B-52 bombers flew over the islands in defiance of Beijing. If circumstances require, the Chinese government could interpret such a move as a US military aggression that could easily get out of hand. Neither Japan, the United States, nor China is prepared to look weak by backing off in the East China Sea.

Both then and now most people place a lot of confidence in the pacifying consequences of international trade. Just as in 1914, the consensus is that the global economy is so intertwined that large-scale military conflict is simply impossible. However, in *The Rhyme of*

History, MacMillan writes that "now, as then, the march of globalization has lulled us into a false sense of safety. The 100th anniversary of 1914 should make us reflect anew on our vulnerability to human error, sudden catastrophes, and sheer accident."[163] Stoking nationalist sentiments may at some point be the Chinese government's strategy to distract citizens from slowing economic growth. And yet, Chinese leaders are very much aware of the fact that provoking a military confrontation in the region would destroy the very foundations of the global order that allowed for its rise in the first place. The risk of war, which would have catastrophic consequences for China's long-term growth trajectory (and that of the rest of the world) thus remains unlikely. A more detailed discussion about whether the future of global order will be peaceful follows below.

Managing China's economic transition

As early as 2007, at the National People's Congress, Premier Wen Jiabao cautioned, "The biggest problem with China's economy is that the growth is unstable, unbalanced, uncoordinated, and unsustainable."[164] Since then, China has been undergoing a highly complex transition from an export- and investment-led economy, too dependent on investment and credit, to one fuelled by consumption. This can be done by measures such as expanding state-funded social security to reduce household savings. In addition, China's state-owned enterprises (SOEs) have easier access to credit than private companies, thus distorting the economy, leading to wasteful investments: a situation aggravated by the fact that the Chinese government insisted on maintaining growth close to 10 percent even after the Western financial crisis, rather than embracing the "new normal" earlier. Wresting control from the more than 150,000 SOEs to ensure better allocation of capital will imply upsetting many people who have greatly benefited from the policy over the past decades. While Chinese policy makers had an aura of always getting it right, the surprise devaluation of the yuan in August 2015 and temporary difficulties to manage stock market volatility suggested the transition would not be as easy as some believed. Indeed, no country has ever managed such a transition without a temporary slowdown. The Communist Party's Third Plenum in late 2013 detailed the economic transition in a 326-point road map, arguing that it would take between seven years and a decade to complete it.

In addition, Beijing faces the challenge of managing a structural shift away from manufacturing and construction activities toward services, which will bring momentous social change. Today, about 55 percent of China's population lives in cities, compared to less than 20 percent in 1978. The World Bank expects this number to surpass 65 percent in the next fifteen years.[165] The challenge is to manage these obstacles along with several others, including a modernization of the financial system and (detailed in chapter 4) an unprecedented drive of international institution-building, which involves internationalizing the Chinese currency. The key dilemma of all these reforms, necessary to modernize China's economy and embrace a global leadership role, is that they will reduce government control, leaving a growing amount of decisions to market forces.

At the same time, it must be noted that the Chinese government has an impressive war chest to steer the economy through this difficult phase. The country's foreign-exchange reserves stand at $4 trillion, which it can use to protect the economy from external turbulence. Another positive aspect is that China is still a relatively poor country, so it will take years before wages reach Western levels. Chinese exports, as a consequence, are likely to be competitive for a long time. Fears that China could turn into another Japan in the early 1990s is therefore misleading, as Japan had already reached GDP per capita levels comparable to Western countries when it stopped growing. China's GDP per capita, by contrast, is only 25 percent of Japan's in 1990, and it has years of growth ahead before it can fully catch up with the West. Rather, in terms of GDP per capita, China today may be compared with Japan in the 1950s, which marked the beginning of near double-digit Japanese growth for the next decades. Another more useful comparison may be South Korea in the mid-1970s, after which South Korea grew above 7 percent per year until the 1990s. In theory, China still possesses a significant latecomer advantage, as it can achieve technological advances via imitation and importation, having to rely less on innovation.[166]

When analyzing global order, this is perhaps the most important argument: even if Chinese policy makers fail to modernize China and bring GDP per capita to Western levels until well into the second half of the twenty-first century, China will be, in absolute terms, economically dominant nonetheless. Such a scenario requires no absolute decline in the West. Due to economic interconnectedness, China's growth trajectory is positively correlated to the West's capacity to recover economically (even though a stronger focus on domestic consumption in China will limit interdependence somewhat). This analysis is not about a contest between the West and Beijing, but rather about the inescapable logic of demography and the fact that China is bound to slowly catch up, which is why it does not include predictions of future economic growth in the West. China has been the most populous country on earth since it became a unified state two millennia ago, and it was the world's largest economy until the middle of the nineteenth century; as such there is nothing extraordinary about its return to the top. With a population more than four times as large as that of the United States, the Chinese economy will overtake the US economy, in absolute terms, as soon as China's GDP per capita exceeds 25 per cent of the US: a fairly easy thing to do. Jian Canrong of China's People University poses an interesting question:

> Britain launched the Industrial Revolution and built a global empire with a comparatively small population, and

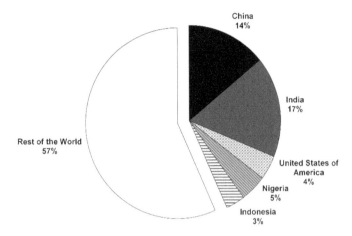

Graph 2.2   Population share in 2050. *Source:* UN[167]

the United States created the myth of the sole superpower with a population on the order of 100 million people (a century ago). What will the industrialization of China, with its 1.3 billion people, mean for the world?[168]

Simply put, the United States' economic preeminence is not its own to keep or lose, and neither should it be the US government's goal to maintain it; maintaining the extreme concentration of wealth and power that allowed the United States and Europe to be so influential (representing only a small majority of the world's population) was, from the outset, only a temporary situation, lacking the necessary equilibrium to sustain itself for much longer. From a global perspective that should be celebrated, as it is the direct consequence of lower levels of poverty around the world. One of the most enduring trends of the past decades is the growing percentage of people living in developed countries. Barring any profoundly unexpected event (such as a global pandemic), this development is set to endure. As Gideon Rachman puts it,

The rise of non-western economies is a deeply rooted historic shift that can survive any number of economic and political shocks. It would be a big mistake to confuse a temporary crisis with a change to this powerful trend. The bursting of the dotcom bubble in 2001 did not mean that the internet was massively overhyped, even though some people jumped to that conclusion at the time. In the same way, today's turmoil will not change the fact that emerging markets will grow faster than the developed world for decades to come.[169]

Considering all that, adopting the second group's position vis-à-vis China—moderate growth between 3 and 4 percent—seems like the most reasonable approach to assess the future of global order. This would be far below the 10 percent growth seen in past decades, but still enough to maintain the overall trend of multipolarization; after all, the United States' and Europe's economies are unlikely to grow at similar rates in the coming years.[170]

In 2015, the US economy was still 83 percent larger than the Chinese economy in nominal terms (China was slightly larger when using Purchasing Power Parity). If the Chinese economy grows at five percentage points higher than the US economy (with no big change in the exchange rate), China will become the world's largest economy in 2027.[171] The scenario chosen for this analysis, thus, expects the transition to occur significantly later, after 2030. This book adopts a notably cautious stance regarding the depth and speed of change, underlining that even such a modest and somewhat pessimistic growth scenario is bound to lead to profound alteration of global order. The IMF predicts that of the eight greatest contributors to global expansion until 2020, only two, the United States and South Korea, are rich countries. While China and India are expected to contribute more than 40 percent, the United States comes third with 10 percent.[172]

Naturally, it is necessary to put today's debate about multipolarization into perspective with previous discussions about US decline and the rise of emerging powers,

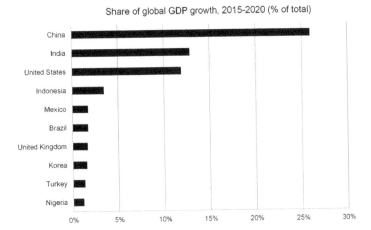

Graph 2.3 The biggest contributors to global growth. *Source:* IMF

and the slowdown of the Chinese economy in 2015 has been a helpful reminder that merely extrapolating Chinese double-digit growth to the next decades is unlikely to be realistic. Declinism has been a constant feature in the American narrative since the 1950s, when the Soviet Union launched the Sputnik. In addition, countries such as Brazil have been called "emerging" as early as the 1960s. In the latter part of the Cold War, some believed Japan could overtake the United States. As Brooks and Wohlforth write, "This will count as the fourth such crisis since 1945; the first three occurred during the 1950s (Sputnik), the 1970s (Vietnam and stagflation), and the 1980s (the Soviet threat and Japan's challenge). None of these crises, however, shifted the international system's structure: multipolarity did not return."[173]

Yet we must also recognize that today's declinist expectation is far more soundly based than its predecessors, and both China and India are more dynamic and stable than the Soviet Union ever was.[174] Thirty-five years ago, China's economy was smaller than that of the Netherlands.[175] In

2014, by contrast, the increment of growth in China's GDP was equal to the entire Dutch economy.[176] In 2013, China became the most important trading partner of the Middle East, and it is already the most important trading partner of the African continent. There is little doubt that it will soon be the key economic partner to all regions and major players in the world, giving it unprecedented influence. As Lee Kuan Yew, the first Prime Minister of Singapore, aptly remarks, "It is not possible to pretend that [China] is just another big player. This is the biggest player in the history of the world."[177] Christopher Layne makes a similar argument in his article "This time it's real: The end of unipolarity and the Pax Americana."

Implications for Global Order: Will Asymmetric Bipolarity be Durable? Will it be Peaceful?

Considering that lower Chinese growth in the coming decades (leading to a slow but continued process of multipolarization) is the most likely scenario, three questions emerge. First, what will the new order look like? Second, will it be durable? Third, will it be peaceful?

There is a relatively broad consensus that, despite economic multipolarization, the United States has the capacity to maintain its dominant position for a considerable time, even with a smaller GDP than China. As Brooke and Wohlforth rightly point out, "The United States spends more on defense than all the other major military powers combined, and most of those powers are its allies."[178] If the United States remains committed to military superiority, no country can seriously challenge it for decades to come.

Yet if China's GDP and economic influence in global affairs will be, after 2030, comparable to that of the United

States, Washington may not be able to keep its vast military advantage over other actors for a long time. Still, for many years, the United States can be expected to remain the only power in the world capable of intervening in nearly any region of the world and deny access to its neighborhood to any outside power, even though China is increasingly likely to develop the capacity to deny access to its own neighborhood.

Toward asymmetric bipolarity

In the coming decades, global order is likely to be dominated by two major powers: the United States and China (before, if current trends persist, other players such as India may transform global order into a concert of powers). John Mearsheimer, a leading realist scholar, expects a classic security competition to emerge:

> We should expect to see proxy wars, in which Chinese and American allies fight each other, backed by their respective patrons. Beijing and Washington are also likely to be on the lookout for opportunities to overthrow regimes around the world that are friendly to the other side. Most of those efforts would be covert, although some would be overt. We should also see evidence of each side's pursuing a bait-and-bleed strategy when there is an opportunity to lure the other side into a costly and foolish war.[179]

In addition, many scholars believe that as great powers rise, they try to extrapolate their domestic rules and norms to the rest of the world—like the United States has done after World War II, leading to an ideological contest between superpowers.[180] Contrary to the four decades of post–Cold War bipolarity, which saw a contest of political ideologies, the global order in the coming decades may turn out to be different. While the United States will continue to promote democracy and liberal values for strategic reasons, China will not respond with an explicit ideological counter-narrative or alternative model. This is partly because unlike the United States, China has become a world power while still facing very basic development challenges at home, with a focus primarily on lifting millions of citizens out of poverty. More important, and again in contrast to the United States, China is not interested in moral progress in international affairs or in changing the basic rules and norms according to which global order operates, nor does it believe in a universalist narrative. Rather, it will seek to turn its mercantilist trade model into a more sophisticated one and assure that other countries are willing to engage economically on China's terms. This may reduce the likelihood of classic Cold-War scenarios, involving the toppling of dictators, theories about supposed "domino effects," and bloody and frequent proxy wars as seen in places like Mozambique, Afghanistan, or in Central America.[181] As Lee Kuan Yew argues,

> Unlike U.S.–Soviet relations during the Cold War, there is no irreconcilable ideological conflict between the United States and a China that has enthusiastically embraced the market. Sino-American relations are both cooperative and competitive. Competition between them is inevitable, but conflict is not.[182]

This will be particularly true as long as China's Communist Party is in power, since it may be best equipped to contain nationalist tendencies, the main ideology that could increase the risk of conflict in the coming years. Second, unlike in the Cold War, when the United States and Soviet Union competed both economically and militarily, the new order may be called "asymmetric bipolarity": the United States is likely to maintain its military dominance, while China's economy may exceed that of the United States, provided that it can successfully avoid the pitfalls presented above. This will create an unusual constellation in the distribution of power. China will not, for now, seek to confront or overtake the United States militarily (it will be inferior for years to come), while the United States will have accepted that it cannot challenge China's economic might. China is thus unlikely to seek open confrontation. Instead, China may rather make it increasingly difficult (by small increments) for the United States to maintain influence in China's neighborhood. What does asymmetric bipolarity mean for the durability and peacefulness of post-Western order?

Will it be durable?

The durability of the bipolar order described above largely depends on two variables: the United States' and China's military power. Will China allow the United States to maintain its military dominance (a scenario that would suggest systemic durability), or will China seek to convert its economic power into military power and challenge the United States' supremacy in the military realm? Conversely, will the United States be capable of maintaining its global lead in the military realm?

Most believe that military power inevitably derives from economic power, so China's economic rise is a mere precursor to its military dominance and hegemony. Nuno Monteiro, on the other hand, has argued that military power is not a side product of economic development but the result of a state's decision to invest a fraction of its wealth into the production of military capacities.[183] China, then, could very well become the largest economy on earth without seeking global military dominance. He says we should therefore refocus our analysis from the determinants of economic growth to those of militarization. Monteiro's argument certainly serves as an important reminder that we need to be careful not to blindly assume that the greater a country's economy, the more it will invest in its military power. For example, France and the United Kingdom, despite their smaller economies, are militarily more powerful than Germany, and policy makers in Berlin do not show any signs of seeking to catch up militarily.

Such cases are particularly likely in highly institutionalized contexts. Germany enjoys ample security guarantees by the United States and thus has few incentives to invest more in its military power.

Yet while smaller powers, or those firmly embedded in institutional security arrangements, may make decisions about military spending independently of economic growth, for great powers with hegemonic potential it seems less likely that investment in military power is independent of economic power. That is largely because economic growth and greater global engagement inevitably expands a great power's spheres of interest. A hypothetical great power that does not trade with the rest of the world and faces no threat in the neighborhood could, in theory, maintain low military spending even though its economy grows at high rates. Yet such powers do not exist in today's highly connected global economy, and strong growth will lead to growing strategic interests and economic involvement in regions that previously mattered little. China's recent decisions to deploy a battalion to South Sudan (where it has significant economic interests) and send military advisors to the Iraqi government show that policy makers consider enhancing military capacity a necessary strategy to protect economic interests, and not a result of a cultural predisposition to dominate the world. If, for example in 2030, a civil war in Nicaragua threatened the operations of the Chinese-financed Nicaragua Canal, there is no reason to believe that China would behave differently from any previous great powers that see their strategic interests at risk. China would deploy troops to impose stability, in a classic example of how the strategic interests of rising states proliferate around the world, forcing them to increase their military power. In addition, China enjoys no security guarantees comparable to those of Germany, and security relations in Asia are not as institutionalized as they are for NATO members, increasing Beijing's incentive to invest in its military capacity.

In addition, those who argue that China may not necessarily seek to catch up with the United States militarily often do not take into consideration how humiliating Western-led order looks from the perspective of Chinese nationalists. A rising and perhaps more nationalistic China is unlikely to accept US military dominance in the long term, especially once its economy is significantly larger than that of the United States. What will policy makers in China respond to nationalistic agitators who point out that US-American destroyers routinely cruise closely along the Chinese coast, suffocating even the slightest Chinese effort to exert strategic influence in its immediate neighborhood? China's current activities in the South China Sea already indicate that China is unlikely to accept being an economic superpower for long without considerable military heft. After all, no aspiring great power gains status or self-respect by ceding responsibility for security in its backyard to a foreign power from far away.[184] China is therefore likely to slowly build up a blue-water navy, something that should not necessarily be seen as a destabilizing factor. In 2014, China increased defense spending to $130 billion, the highest figure in recent years despite an economic slowdown.[185]

A related question is whether the rest of the world will accept the United States as the legitimate provider of security once China increasingly dominates the world economically and wields growing influence in the domestic political affairs of other countries. In the case of Taiwan in particular, it must be pointed out that China is just 130 kilometers away from the island; contrast this with the distance to the nearest point in the United States, Hawaii, which is almost 9,000 kilometers away. This makes it much harder for the US Navy to maintain its superiority.

The presence of nuclear weapons is also often thought to reduce the possibility of China seeking to catch up with the United States in the realm of conventional military power. As Nuno Monteiro writes,

For world politics, the implications of the nuclear revolution are momentous: systemic change is now even harder than in the past. Put simply, with great-power peace may come the perpetuation of the US-led liberal hegemonic order. Seen in this light, the longevity of the *Pax Americana* would have little to do with any "normative packages" or the palatability of the way Washington runs the international system. Instead, it would be the consequence of a lack of mechanisms for change short of risking a conflict that would be in no challenger's interest because it would threaten its own survival.[186]

There is no question that the existence of nuclear weapons affects the logic of change and order. It would be premature to argue, however, that this makes great power transition less likely, thus assuring that US hegemony is here to stay. After all, one could think of many possible scenarios in which China would gain more power and profoundly change global order without any large confrontation between Beijing and Washington. While this scenario is unlikely at this point, China could succeed in convincing its neighbors to bandwagon and accept Chinese security guarantees. Under such circumstances, even the announcement of a Chinese Monroe Doctrine would not necessarily lead to a conflict. While unlikely in the coming decades, the AIIB could substitute for the World Bank as the world's leading lender—not by force, but by having member countries vote with their feet and simply prefer to borrow from and lend to the new institution. China could, in theory, start providing security guarantees to countries around the world, without ever raising the specter of hegemonic war. It is only rarely considered that China would embrace and dominate global structures from within, and eventually assume leadership without resorting to violence.

Even under conditions of continued US military leadership, China's political influence is likely to increase markedly. In Latin America, for example, Chinese credit already exceeds that of the World Bank and the Interamerican

Development Bank combined.[187] In principle, this puts China in a good position to strengthen its projection even in the Western Hemisphere.

Monteiro argues that the key question is whether the economic benefits of power preponderance exceed the cost generated by military conflict the United States has to engage in to maintain its dominant position. According to Monteiro, as long as the US pursues a strategy of defensive accommodation (maintaining its dominant position but allowing rising powers to grow economically), the advantages of US military power preponderance far outweigh the conflict costs—pointing out that defense spending over the past two decades never exceeded 5 per cent of GDP (no more than during bipolarity). Therefore, he expects the current US preponderance in conventional military power to remain largely unchanged for "as far as the eye can see" even if the United States loses its status as the world's largest economy.

Yet once the United States' GDP and economic influence in global affairs is similar to that of China, how will policy makers in Washington convince voters worried about health care, education, and infrastructure to support maintaining more than 1,000 military facilities in more than 140 countries, in which more than 200,000 military personnel are stationed? What will they respond to those who argue for systematic retrenchment (as already happens now), or those who say that China should finally "step up to the plate" and start providing international security? We may witness a growing number of "happy declinists" such as Charles Kenny, who argue that the lives of US citizens would not necessarily be negatively affected if the United States were merely one of several poles in a multipolar system. As he writes, "The link between the absolute size of your economy and pretty much any measure that truly matters is incredibly weak. Whenever China takes over the top spot, it will still lag far behind the world's leading countries on indicators reflecting quality of life."[188]

There is an aggravating factor that will dramatically increase pressure on US policy makers to bring the troops home permanently: Monteiro predicts that the significant level of conflict and US military action the world has witnessed over the last two-and-a-half decades will continue for as long as US power remains preponderant. There is little the United States can do to avoid this: any military strategy by the unipole—engagement or disengagement—will set in motion specific paths leading to confrontation and, quite frequently, war. Unipolarity, the author writes, "is a damned-if-you-do, damned-if-you-don't situation, in which conflict is hardly avoidable."[189] Technological advances (drones, etc.) may reduce the political cost of US warfare—and indeed, many US-Americans are not even aware of the fact that the US military is at war in places such as Pakistan and Yemen. Yet there are few signs that technology will do away with the messy, expensive, and bloody conflicts in which the United States engaged in Iraq and Afghanistan during the past decade.[190] Frequent wars, even undeclared ones, are certain to generate considerable costs and will thus be vulnerable to budget hawks, particularly during economic difficulties.

I therefore do not believe that there is any systemic logic about why US military dominance will endure. Particularly when analyzing great powers or those with ambitions to become one, military power often grows as a function of economic growth. Provided that China continues to grow annually between 3 and 4 percent or more in the coming years, we will witness a continued rise in the country's military power. The asymmetric bipolarity described above is thus not inherently durable and may not last much longer than US-led unipolarity, as the coming decades may be dominated by an ongoing process of renegotiation between the two great powers.

At the same time, it is worth remembering that the United States became the world's largest economy around the turn of the twentieth century, but it took several decades before it became the world's only uncontested

military power. I therefore agree that US military supremacy (and asymmetric bipolarity) may exist for several
decades. Still, the situation will not be systemically stable;
it will be marked by a constant renegotiation of terms on
which China and other emerging powers engage in the
existing order. The speed of this renegotiation will depend
on how quickly China's military power will grow as compared to that of the United States.

Will it be peaceful?

The general consensus is that the rise of non-Western
powers, led by China, will cause growing instability. Liberal
internationalists often implicitly or explicitly equate
Western-led liberal order to peace, so the erosion of the
Western-centric concentration of power carries many risks.
Mearsheimer, a realist, argues that the bipolarity of the
Cold War was a more peaceful architecture of power than
the unbalanced multipolarity of the twenty-first century.[191]
To some extent, US thinkers are emulating their British
counterparts a century earlier. As policy makers in London
realized that the days of the British Empire were numbered,
the diplomat Lord Salisbury famously argued, "Whatever
happens will be for the worse.... Therefore it is our interest
that as little should happen as possible."[192] Indeed, with
very few exceptions, the vast majority of leading opinion-
makers does not believe that a more bipolar or multipolar
twenty-first century will be as peaceful, or even more peaceful than unipolarity.[193]

There is no certainty, however, that this order will be
more violent than Cold War bipolarity or post–Cold War
unipolarity, which was marked by military struggles in the
so-called periphery—examples include Inchon, the Mekong
River delta, Luanda, Iraq, Iran, and Afghanistan. Although
the arrival of unipolarity eliminated the prospect of great-
power competition, the structure of a unipolar world does
not have a clear beneficial impact on the overall prospects
for peace. That is because unipolarity allows for frequent

conflicts between the hegemon and obstinate minor powers and conflict between small powers, which are more difficult to keep in line by great-power allies.[194] Unipolarity poses no structural limitations on the hegemon, which leaves the door open to adventurism and hubris, as seen in 2003, when the United States invaded Iraq. Hence, unipolarity is prone to witness asymmetric and peripheral conflicts such as US wars against Iraq, but also smaller wars such as the one between Peru and Ecuador in 1995 or between Russia and Georgia in 2008. Finally, there is no clear evidence that unipolarity has any impact on the frequency and intensity of intra-state war.

These findings have important consequences for both academics and policy makers. Since unipolarity is not any more benign to an international system than bipolarity or multipolarity, it is far from certain whether the maintenance of today's unipolar order should be a goal of US foreign policy. Put differently, it is simply not clear whether unipolarity in a nuclear age is better—for either the United States or the world. Even from a purely US-centric perspective, the return of bipolarity may not be bad news. After all, it is far from obvious whether US unipolarity has helped Washington project its influence better than prior to the collapse of the Soviet Union. A bipolar order is possibly better at keeping trouble-making small powers such as North Korea in check. At the same time, due to the absence of an ideological component in US–Chinese bipolar order, the number of proxy wars is likely to be far lower than during the Cold War. Due to the nuclear revolution, the chances of a great-power confrontation are negligible. Finally, a bi- or multipolar order may actually improve the United States' reputation around the world, as is already the case in Latin America, where anti-Americanism is increasingly tempered by the fear of a rising China.

In the same way, the often-used argument about the need for a hegemon to sustain international order is contested. Reich and Lebow argue that a hegemon is unnecessary for international stability. They go so far as to say that, in an increasingly multipowered world, the idea of a hegemon is "inappropriate."[195] Acharya writes that global order will be more decentered than before, providing regional powers with greater scope for local and regional approaches. That sounds like bad news to many US policy analysts, but the author rejects predictions that multipolarity will be messy and unstable. Quite to the contrary, he says, a multiple-power system could lead to greater international cooperation. Given the many diverse perspectives that need to be taken into account when making decisions of global importance—for instance, regarding climate change—a bipolar or multipolar order may be far more adequate than a Western-centric order.

Acharya argues that "no major Western analyst ... accepts that the US decline might be good for international order either in general or in specific areas such as development, governance, and international justice."[196] At the same time, the analysis above shows that the predictions that multipolarity will lead to instability cannot be backed up by solid historic or theoretical evidence. From a US perspective, investing a lot of time and energy in the maintenance of Western-led order thus risks being interpreted by other powers as being self-interested, not a product of a larger concern for global stability. As van der Putten argues, "it is not in Europe's interests to support the perpetuation of US global leadership at all costs, if this involves the danger of long-term global instability [and] the paralysis of global governance."[197]

A key example of such a short-sighted policy was the United States' attempts to thwart the creation of the Chinese-led Asian Infrastructure Investment Bank (AIIB) in 2015, which was, in the eyes of developing countries, little more than an attempt to perpetuate the control of the world's key development banks without much concern for the provision of global goods. Acharya also calls for a fresh look at regionalism in the post-unipolar order, pointing out that most powers will be unable to project meaningful influence beyond their respective regions, and that regional organizations such as ECOWAS and ASEAN have become more sophisticated multipurpose organizations. NEPAD, the AU, ECOWAS, and UNASUR have begun to establish peer-review mechanisms that may have led to the punishment, suspension, and even intervention in member states that did not respect democracy or human rights. Even ASEAN, against all odds, has set up an intergovernmental human rights mechanism. The author argues that regionalism has remained "open" and supportive of multilateral regimes, so worries about competitive "bloc" formation are usually exaggerated. Rather, Acharya writes, the proliferation and broadening functions of regional institutions may "introduce a healthy diversity and leadership into the emerging world order instead of the singular dominance of American power or the EU's legalistic and centralized model of cooperation."[198] Looking into the future, the author does not believe that any rising power will be able to replace US hegemony; rather, they will assume regional leadership in a concert model.

Mainstream thinkers in the United States will ask what China has done over the past years to provide global public goods, arguing that a US military retreat from Asia would cause several of China's neighbors to acquire nuclear weapons. Who will secure global sea lanes? In the same way, they will point out that without US military power, the world would have been unable to stop genocide in Kosovo.

There is no question that the United States remains indispensable when it comes to specific public goods such as military intervention to stop genocide (pillar three of the responsibility to protect, R2P). In the same way, Europe and the United States accept far more refugees (for instance, from Syria and Iraq) than rising powers such as China. And still, China's contributions have grown considerably over the past decade—quite remarkably in some instances, considering that China is still at a far earlier stage of its development process. Beijing is already actively involved in the fight against piracy, and the creation of a fully operational blue-water navy will enhance its capacity to provide maritime security. When it comes to sovereignty vs. human rights, Beijing's stance has become more pragmatic. In the past years, Beijing has supported several UNSC resolutions on Syria, including those mandating the UN Observer Mission, the destruction of Syria's chemical weapons, and a humanitarian aid access plan. There is plenty to criticize in Beijing's foreign policy, and the impact of China's rise on global human rights norms is a valid concern, but China can no longer be easily accused of failing to contribute global public goods any more than established powers.

How will such a scenario affect US–Sino relations, by far the most important relationship in the world in the coming decades? Pointing to the centrality of the relationship for the future of global order, Kissinger writes that, despite their importance for global order, both China and the United States are profoundly ambivalent about the international system. While Beijing has never enjoyed so much influence in modern times, the United States has little experience dealing with another actor of comparable power.[199] He also rightly points out that Washington and Beijing have a lot in common; both consider themselves to be unique, even though US exceptionalism also amounts to a moral obligation to support and promote values around the world for reasons beyond raison d'état.

Most likely, we will witness a "managed rivalry" in constant flux, that will require continuous adaptation to the changing terms of the relationship, implying an ongoing renegotiation and adjustment—quite unlike the early post–Cold War years, when the US–China relationship was relatively static. As Michael Mastanduno says, since the financial crisis in 2008, it is no longer possible to reach a "grand bargain," tacit or explicit, for an extended period of time.[200] Since China will seek to emphasize domestic consumption, the economic ties between the two will no longer be as close as before, even though the principle of "mutually assured economic destruction," for example, if China would sell off its dollar reserves, will still hold.

Despite this rivalry, large-scale conflict between the two is unlikely for a series of reasons. First of all, there is no mainstream support in the United States for containing China. John Mearsheimer recommends that US policy makers should "seek to form a balancing coalition with as many of China's neighbors as possible. The ultimate aim would be to build an alliance structure along the lines of NATO, which was a highly effective instrument for containing the Soviet Union during the Cold War."[201]

If the United States sought to create and lead an anti-China alliance in Asia, however, it would face three obstacles. Not only would it contain states that do not trust each other (for example, Japan and South Korea), which may lead to collective action problems (free-riding), but all countries participating increasingly depend on China's economy, reducing their willingness to oppose Beijing (even though, in principle, they are more likely to balance China and bandwagon, as it poses a greater threat than the United States). Finally, given the geographic distance between alliance members, the United States would have to spend a lot of time and energy to coordinate a containment strategy. Countries in the region would most likely opt for a hedging strategy, maintaining the United States as a security ally, but benefiting from broader economic integration with China. As a consequence, countries such as Vietnam and the Philippines could emerge as the greatest beneficiaries of this dynamic, provided that they play their cards right. Irrespective of what the United States chooses to do in the region, it seems certain that the multitude of relatively strong neighbors will significantly delay Chinese global ambitions—unlike the United States, it does not have the privilege of declaring its own "Monroe Doctrine" early on.

Some alarmists believe that trade could increase the risk of conflict rather than reducing it. Aaron Friedberg, for example, regards trade as a potential cause for friction, arguing that "if disputes over trade imbalances, exchange rates, investment flows, access to and control

over scarce commodities become increasingly vitupera-
tive, ... the entire relationship could unravel with surpris-
ing speed."[202] However, the cost of a military conflict
with the United States, even if limited to conventional
means, will be prohibitively high for China for decades
to come. Growing trade ties will add a further layer that
makes military conflict less likely (although examples such
as the conflict between Germany and the United Kingdom
in World War I show that trade does not make conflict
impossible). There is little evidence for increased systemic
tensions.

Conclusion

This analysis is by no means exhaustive and does not claim
to "solve" the complex debate about the future of global
order. Rather, it seeks to strike a calmer note and question
the multitude of alarmist accounts that depict the end of
Western global leadership as something to fret about. As
the analysis above shows, the most likely scenario in the
coming decades is so-called asymmetric bipolarity, in
which the United States will dominate militarily, while
China will be the world's most important economy. The
dynamics that will shape such a system are understudied,
and it is far from certain whether such a system will be
durable or peaceful. Even though it may persist for decades,
it will not be inherently stable. Rather, it will be subject to
ongoing renegotiation, provided that China can sustain its
economic leadership position. More important, however,
the analysis suggests that warnings of imminent post-
unipolar chaos and instability are exaggerated, and likely
the result of a Western-centric worldview rather than an
objective analysis.

– 3 –

The Future of Soft Power

Considering the spread of hard power described in the previous chapter, a crucial question is whether soft power in the emerging world has risen commensurately. Can emerging states' soft power rival that of the West as they expand their global presence, and will other states be more willing to follow their lead and defer to their wishes? Are the BRICS countries capable of challenging the West's attractiveness and capacity to shape the global agenda? Will states seek to emulate rising non-Western powers and view their policies, values, or institutions as desirable and worthy of imitation? The most common answer to these questions is no, and there is evidence that the West exudes far more soft power than any non-Western power. This, in turn, is thought to prolong the West's global dominance.

And yet, I argue that the degree to which soft power preponderance is based on hard power sources is greater than generally recognized. As a consequence, economic multipolarization will allow non-Western powers such as China and India to catch up significantly in the soft power realm. For example, the United States' key alliances in Asia today (such as Japan and India) are not the product of Western soft power alone, but of security guarantees.

Issues related to soft power, such as reputational disasters like the Iraq War, have only a very limited impact on the foundations of US standing in the world. In the same way, as China and other emerging powers rise economically, they will have the potential to gain allies and create globally popular policies, such as financing the "New Silk Road," a train connecting Brazil to the Pacific, or large-scale investments in green energy. Put differently, while the West's leadership in the realm of soft power is real, a greater part of it is susceptible to shifts of economic power than we think, and much of it could not be sustained without hard power.[203] While soft power can in some instances be converted into hard power (for instance, attracting talented immigrants who help grow the economy, promoting innovation in a environment of free speech), the latter is still decisive when discussing the future of global order. Thus, emerging powers' relative disadvantages in the realm of soft power are of less importance to the future of global order than generally thought.

The discussion about soft power is complicated by the theoretical limitations of the concept invented by Joseph Nye in 1990.[204] The concept is somewhat vague, and this combined with the Western-centrism of many who used it (often distorting Nye's original idea) means that analyses employing it can reach differing conclusions. Still, despite these problems, there are undeniably important sources of power other than economic or military strength, and they deserve to be studied in detail in the context of growing multipolarization. The debate about rising non-Western state actors and soft power points to intriguing questions about rising powers' capacity to increase their global influence and shape the international agenda. This dispute is far from settled, and there is no consensus on how the lack of political freedom in Russia and China, high levels of poverty (India) or violence (Brazil) affect their capacity to influence others beyond traditional forms of power. Indeed, the fact that the world is increasingly becoming dominated by economies with a relatively low GDP per capita and internal challenges typical of developing countries complicates discussions about who can serve as a model in the future, and about whom poor countries will look toward for orientation, inspiration, and emulation.

There is no doubt that, despite remarkable economic growth during the first decade of the twenty-first century, China's and other rising states' capacity to enhance their soft power is highly uneven, and they still struggle to rival established Western powers in most of the concept's dimensions. Still, many of the arguments used by analysts about why China's soft power is limited—often made from a Western-centric perspective—are bound to weaken once China's economic weight increases.[205] It is true that China currently has few friends, but that will change as China will increasingly be able to support economically a growing number of countries or provide them with security guarantees. In the same way, the alliances countries will entertain with the United States may weaken. Even though the rise of an anti-China alliance in Asia is a possibility, neighbors will also be influenced by Beijing's economic power. China's recent diplomatic success, when even countries skeptical of Beijing's intentions sought membership in the new Asian Infrastructure Investment Bank, seems to support that argument. Chinese leaders' constant efforts to expand economic cooperation may have a greater effect on societies in the region than the United States' approach, which is centered on security guarantees. As Harrington writes,

> Since 2000, bilateral trade between China and the ten members of the Association of Southeast Asian Nations has grown tenfold, from $32 billion to $350 billion last year, and could reach $500 billion in 2015. As China has risen to become Southeast Asia's largest trading partner, the US has slipped to fourth place, with only $206 billion in total trade with ASEAN last year.[206]

Economic power is thus a fundamental precondition for a global soft power projection—and it was largely due to the West's economic rise that it was able to gain soft power, as detailed in chapter 1. Though there may be a delay in translating hard power into soft power, China, or any other rising power, for that matter, is likely to strengthen its capacity to improve its image in global affairs and offer competing narratives about global order in both the past and present. Naturally, the growth of China's soft power will also depend on the speed at which average citizens' living standards improve, being currently still far lower than those in the rich world.

In the coming decades, China's economic dominance may thus allow it to rival the United States not only militarily but also in its capacity to act as an agenda-setter and global manager, partly through the new institutions described in chapters 4 and 5, which help China institutionalize and legitimize its growing influence. At a later point, although this may be decades away, it may even begin to compete with the United States in its capacity to attract the world's leading researchers and be seen as culturally attractive (as it had been up until the mid-nineteenth century), provided that its per capita GDP approaches that of rich countries. For many in the West, this will sound counterintuitive, convinced as they are that Westernization is the only possible course of history. However, sinicization and China's growing influence in all aspects of global relations are likely to become widely discussed phenomena—if not culturally, at least regarding things like technology or urban planning. This does not mean that autocratic forms of government will ever be more attractive than democratic ones—far from it. It does mean, however, that a greater share of soft power than is often believed can be attained through hard power means, ranging from the provision of global public goods (such as in the realms of maritime security, climate change, global health, and financial stability) to the financing of large-scale infrastructure projects around the world.

The Limitations of Soft Power

The concept of soft power is one of the most notable innovations in the discipline of international relations since the end of the Cold War. It is one of the few ideas developed in academia that has successfully been adopted by policy makers around the world. Indeed, it is hard to overestimate the speed with which soft power has diffused from academia to practical political discussions. Hillary Clinton has been called the "soft power Secretary of State" for fully embracing the concept, and India's former Minister of External Affairs Shashi Tharoor frequently used the idea to frame India's place in the world.[207] Even the Chinese government has made soft power a central theme of its foreign policy. Moreover, consulting firms have established soft power indexes to rank countries.[208] Brazilian foreign-policy makers have made soft power one of the trademarks of their foreign-policy strategy.[209] Even Russia, seen as a country without any soft power by many in the West, has embraced the concept. In 2014, Russia outlined a new soft power doctrine entitled "Integrated Strategy for Expanding Russia's Humanitarian Influence in the World." The plan, according to Foreign Minister Sergey Lavrov, was to counter "unprecedented measures to discredit Russian politics and distort Russia's image."[210] Examples include humanitarian aid, such as the financing of the Serbian-Russian Humanitarian Centre, opened in 2012 in the southern Serbian city of Nis as a disaster-response center with regional reach.[211]

The broad interest in soft power strategies rests partly on the fact that exercising soft power is cheaper than more traditional ways of enhancing power. The concept undergirding soft power is that nations will voluntarily support the wishes and interests of a nation because it has somehow cultivated their loyalty and support through actions, qualities, and policies that garner admiration and respect.

Power, Nye often points out, is "the ability to influence others to get the outcomes one wants."[212] Soft power, then, is the use of "attraction and persuasion rather than the use of coercion or force in foreign policy. It arises from the attractiveness of a country's culture, political ideals and policies." It is thus a country's ability to get what it wants by attracting and persuading others to adopt its goals. Soft power involves leading by example. As Hall explains, "Whereas hard power changes the external costs or benefits facing an actor, soft power alters an actor's perception of what is desirable or undesirable in the first place."[213] It differs from hard power, the ability to use carrots and sticks of economic and military strength to make others follow your will.

While the concept is embraced by policy makers, several historical examples raise questions about the actual impact of soft power. For example, after World War I, Woodrow Wilson was perhaps, on a global scale, the most popular US president in history. His speeches about self-determination and global peace inspired millions in Europe and the Global South. Across the European continent, he was greeted like a global celebrity, and hundreds of thousands lined the streets to see him. He possessed almost unlimited soft power, and yet, during the negotiations in Versailles, Wilson failed to have it his way.[214] Clemenceau and Lloyd George, two seasoned political operators, were tenacious defenders of their nations' interests. Wilson's soft power seemed to be of little help. To make matters worse, Wilson's incapacity to fulfill his promises in Paris led to anti-American protests across the world, including in Egypt, Korea, and China.[215] One must also point out the "hard sources" of Wilson's soft power: he was the first US president to hire a professional marketing team; it built an unprecedented global propaganda network during World War I to promote Wilson's rhetoric of self-determination. More important, he was the leader of the nation that had played the decisive, victorious role in World War I.

Emulation—being copied by other countries—is seen as an especially potent manifestation of soft power. Yet the example of the Meiji Restoration in the nineteenth century complicates this statement. Western ideas and values were extremely popular and influential in Japan at the time, but they failed to align Japan to the West. To provide a final example, Hamas's embrace of democracy has in no way turned it into an ally of the West. This should serve as a warning to all those who argue that China's democratization would end the risk of confrontation with the West. Quite to the contrary, a democratic China could adopt a far more nationalistic and aggressive foreign policy, actively confronting the United States' military presence in Asia. In the same way, it raises important caveats to the assertion that China's limited soft power will keep it from exercising global influence.

The importance of public opinion, another issue often mentioned in the context of soft power, must also be assessed carefully. Taking the example of Brazil, Bruk writes, "Brazil is the state where soft power plays a primary role. For the most part, the general perception of the country abroad is positive: Brazil is viewed as a state with a rapidly developing economy and social sectors, an attractive and exotic culture, and rich natural resources."[216] A 2013 study by a leading business school, INSEAD, noted that "Brazil is an attractive country in the traditional soft power sense. It has an appealing popular culture and a multicultural society whose people interact well with others."[217] Indeed, the Brazilian government itself has embraced this narrative.

Yet, as mentioned above, the challenge scholars face is to provide evidence of how this generates any tangible benefits for Brazil's national interest. Superficial evaluations like the ones above are unaware of Brazil's unattractive sides. For example, Brazil is one of the most dangerous countries in the world for journalists: 65 percent of journalists murdered in Brazil since 2011 had been reporting on corruption, and government officials are suspected to be perpetrators in 52 percent of the cases.[218]

Finally, calling Brazilian culture "exotic" is a Western-centric view unlikely to generate much support in Latin American countries. Brazil's soft power is strong in some countries, but not in others, and particularly strong among those whose notion of Brazil is based on relatively superficial knowledge.[219]

In the same way, Western analysts often confidently assume that China will never be as attractive as democratic regimes, yet populations in Africa or other parts of the world may not necessarily agree. As Trevor Moss points out,

> In many states, China probably is wasting its time and resources when it tries to get people to watch CCTV, piles newsstands with English versions of *China Daily*, or part-funds its Confucius Institutes. These initiatives are doomed to fail in certain contexts. But these same activities can work beautifully elsewhere.[220]

All this shows that soft power is inherently relational. China and the BRICS countries' development model may seem attractive to several African countries, while their low GDP per-capita and their profound socioeconomic challenges are unlikely to generate much appeal in Europe. Indeed, while the BRICS grouping may be seen as an odd phenomenon of little consequence in the rich world, the opposite is true in poorer countries, and many governments—ranging from Turkey, Mexico, Sudan, Iran, Egypt, and Argentina to Nigeria and Indonesia—have expressed interest in joining the grouping. From a Chinese perspective, however, enjoying soft power in its neighborhood and in other developing countries may be equally or even more important than European or US opinions on the matter, as China is conscious of the fact that it would be almost impossible for a poor country to be admired or emulated by rich countries.

Nye himself sometimes cites economic assistance as an example of soft power, even though it requires financial means, which, in turn, are an element of hard power. Rich countries can provide economic aid, poor countries cannot. In fact, several BRICS countries have, over the past decades, turned into donor countries. Some of that is likely to have enhanced their attractiveness vis-à-vis poor countries' governments. This strategy amounts to little else than buying influence, which, in essence, is a manifestation of traditional economic power.

Nye writes that soft power is intangible, but economic credibility, though intangible, very much depends on tangible sources, as is the threat generated by a large army. Even shrewd diplomacy, seemingly an intangible good, requires a global network of embassies, which requires financial resources to sustain. The degree to which hard power is a prerequisite of soft power is illustrated when we think about emerging powers. Many observers wrote about the BRICS' growing soft power during the first decade of the twenty-first century, yet this was largely a product of their fast economic growth, an expression of their (real or expected) hard power. In the same way, many observers pointed to the West's declining soft power, precisely because of its stagnant economy. Soft power thus blurs a complex relation among behaviors, resources, and strategy, and it falsely implies using hard power as a synonym for command power and hard power resources, and soft power as a synonym for co-optation power and soft power resources. As a consequence, rising powers like China and India, provided that they play their cards right, possess far more soft power potential than is generally assumed; for example, China could play a leading role in maritime security (combating piracy), peacekeeping (it is already a major troop provider), and climate change, which would strongly enhance its soft power. Indeed, several of the institutional examples shown in chapters 4 and 5, such as the New Development Bank, are examples of how emerging powers are seeking to transform hard power into soft power.

Soft Power and Western-Centrism

Applying the idea of soft power to the case of China shows how the concept is tainted by our Western-centric world-view. Nye has criticized China's efforts to acquire soft power through centralized schemes, such as the spread of Confucius Institutes or the establishment of the China Public Diplomacy Association.[221] Despite "spending billions of dollars to increase its soft power...China has had a limited return on its investment,"[222] he writes. Yet while the popularity of artists such as Andy Warhol around the world is seen as an example of US soft power, few would say Ai Weiwei's popularity in the West is an example of Chinese soft power.[223] This tends to suggest that we too downplay non-Western sources of soft power.

Finally, the case of Brazil (one of the few countries with global ambitions that has decided not to pursue hard power) seems to suggest that hard power is still far more important than is generally thought. Stolte argues:

> Role expectations for Great Powers and aspirants to this status have changed. The Great Power privileges of using force and deciding on the world's most crucial issues are no longer conquered through violence and military superiority but are earned by persuasion and the demonstration of the worthiness to receive this status.[224]

Yet three examples may illustrate how hard power still matters more than anything else. First, while Brazil decided to sign the NPT in 1998 and become a "good global citizen," India refused to sign, and tested nuclear weapons in the same year. Today, the United States has not only recognized India's nuclear power status, but it also officially supports India's candidacy for a permanent seat on the UN Security Council—while Washington merely "appreciates" Brazil's desire to join the UNSC on a permanent basis (a difference that can largely explained by the

United States' belief that India is a crucial element in balancing the rise of China). The second example is Brazil's attempt to reach a nuclear deal with the Iranian government in 2010, which was met with broad rejection in the West, largely because it did not believe Brazil possessed the legitimacy to negotiate a deal. The final example is the P3's rejection of Brazil's and India's concerns about the implementation of UNSC Resolution 1973 regarding the intervention in Libya, a topic which, according to policy makers in London, Paris, and Washington, was far too weighty to be discussed with perceived lightweights such as Brazil. In each of the three cases, the lack of hard power posed decisive limits on Brasília's great-power ambitions.

Emerging Powers and Soft Power

When applying emerging states' power potential in three key areas related to soft power—cultural diplomacy, international legitimacy/ agenda-setting capacity, and the attraction of each society—it becomes clear that the grouping's performance is highly uneven, but that the limitations are not entirely structural, as most observers would intuitively believe.

Cultural diplomacy, an exchange of ideas, information, art, and other aspects of culture among nations and their peoples in order to foster mutual understanding, is a tool used increasingly often by rising states to enhance their image abroad. Language instruction, academic exchange, and tours by artists are the hallmark of cultural diplomacy, a strategy pursued by all rising powers, even though China is the only rising power that has the financial capacity to do so in a systematic way. In 2011, for the first time in fifteen years, the sixth plenary session of the Seventeenth Central Committee of the Communist Party focused on several cultural aspects, and spoke of the need for China to promote "its cultural sector to boost its soft power."[225] As the *New York Times* reported,

At a time when most Western broadcasting and newspaper companies are retrenching, China's state-run news media giants are rapidly expanding in Africa and across the developing world. They are hoping to bolster China's image and influence around the globe, particularly in regions rich in the natural resources needed to fuel China's powerhouse industries and help feed its immense population.[226]

In 2009, China launched a project with a $6.58 billion budget called *waixuan gongzuo*, which can be translated as "overseas propaganda."[227] Hillary Clinton, citing the growing presence of state-backed outlets such as Russia Today (RT) and CCTV, argued during a Congressional committee meeting that "We are engaged in an information war, and we are losing that war."[228] In addition to RT, Russia reorganized the RIA Novosti news agency and laid off a significant part of its staff, including its relatively independent management. The agency's new leader then announced the launch of Sputnik, a government-funded network of news hubs in more than thirty countries with 1,000 staff members producing radio, social media, and news-wire content in local languages.[229]

Like Russia and China, the United States and European countries have ample experience with cultural diplomacy, financing broadcasters such as Voice of America, BBC, France Info and Deutsche Welle. In the same way, they finance cultural programs through the British Council, the Alliance Française, the Goethe Institute, the Instituto Cervantes, and so on. In that sense, there is nothing exceptional about emerging powers' strategies.

Despite the rise of non-Western news networks such as RT and CCTV, emerging powers will struggle enormously to create news sources that can challenge established Western players and the narratives they develop. It is here that the West's power is most resilient, and change in this area is likely to be far slower. CNN and BBC will be difficult to challenge, since evidence shows that neither CCTV nor RT enjoy the same levels of trust Western broadcasters enjoy.[230] Still, the rise of Al Jazeera shows that non-Western media outlets can, in principle, generate global visibility and earn significant credibility.

Many Western observers will regard the rise of non-Western powers capable of challenging the current distribution of power as dangerous, and the end of unipolarity as an existential threat to the cosmopolitan project and to universalist Western rhetoric, as the West will lack the material superiority to get away with openly seeking to remake the world in its image. In that context, revisionist rhetoric by rising states does not, of course, enhance their soft power in the West. In the same way, when Nye explains the role of soft power in the United States' effort to build post-World War II order, his ideas are, quite naturally, US-centric, and essentially a supporting narrative for US hegemony:

> The US is certainly not above using force. It has been at war with one country or another for much of the past century. But soft power has provided a narrative. Many people—though certainly not all—believe America acts out of decent intentions and is basically a benign power. That is quite a trick. China by contrast has had few wars in recent decades. Yet it is generally held in suspicion.[231]

Rising states and many developing countries may disagree, and regard multipolarization and the contestation of US hegemony as a necessary change to assure that rules and norms will be respected, so Russian revisionist rhetoric may strengthen rejection among US-Americans and Europeans, but enhance Russia's image in places like Venezuela or Ecuador, where anti-Americanism is rife. Many policy makers in the emerging world would agree with Reich and Lebow when they argue that "the United States has violated the responsibilities and roles assigned to a hegemon...constituting as much a threat to global order and stability as it is a possible pillar of its preservation."[232] That explains why Venezuela and Cuba, two countries with little soft power in the West, still enjoy considerable soft power across Latin America despite their failing economic models and human rights problems. As Tomila Lankina and Kinga Niemczyk point out,

> Soft power, as Nye reminds us, is about attraction. Underestimating the true magnitude of Russia's attraction to a variety of constituencies and audiences risks further miscalculations of Russia's intentions by Western policy makers. One reason for the relative neglect of Putin's brand of authoritarian soft power is the earlier assumption by many observers...of a teleological process of a gradual diffusion of democracy and associated values among post-communist nations....The underlying premise in the Russian Foreign Policy Concept of 2013 is the perception of the West as a source of instability and danger in the international system—be it through causing economic and financial crises; intervening in regional crises without a UN mandate; or meddling in the internal affairs of sovereign states in the name of democracy promotion.[233]

The discussion about legitimacy, a key source of soft power, is thus marked by strongly differing views of whether the status quo—the current distribution of power and hierarchy—is legitimate or not. Every single country embraces its own particular values, and rather than adopting a genuinely new foreign-policy strategy to enhance their soft power, policy makers tend to merely present their already defined policies in soft power terms. Describing something as a soft power resource can "serve as an endogenous validation of the policies and national discourses that political practitioners advocate."[234] Thus, soft power has political utility in serving to reaffirm the policies and values that political actors already work on.

Many of the arguments used by analysts about why China lacks legitimacy (and hence why its soft power is limited), and why the world will see through any Chinese "charm offensive,"[235] are bound to weaken once China's economic weight increases. It is true that China currently has few friends, but that will change if China is increasingly able to support economically a growing number of countries or provide them with security guarantees. In the same way, the alliances many states will entertain with the United States may weaken, as seen already in places such as South Africa, Russia, and Venezuela. In fact, there is considerable evidence showing that China's hard power alone is already having a considerable impact, allowing China to "have it its way." For example, many world leaders have recently spurned or downgraded meetings with the Dalai Lama due to pressure from China. This is very much a consequence of Beijing's growing capacity to threaten and punish those who might defy it.[236] Western analysts, however, still generally see Western soft power strategies as more genuine and honest than those of non-Western and non-democratic regimes such as China.[237]

For instance, most Western analysts regard China's (or any emerging powers') behavior in Africa to be ruthless and largely egoistic.[238] In a Chatham House paper entitled "Brazil in Africa: Just another BRICS country seeking resources?," Christina Stolte asks "Is Brazil just 'another emerging power in the continent', disguising its economic interests by offering aid projects to its partner countries?"[239] It is far from clear, however, whether China's or India's impact in Africa are any more harmful than France's or Britain's. Yet as Kenneth King writes in *China's Aid and Soft Power in Africa*, China's soft power strategy may be far more successful in Africa than in the West.[240] He describes how the number of Africans receiving scholarships in China has increased dramatically over the past years, and how the West's negative image of China in Africa is often contrasted with a more nuanced view by Africans. As Trevor Moss writes, "These educational efforts are packaged respectfully—they are an attempt to show Africans how China does things, not a means of lecturing Africans about how they should do things."[241] Deborah Brautigam's *The Dragon's Gift*—perhaps the most detailed analysis of China's presence in Africa—comes to the same

conclusion: that China's reputation in Africa is not as negative as the West generally believes.

Very similar dynamics apply to Latin America and the
Middle East, and Western analysts often falsely assume
that their qualms about China are shared in the developing world. Indeed, polls show that opinions of China's
influence are positive in much of Africa and Latin America,
but predominantly negative in the United States and
Europe.[242] Considering that the West has the most to
lose from China's rise in relative terms—its geopolitical
predominance—worries in the United States and Europe
may be natural and inevitable. Opinions in Africa and
Latin America, then, may be far more representative of
whether China has soft power or not, as these regions
regard China's rise without the threatening connotation
so ingrained in the West.

For China, the most immediate concern will be to
what extent its soft power initiatives have an impact in its
immediate neighborhood. In this context, soft power may
contribute to reducing more explicit balancing behavior
against Beijing. Anecdotal evidence suggests that even
countries with a record of loathing Chinese influence, such
as Indonesia, are opting for rapprochement. In Indonesia
a growing number of schools included Mandarin in the
curriculum, and China sends professors to many countries
of the region.[243] The potential for a more concerted soft
effort in the region is significant, as millions of ethnic
Chinese live in neighboring countries.

Rising Powers and Agenda-Setting Capacity

When it comes to agenda-setting capacity, established
powers remain relatively dominant, even though China has
made considerable progress. Partly thanks to the control of
existing institutions, the West, led by the United States and
Europe, is still able to set the agenda in the international
debate and engage on a global scale. Setting the agenda

is the result of initiating, legitimizing, and successfully advocating a specific policy issue in the economic, security, or any other realm. When considering the three key issues that dominated global affairs in 2014 (Ukraine, ISIS, and Ebola) it becomes clear how little emerging countries assumed a leading position. Where do the ideas that shape the way we think and act upon these challenges come from? What have policy makers in Brasília, New Delhi, and Beijing said about their countries' role in providing tangible solutions, and how have those views affected global opinion and policy?

International agenda setting is an arduous and uncertain process. It requires a specific combination of factors. The first is brainpower: the intellectual capital to develop an innovative initiative or response capable of helping the international community address a global challenge. Second, it requires a national leader willing to invest political capital. Third, it requires some international credibility. That is not a matter of hard power—small countries such as Norway have succeeded in setting the agenda on specific issues—yet the initiative's backer must have the necessary standing (for example, a successful domestic model of addressing the issue) to be seen as legitimate. Finally, it needs the logistical diplomatic structure to promote the initiative on a global scale. That requires fine-tuning global communication, involving embassies around the world, identifying allies early in the process, anticipating where resistance will emerge, and engaging global public opinion. It also involves policy makers and diplomats responding to media inquiries and writing convincing op-eds, and going on local TV to promote the idea. At home, it requires engaging opinion-makers, academics, and journalists to explain and defend the idea. Yet notably, it does not necessarily require economic or military power.

To what extent can emerging countries convert hard power into global influence? Can China set the agenda in the global discussion, introduce and implement new ideas about managing global order, and be seen as a model? Will

China's rise challenge the West's dominance over the ideas that shape global order?

There are some examples that show how emerging powers are seeking to set the global agenda. In Central Asia and other parts of China's neighborhood, Beijing may be increasingly able to dominate the debate about economic development, being the region's leading trade partner. In 2011, Brazil briefly turned into a norm entrepreneur in the area of humanitarian intervention when it launched "Responsibility While Protecting" (RwP). In 2014, it organized a global summit on the future of internet governance. During the Lula years, Brazil introduced new ideas about regional integration in Latin America, and, on a broader scale, promoted a discussion about the challenges of poverty and inequality. China has assumed an important role in the stabilization of Sudan, placing soldiers in the volatile region. Still, Western powers are far ahead when it comes to agenda-setting capacity.

Democracy, GDP Per Capita, and Soft Power

Finally, what is the capacity of emerging powers' societies to generate global attraction? This is, without a doubt, China and India's greatest obstacle to greater soft power: their inability to attract talented immigrants. Considering their much lower GDP per capita, this seems natural. For the vast majority of citizens, life in the West is more comfortable than in developing countries, and no rich society would ever seek to emulate a poorer, more unequal one. Other factors further reduce China's soft power potential. The lack of free speech and democracy in China will inevitably make it difficult for Chinese newspapers to be seen as trustworthy and impartial abroad, reducing their influence in global affairs. It will also keep the world's leading minds from accepting offers from Chinese universities, which are unable to innovate as much as Western educational institutions due to government censorship. China's innovative capacity, as a consequence, will hardly reach that of democratic societies.

Immigration to China is smaller as a result, negatively affecting China's capacity to attract innovative industries. More seriously, it will keep Chinese students and future elites isolated from international debates, making it more difficult for them to set the global agenda later on. The result is unattractive: as Jiang Guerin notes, China's best schools produce the world's best test-takers, but the United States' best schools produce the world's most creative talent.[244] There are few signs that this will change in the near future. In 2012, rather than relaxing limits on freedom of speech, then–Vice President Xi Jinping visited China's leading universities to call for *increased* party supervision of higher education.[245] The reason is that in the Communist as in the Confucian tradition, intellectual elites were seen as an appendage of the state rather than as independent groups with their own forms of organization and power. Indeed, the absence of a civil society and an autonomous public realm in Communist China is not a new phenomenon: China has never had them.[246]

Not everyone agrees that China's authoritarian system will reduce its capacity to innovate. As Francis Fukuyama argues,

> China has changed far more than anyone imagined since the Cultural Revolution and it has a long history of institutional transformation. Although much of China's recent economic and intellectual progress has been a form of catch-up. China is a vast country with many smart people. I would not assume that just because China lacks great political freedom that this means China isn't going to be able achieve astounding progress, to innovate in technology and institution building.[247]

Russia's attempt to improve its international image makes use of Western tools: it hired Ketchum, a US agency, to design what President Putin officially calls a "soft power strategy." While opposing the West, Russia nevertheless frames its own demands in the Western language of democracy. These acts of mimicry seeking to "catch up" with the West are signs of normative dependency on it; they reveal incapacity to come up with any distinct ideological platform.[248]

The Skolkovo-E&Y Institute has compiled a soft power index, which includes categories such as immigration, universities, and political freedom. Naturally, the United States received a far better evaluation than emerging powers. The US scored high in eight of ten categories: immigration (percentage of foreign-born immigrants), universities (quantity of internationally ranked universities), and media exports (the fees earned from exporting goods such as music, films, and books) provided the biggest boost to US soft power. These are followed by political freedom, iconic power (*Time* magazine's 100 most influential people), most admired companies, rule of law (the quality of a nation's institutions), and inbound tourism (global interest in the host country). The US scored low in only two categories, CO_2 emissions and voter turnout.[249] While one may criticize the way this index is set up (*Time* is certainly a Western-centric publication and may be less likely to include non-Western actors), all these aspects without a doubt provide tough challenges for the Chinese government.

Most soft power rankings cite the United States' unmatched capacity to attract the best and the brightest from all over the world. There is no emerging power that comes anywhere close regarding their capacity to attract highly qualified immigrants, who strongly enhance a society's vigor and innovative capacity. In fact, the BRICS countries are largely unable to attract any immigrants beyond their immediate region. The share of foreign-born people who live in Brazil (0.3 percent), India (0.4 percent) and China (0.1 percent) is extremely low when compared to Europe or the United States, where the figure often stands around 10 percent.[250] The same is true for Western universities, which attract a far greater number of international students than leading institutions from emerging powers, like Peking University of Tsinghua. The West's intellectual leadership—its first-mover advantage in creating a network of globally leading universities, research institutes, and news networks—is far harder to challenge than economic or even military leadership. Even several decades from now, many of Asia's leading politicians will have studied in the United States, and not vice versa.

Su Changhe writes that students who have studied abroad are "a force which must not be ignored in the process of promoting US culture."[251] Yet it would be misleading to believe that cultural attraction is the only way to explain such data. Students who seek to pursue education in the United States may do so because they are attracted to Western culture, yet others may decide to apply because it provides them with the best career chances upon returning to their home country.

Elites from around the world have studied at Western universities for a long time, and understanding how that shaped their respective countries' views and foreign-policy strategies vis-à-vis the West is a fascinating topic of research. Yet it is certain that there is no easy answer, and there are several historical examples of leaders who have worked or lived in the West but who later on adopted critical positions vis-à-vis their former host countries, such as several of the Indian independence leaders.

Conclusion

Over the past two decades soft power has become one of the most important new ideas in the discussion on global affairs. As this analysis has shown, the concept is somewhat problematic as its meaning has become quite broad through frequent usage. The concept's weakness becomes particularly obvious when the idea is applied to rising non-Western powers, whose foreign-policy strategy is not based on a liberal internationalist hegemonic narrative like that of the United States. Yet despite its conceptual fuzziness, the idea of soft power points in an important direction, and economic and military strength are not the only types of power that matter. The concept of soft power is of great importance in gaining a better understanding of the less visible sources of power.

Rising states' soft power potential differs greatly, but its perceived effectiveness is also based on the observer and on the times. China may be regarded unfavorably by the Japanese in one moment (say, after a controversial state-ment by a politician), but that perception may change several months later. Europeans may see Brazil in a posi-tive light during the World Cup but negatively only months later. Russia may possess great soft power in Hungary but not in Poland. Still, based on the brief analysis of some of the elements that are related to soft power, it becomes clear that all emerging powers still face considerable obstacles as they seek to rival the West's soft power.

It is in this realm that an important contest between China and the United States may take place over the coming decades. The financial crisis of 2008, the delegiti-mization of the US-led financial system, and China's ability to continue its growth story seemed to presage a world in which legitimacy and influence is openly contested. This change of guard became most visible in Africa, where an increasing number of leaders seek to emulate China (or, in Rwanda's case, Singapore) rather than trying to copy a Western power.

Despite its political deadlock and serious problems such as economic inequality, the United States still enjoys far more legitimacy and influence in international affairs than any emerging actor. That is largely due to political trans-parency and freedom as well as its continued capacity to innovate, which China will struggle to match.

In the same way, the West's intellectual leadership, based in its first-mover advantage in creating a network of glob-ally leading universities, research institutes, and news networks, is far harder to challenge than economic or even military leadership. In addition, despite the rise of non-Western news networks such as Al Jazeera, RT, and CCTV, emerging powers will struggle enormously to establish news sources that can challenge established Western players and the narratives they develop. It is here that the West's power is most resilient, and change in this area is likely to be far slower. As a consequence, the West is likely to be able to influence global affairs for a long time to come despite its possibly weakening economic and military standing.

Still, these advantages are only one element of soft power, and China can be expected to make enormous progress in others, thus dramatically enhancing its soft power around the world, and particularly so in developing countries. Economic power is a fundamental precondition for a global soft power projection, and China's status as key economic partner in Latin America, the Middle East, Central Asia, and Africa will allow Beijing, to an important degree, to shape the way people view China's rise.

— 4 —
Toward a Parallel Order: Finance, Trade, and Investment

Rather than making general guesses about what global order may look like in the future, this chapter and the next present more than twenty initiatives, the majority led by China, though some by other emerging powers. These initiatives are, in their entirety, creating a parallel structure that will reduce the universal claim of several Western-led institutions. Unlike many alarmists who unrealistically expect China to destroy existing structures in the near future, however, the chapter makes a more nuanced argument: policy makers in Beijing (and Delhi and Brasília) can be expected to continue to invest in Western-dominated structures and push for their reform. Yet at the same time, they quietly expand networks in many different areas, ready to engage those who feel today's institutions fail to satisfy their needs, or those who seek to increase autonomy from the United States.

China's stance vis-à-vis existing order is thus not openly aggressive. Most of the structures it sets up are complementary or parallel to existing ones, rarely challenging them head-on—for now. They include initiatives in the realms of finance, currency, infrastructure, diplomatic dialogue, trade and investment, and security. One of the main goals of establishing parallel structures is to slowly enhance strategic autonomy and reduce China's dependence on Western-controlled structures. Strengthening the role of China's currency and establishing a China-centric global payment system could be an example of one of these. Still, risk-averse and conscious of its limitations, China continues to actively support existing structures, making it harder for the West to accuse China of actively undermining current order. In addition, initially and perhaps permanently, several key sinocentric structures have been established within the existing liberal logic, such as the BRICS Contingency Reserve Agreement and the Chiang Mai Initiative Multilateral (CMIM), which are both embedded in the IMF system. In the same way, the BRICS grouping, in more general terms, remains embedded in international capitalism and global security structures. This shows that, at least for now, new institutions are unlikely to fundamentally challenge the logic that undergirds current order. Rather, the new structures are created as a parallel hedge serving not only China but also actors such as Brazil, India, South Africa and Russia, which can reduce their dependency on existing structures without openly reducing their support for them. As power is shifting toward emerging powers, these structures are an attempt to institutionalize their growing weight, project their power, and, as described in the previous chapter, enhance their soft power by assuming greater international responsibility. For the West, the major question is to what extent it wants to become a stakeholder in Chinese-led projects, or whether to undermine the new institutions.

This analysis largely focuses on China as it is the only non-Western power today with a concrete global project—unlike other emerging countries, which harbor global ambitions but still lack the power to implement them.

Tables 4.1 to 4.5 indicate the international institutions led by non-Western powers in the areas of finance, trade and investment, security, diplomacy, and infrastructure, which I will analyze in this chapter and the next. In the right column of the graph appears the existing institution that is most comparable to the new institution.

Table 4.1 The Parallel Order: Finance

Non-Western Institutions	Traditional Institutions
The Asian Infrastructure Investment Bank (AIIB)	Asian Development Bank
The BRICS-led New Development Bank (NDB)	World Bank
BRICS Contingency Reserve Agreement (CRA)	IMF
Global infrastructure to internationalize the Yuan	US-dollar
China international payment system (CIPS)	CHIPS
China Union Pay	VISA and MasterCard
Shanghai Global Financial Center (GFC)	Traditional financial centers
Universal Credit Rating Group	Moody's, Standard & Poor's
Chiang Mai Initiative Multilateral (CMIM)	IMF
ASEAN+3	
ASEAN+3 Macroeconomic Research Office (AMRO)	OCED

Table 4.2 The Parallel Order: Trade and Investment

Non-Western Institutions	Traditional Institutions
Regional Comprehensive Economic Partnership (RCEP)	Trans-Pacific Partnership
Free Trade Area of the Asia Pacific (FTAAP)	Trans-Pacific Partnership

Table 4.3 The Parallel Order: Security (Chapter 5)

Non-Western Institutions	Traditional Institutions
Conference on Interaction and Confidence Building Measures in Asia (CICA)	Asian Regional Forum
Shanghai Cooperation Organization (SCO)	NATO in Central Asia
BRICS national security advisors (NSA) meeting	

Table 4.4 The Parallel Order: Diplomacy (Chapter 5)

Non-Western Institutions	Traditional Institutions
BRICS Leaders Summit	G7 (formerly G8)
BRICS and IBSA working groups and other structures	OECD
Boao Forum for Asia (BFA)	World Economic Forum

Table 4.5 The Parallel Order: Infrastructure (Chapter 5)

Non-Western Institutions	Traditional Institutions
Silk Road Fund / One Road-One Belt (OBOR)	
Nicaragua Canal	Panama Canal
Trans-Amazonian Railway	

Finance: The Asian Infrastructure Investment Bank (AIIB)

When China's Xi Jinping first mentioned his idea of a new China-led development bank for the region, some of his own officials were surprised that he had already aired the concept publicly. At the time, in October 2013, policy makers in Beijing had designed little more than the basic structures and guidelines of the bank. This is part of a greater trend of undeniable demand for additional capital to modernize infrastructure across the Asian continent. In a much-cited study, the Asian Development Bank (ADB) said that the region needed $8 trillion of investments in infrastructure in the current decade to put Asia on a sustainable growth trajectory.[252] Poorer countries such as Myanmar, however, lack the means to do so, and existing institutions such as the Asian Development Bank cannot satisfy existing demand. The ADB lends little more than $10 billion a year for infrastructure development. Its president is traditionally named by Japan, even though China is by far the region's largest economy. At the same time, Beijing was looking for ways to strategically deploy its large foreign exchange assets, making the creation of a new bank look like an attractive option.

In the following year, the United States and Japan undertook a regional diplomatic offensive to convince Indonesia, South Korea, and Australia, among others, to reject China's invitation to join the AIIB, thus reducing the new institution's respectability and making it look like a sino-centric institution: precisely what Beijing sought to avoid, so as not to be seen as a regional bully. US motivations were clear: a potent AIIB with broad regional support would reduce the influence of both the World Bank and the Asian Development Bank, dominated by Washington and Tokyo respectively. Indeed, despite the risks, the rise of a China-led development bank, US policy makers reckoned, would increase both China's influence and its soft power in the region, a trend that could dramatically limit Washington's capacity to build alliances in Asia based on the common aversion to Beijing.

The arguments used by US policy makers were largely unconvincing, and it was only after severe diplomatic pressure that Indonesia, Australia, and South Korea initially decided not to join the AIIB. In all three countries, however, powerful voices began to argue that rejecting China's invitation would deprive them of influencing the way a key regional institution would be run.[253] Shortly thereafter, the critics won the day, and Japan became the only major player not to become part of the new institution in the region.

Washington's opposition to the AIIB was not only futile, it also hurt US national interest: citizens across Asia recognized that the United States sought to maintain influence in the region, while caring little for the well-being of Asia's poor. The argument that the AIIB would not recognize the environmental and governance standards the World Bank or the Asian Development Bank adhere to may have some truth to it, but rejecting the institution for that reason was inadequate. A more coherent response would have been to embrace the new initiative, but incentivize member countries (many of which are US allies) to push for more rigorous standards. Paradoxically, by pressuring Seoul and Canberra to stay out of the new institution, Washington accepted losing two actors through which it could have indirectly influenced the AIIB.

The episode underlined how insincere US foreign-policy makers' calls on rising powers to become "responsible stakeholders" were. After all, there are few better examples of China "stepping up to the plate" than providing $50 billion for regional infrastructure development. While surprising to some in Washington, China's move made it obvious that rising powers want to assume responsibility on their own terms rather than accepting the rules and norms established by US-led institutions. Similarly, in 2009, Washington was furious when it learned about Brazil's and Turkey's decision to negotiate a nuclear agreement with Iran—a move that challenged the West's monopoly on discussing nuclear proliferation in the Middle East, another decisive issue in global affairs.

A few months later, in a rare open disagreement between London and Washington, aligned on virtually every major foreign-policy issue over the past decades, Britain became the first major Western government to apply for

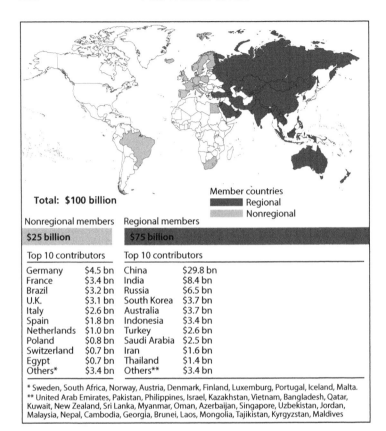

Total: $100 billion			Member countries
Nonregional members	Regional members		Regional
$25 billion	**$75 billion**		Nonregional

Top 10 contributors		Top 10 contributors	
Germany	$4.5 bn	China	$29.8 bn
France	$3.4 bn	India	$8.4 bn
Brazil	$3.2 bn	Russia	$6.5 bn
U.K.	$3.1 bn	South Korea	$3.7 bn
Italy	$2.6 bn	Australia	$3.7 bn
Spain	$1.8 bn	Indonesia	$3.4 bn
Netherlands	$1.0 bn	Turkey	$2.6 bn
Poland	$0.8 bn	Saudi Arabia	$2.5 bn
Switzerland	$0.7 bn	Iran	$1.6 bn
Egypt	$0.7 bn	Thailand	$1.4 bn
Others*	$3.4 bn	Others**	$3.4 bn

* Sweden, South Africa, Norway, Austria, Denmark, Finland, Luxemburg, Portugal, Iceland, Malta.
** United Arab Emirates, Pakistan, Philippines, Israel, Kazakhstan, Vietnam, Bangladesh, Qatar, Kuwait, New Zealand, Sri Lanka, Myanmar, Oman, Azerbaijan, Singapore, Uzbekistan, Jordan, Malaysia, Nepal, Cambodia, Georgia, Brunei, Laos, Mongolia, Tajikistan, Kyrgyzstan, Maldives

Graph 4.1 Capital Stock in the AIIB. *Source:* Asia Infrastructure Investment Bank

membership in the Chinese-led Asian Infrastructure Investment Bank (AIIB). By announcing Britain's intention to join, David Cameron made a bold move that is proof of a far more sophisticated understanding of global affairs than on the other side of the Atlantic.

Other major economies such as Germany, France, and Brazil soon followed Britain's lead. In late June 2015, representatives from fifty countries gathered in Beijing to participate in the signing ceremony of the articles of agreement of the Asian Infrastructure Investment Bank. The significance of the event for both Asia and the global order could hardly be overstated. It represented the definitive end of China's traditional strategy of "Hide your strength, bide your time" articulated by Deng Xiaoping. China's claim to a global role was now fairly explicit, and for the first time, the country opted for the creation of a new global institution to cement its leadership ambitions.

The AIIB's articles, agreed to by the bank's fifty-seven founding member countries, call for the bank to be overseen by an unpaid, nonresident board of directors (unlike the World Bank, the African Development Bank, and the Asian Development Bank). Using English as its operating language, the bank will open bidding for projects to all, unlike the ADB, which limits contracts to member countries. Several differences with existing institutions will emerge and are likely to create healthy competition among ideas, which may strengthen the effectiveness of lending practices across the board.

Implications

The creation of the AIIB was good news for three reasons. First, the membership of countries from around the world will force China to operate according to a clear set of rules and norms. If other countries start to sharply disagree with the way China leads the institution, they would leave, creating an embarrassment Chinese leaders will seek to avoid. For developing countries, receiving loans from the AIIB will be far safer than dealing with China bilaterally. More broadly, China's decision to opt for multilateralism is to be welcomed, affirming the basic principles of today's global order.

It is also a sign of Chinese maturity in the international realm. That is significant because, as Henry Kissinger once argued, the Hu Jintao–Wen Jiabao administration (2002–2012) was the first Chinese leadership who governed China as a full and equal member of international society.[254]

China will hold 26.06 percent of the votes in AIIB, giving it an effective veto over major decisions, followed by India with 7.5 percent and Russia with 5.92 percent. Countries defined as "within the region" will hold a combined 75 percent stake in the bank's $100 billion capital base. And yet, as Amitav Acharya rightly wrote in a recent op-ed, "The AIIB...puts China's leadership capacity to its most severe test to date."[255]

Second, Asia badly needs greater investment in infrastructure, and none of the existing banks have been able to satisfy such a massive demand. Together with the World Bank, the New Development Bank, the Asian Development Bank, and others, the AIIB is a boon for Asian economies, which—in their entirety—are set to become the center of the global economy during the twenty-first century. The AIIB therefore does not represent a threat to any other institutions, including the BRICS-led New Development Bank, described below.

Thirdly, a new large organization like the AIIB, which will greatly benefit from existing knowledge generated at the World Bank and elsewhere, may itself produce new ideas and best practices that take the global debate about development further.

The BRICS-led New Development Bank (NDB)

Less than a month after the official creation of the China-led Asian Infrastructure Investment Bank (AIIB) in Beijing, another global financial institution was launched 1,200 kilometers further south. Based in Shanghai, China's financial hub, the New Development Bank's creation marks a remarkable step in the history of the BRICS grouping. After being a mere investment category between 2001 and 2007 and an informal platform between 2008 and 2014, the launch of the NDB is the beginning of a new era for an unlikely grouping that has been confronted with broad skepticism and rejection in the Western media since its beginnings. While the Asian Infrastructure Investment

Bank has received far more media attention, the NDB will begin with the remarkable initial capital of $50 billion. The five BRICS countries all have equal voting shares.

With regard to ties between member countries, the creation of the bank along with the Contingency Reserve Agreement (CRA) is set to strengthen the relationships among central banks, national development banks, and finance ministries. Yet the existence of the bank should be used to generate additional ties not only between governments but between societies that have scarcely interacted in the past. The NDB's impact on lending practices will only become evident in the coming years. Kamath, the bank's first president, pledged to move the bank "from best practices to next practices," adding that traditional development lending was often "too rigid, inflexible, and slow."[256]

The NDB's impact on global governance remains perhaps the most interesting question, even though it will take years before we gain a clearer understanding of whether and how it will affect existing structures. Many observers see the bank as proof that the BRICS have a revisionist agenda. Varun Sahni, for example, argues that the establishment of the NDB is "a strong example of revisionist power aggregation, insofar as it challenges the structures and legitimacy of the World Bank and the International Monetary Fund."[257] Others point out that the bank is a natural reaction by emerging powers to an order that has been unwilling or unable to include them adequately. Kamath insists that "our objective is not to challenge the existing system as it is but to improve and complement the system in our own way." Even though the bank's website states the NDB is "operated...as an alternative to the existing U.S.–dominated World Bank and International Monetary Fund," calling the BRICS countries revisionist would be misguided. The NDB's launch actually underlines the BRICS' willingness to help fix a system that no longer satisfies existing demands. As mentioned above, only those who regard US leadership, rather than the system's rules and functionality, as the decisive element of today's order will call the BRICS revisionist.

The launch of the NDB is a success for the BRICS grouping, but the grouping's greatest challenges lie ahead. Creating a globally active development bank is difficult, and the BRICS will be wise to draw from existing institutions' experiences. In a sign of welcome pragmatism by member countries, the bank's key decision makers, such as Kamath (with a history in private banking) and Nogueira Batista (from the IMF), possess expertise from established bodies. While the new institutions must first show that they can make a tangible contribution to addressing international development challenges, the NDB, along with the AIIB, may serve as symbols of a very different global institutional landscape: more complex, less Western-centric, but ultimately better for a multipolar world.

Still, it is necessary to put the NDB's dimensions into perspective. India and China are the World Bank's two biggest borrowers. Together with Brazil, they have $66 billion in outstanding loans, more than the entire initial subscribed capital of the new BRICS-led bank.[258] While the BRICS grouping had been, until 2014, largely marked by its lack of binding rules, a joint development bank and a Contingency Reserve Arrangement can be interpreted as the initial stage of institutionalized financial cooperation. In addition, they will require the BRICS countries to develop rules and norms that guide both initiatives' actions. For example, how will loans be tied to a monitoring and surveillance mechanism and policy conditionalities? What will they look like? If not following a World Bank–inspired logic, along which lending and governance paradigms will they be developed? The BRICS' policy rhetoric leaves little doubt that they are keen to bring change to a global system that no longer reflects today's distribution of power. Do the BRICS aspire to do more than simply occupy positions of power and leave the system otherwise unchanged? As Radhika Desai argues,

The BRICS countries do have a mortar that binds them: their common experience, and rejection of the neoliberal development model of the past several decades and the western-dominated IMF and the World Bank that still advocate it.... They have long called for the reform of the IMF and the World Bank only to meet with resistance. Rather than waiting, they have decided to act.[259]

Yet what do the BRICS seek to replace the neoliberal development model with, and what role should institutions such as the BRICS Development Bank and agreements like the BRICS Contingency Reserve Arrangement play in a world envisioned by the BRICS? For many thinkers in the Global South, the creation of both institutions— BDB and CRA—represents a "significant move by emerging economies to break away from the traditional donor-recipient model advocated by Western nations for more than six decades."[260] Likewise, Pravin Gordhan, South Africa's Finance Minister, argued that "we should see the BRICS bank as part of a new paradigm to share resources and...achieve a win-win outcome."[261] But what exactly does that mean in practice?

The establishment of more institutionalized structures will force the BRICS to articulate with greater clarity their fundamental views on how to achieve financial stability and economic development and assure a sound future for the global financial and economic system. As Narlikar argues, the creation of these institutions "could be the first step towards more proactive agenda-setting by the BRICS," and a chance for the BRICS to go beyond a reactive stance and engage more assertively.[262] It will also force the BRICS to decide how much they seek to challenge the status quo.

The narrative that South–South cooperation is different from North–South cooperation is not uncontested. Critics of this assumption, and of the idea that the rise of the BRICS is beneficial for all those involved, have pointed to what they call the BRICS' "Scramble for Africa," indicating that South–South cooperation is increasingly similar to economic interaction between the North and the South. After all, they argue, emerging powers such as Brazil, India, and China are transforming themselves into major pillars of the global economy, and thus the disparities within the Global South are set to increase.[263] Like the Africa Conference in Berlin in 1884–5, writes Bond, the Fifth BRICS summit that took place in March 2013 in Durban—during which the BRICS decided to create their own development bank—sought to "carve up Africa," unburdened by Western concerns about democracy and human rights.[264]

BRICS Contingency Reserve Agreement (CRA)

At the Fifth BRICS Summit in Durban in 2015, the leaders of the BRICS decided to create a $100 billion Contingency Reserve Arrangement (CRA) to tackle any possible financial crisis in the emerging economies. Unlike the BRICS Bank, the idea of the CRA is relatively recent and was first discussed among BRICS leaders during a meeting on the sidelines of the G20 in Los Cabos in June 2012.

Unlike the Development Bank, the contingency fund requires far fewer political negotiations and has been fully operational since 2015. The set-up of the CRA reserve pool was easier because it required no physical structure to operate. Reserves are not physically collected in a common fund but are instead held by national central banks, earmarked for that purpose. Only in moments of crisis in one of the member countries' economies will the contingency fund begin to operate, acting as a cushion or backup. Considering the increasing frequency and magnitude of global financial crises over the past decades, the addition of another fund that major countries can rapidly mobilize in times of crisis is likely to boost investor confidence.

China contributes a share of $41 billion, followed by Brazil, Russia, and India with $18 billion each, and South Africa with $5 billion.[265] For several observers, the creation of a $100 billion contingency relief arrangement is a bid to sow the seeds of an alternate financial structure for developing countries, arguing that it could present a direct challenge to the IMF. After the Fifth Summit, the Indian media hailed the creation of the CRA as "a major win for India's campaign to reform global financial architecture." Putin argued the CRA "creates the foundation for an effective protection of our national economies from a crisis in financial markets."[266] Yet such an interpretation is largely unfounded, for now. This is mainly because a $100 billion fund is relatively small by global standards. China can borrow $6.2 billion from the CRA without approval from the IMF; for the other participants the number is smaller. By comparison, the IMF approved $38 billion in loans to Russia in the 1990s, and $15 billion in standby credit to Brazil in 2002. For now, a CRA of $100 billion is thus little more than a stepping-stone to something larger.

Most important, the BRICS' CRA includes an IMF linkage. Only 30 percent of a member's quota is accessible without an IMF program. For the remaining 70 percent the member state must agree to an IMF program, including its policy prescriptions. In this sense the BRICS CRA is far from a counterweight to current IMF-led order. In fact, it will be nested within the current system.

Chiang Mai Initiative Multilateral (CMIM)

The Chiang Mai Initiative (CMI) is an agreement signed in May 2000 between the Association of Southeastern Asian Nations (ASEAN) countries as well as China, Japan, and South Korea.[267] The aim of the initiative is to strengthen the region's capacity to protect itself against risks in the global economy.[268] It is intended to provide a supply of emergency liquidity to member countries facing currency crises—and avoid the need to depend on the IMF, which is seen as having abused its power in its emergency loans during the Asian financial crisis of 1997–8.[269] The CMIM does give its more weighty member economies more voting power, but no veto (such as the US has at the World Bank), and it is designed to benefit smaller economies.[270] ASEAN+3 finance ministers reviewed the CMI in 2004–5 and launched its "stage two," doubling the nominal size of the swaps. After establishing a headquarters in Singapore in 2009, the CMI was renamed the Chiang Mai Initiative Multilateralization (CMIM). By multilateralization, the member countries mean collectivization on a regional basis, the creation of formal reserve pooling arrangements, a weighted voting system for disbursement of funds, and enhancement of surveillance capabilities. Today, it provides its members access to $240 billion of emergency liquidity to shield the region from global financial shocks. While participating states had considered pooling reserves into a single account that could be held, managed, and disbursed by a secretariat, as is the case with the IMF, it was decided to earmark reserves for a common fund and instead retain them in the accounts of national central banks and finance ministries.

Proof that the CMIM is not a threat to the IMF for now, however, is the rule that a country under the CMIM umbrella could only access a small proportion of its line of emergency credit without being forced to enter into negotiations with the IMF for a standby agreement. Only 30 percent of a member's quota is accessible without an IMF program—like the BRICS' CRA described above. To receive the remaining 70 percent, the member state must agree to an IMF program, including the much-loathed policy prescriptions. This linkage to the IMF was criticized early on, such as when Malaysia advocated for complete independence of the CMI from the IMF.[271] Additionally, the CMIM is designed as a US-dollar liquidity support arrangement, thus excluding local currency swaps.[272]

Some depicted CMIM as a major step toward the creation of an Asian monetary fund (AMF) that would be fully autonomous from the IMF.[273] Yet, because severance of the IMF linkage would have required the creation of a regional surveillance mechanism, participating members decided that the swap arrangements should remain complementary to the IMF facilities. At the time, Japan in particular pushed for the IMF linkage to lend credibility to the new initiative. Malaysia, however, only agreed to the linkage under the condition of setting up a study group that would assess ways to eventually remove the IMF linkage. Meaningful steps in this direction have not been taken since then. This is largely attributed to a lack of trust among participant countries.[274] The CMIM is thus a "parallel line of defense" to IMF financing.

Global infrastructure to internationalize the yuan

Since 2009 China has been promoting controlled internationalization of the yuan. The creation of the China International Payments System (CIPS) is a key element of this strategy, as is the plan to transform Shanghai into a global financial center. As Hu Jintao explained in 2011, "The current international currency system is the product of the past."[275] The reasons for such a strategy are clear. The global dominance of the US dollar provides the United States with a tremendous privilege. It costs less for US-Americans to borrow, allowing the government to fund deficits and firms to raise money that would otherwise not be possible. Put differently, the United States has to work less to retain the confidence of global investors, and the pressure to reduce government debt is lower than in economies whose currencies matter little in the international system.

As Christopher Layne puts it,

America's geopolitical preeminence hinges on the dollar's reserve currency role. If the dollar loses that status, US hegemony will literally be unaffordable. The dollar's reserve currency status has, in effect, been a very special kind of "credit card." It is special because the United States does not have to earn the money to pay its bills. Rather, when the bills come due, the United States borrows funds from abroad and/or prints money to pay them.... Without the use of the "credit card" provided by the dollar's reserve currency status, the United States would have to pay for its extravagant external and internal ambitions by raising taxes and interest rates, and by consuming less and saving more; or, tightening its belt and dramatically reducing its military and domestic expenditures.[276]

In addition, it allows Washington to wield its political influence more effectively. The United States can impose sanctions many countries are forced to follow. After all, most international banks need access to the US-American banking system, which requires a license. Therefore, banks worldwide have to accept whatever sanctions the United States imposes, as evidenced by Iran and North Korea.

Even though the Chinese government's goal is to limit US-dollar dominance and create "currency multipolarity" in the medium or long term, the internationalization of the yuan will take place in small and experimental steps, as those are less likely to generate instability or anxiety in the domestic or international economy. Giving the yuan more freedom could weaken the currency, potentially spurring capital flight. Since Beijing started pursuing its yuan internationalization, the use of the currency to settle trade with China has increased greatly. Almost 30 percent of China's global trade is now settled in yuan.

Perhaps the most important moves to internationalize the yuan are the numerous swap agreements with central banks and the Renminbi Qualified Foreign Institutional Investor (RQFII) program to liberalize capital markets. In March 2015, China named the China Construction Bank Co. its first clearing bank in Latin America and allocated 50 billion yuan ($8.1 billion) in RQFII quotas. The RQFII program, which started in late 2011, allows yuan raised offshore to be used to purchase stocks and bonds in China's onshore markets. The global outstanding RQFII quota in late 2015 reached 920 billion yuan.[277] Since 2008

China has also agreed to $500 billion in currency swaps with nearly 30 countries, including Argentina, Canada, and Pakistan.[278] In 2013, Brazil signed a three-year, $30 billion currency-swap agreement with China.

At an IMF board meeting in late 2015, the Chinese yuan joined the elite basket of currencies used to value its own de facto currency. It was the first important change to the institution's Special Drawing Rights (SDR) basket since the euro's inclusion fifteen years ago. The IMF's preconditions to be included and be recognized as a global currency is that a currency must be "widely used" and that it is "freely usable." The decision, long overdue given the size of the Chinese economy, marked a milestone in the Chinese government's efforts to increase the global role of its currency. Central banks around the world are now far more likely to add the yuan to their reserves.

As with any such momentous policy changes, decision-makers in Beijing are far from united regarding the internationalization of the yuan. State-owned enterprises and banks are generally reluctant to internationalize the Chinese currency, as the necessary liberalization would reduce their control over key decisions that affect China's export-led development model.[279] In the same way, the Ministry of Finance, the National Development and Reform Commission (NDRC), and the State Asset Supervision and Administration Commission (SASAC) are not among the move's supporters. On the other hand, liberal forces led by the People's Bank of China (PBoC) are in favor of internationalization, as this would help them push through important domestic financial and monetary reforms. That may be a dangerous strategy. As Mallaby and Wethington argue,

Only once the domestic financial system has been fortified in this manner is it safe to open the economy to foreign capital inflows, allow the exchange rate to float, and let the country's money circulate offshore. Currency internationalization should be the endpoint of reform, not the starting point.[280]

The speed of internationalization thus depends not only on China's growth trajectory but also on internal power dynamics. There are sound economic arguments that transforming the yuan into a global reserve currency could have downsides for China's economy, too: it would lead to foreigners buying and holding massive amounts of yuan, which could lead to a permanent appreciation, thus hurting Chinese exports. In addition, if the US dollar ever lost its role as an uncontested reserve currency, depreciation would almost certainly ensue, negatively affecting the value of China's dollar reserves.

It is too soon to say whether the yuan may ever be able to challenge the US dollar as the world's main reserve currency, however. The challenges China faces are formidable. Not only must the yuan be universally convertible, the country would also have to create a transparent and liquid bond market. Government intervention during market turmoil in July and August 2015 shows that China is still a long way from allowing the markets to self-regulate. In the same way, it is hard to imagine how the yuan could compete with the dollar without a more transparent legal system, which would enhance trust in the government. Injoo Sohn points to additional difficulties:

> The absence of formal alliances also seems to constrain the scope of China's political leverage to internationalize its currency. The dollar internationalization of the early postwar years was supported not only by the United States but also by key Western European allies— China does not enjoy such support as it pursues RMB internationalization.[281]

During the transition from the British pound to the US dollar in the mid-twentieth century, risks were manageable largely because both the pound and the dollar were convertible into gold at fixed rates. Policy makers in Washington and London were aligned on many broader issues concerning global order as well. Washington and Beijing, by comparison, think of their bilateral relationship more in the context of ambiguous mutual dependence and suspicion, making a frictionless transition less likely. Still, China's plan should be welcomed and encouraged: As Barry Eichengreen says, "Given the advantages of having more than one emergency lender and multiple sources of international liquidity, this can only be a good thing for the rest of the world."[282]

The desire to turn the yuan into a globally traded currency is natural for a country whose economy is about to become the world's largest. The yuan already accounts for nearly 9 percent of all trade finance deals worldwide, the second largest behind the US dollar. The Chinese currency is also the fifth most-used payments currency in the world, behind the dollar, the euro, the pound sterling, and Japan's yen. Still, the yuan is not yet close to threatening the dominance of the US dollar. Less than 3 percent of global payments involve the yuan, compared to over 40 percent that involve the US dollar.

China International Payment System (CIPS)

A key step in the creation of a parallel order is China's international payment system (CIPS) to process cross-border yuan transactions, thus greatly increasing global usage of the Chinese currency due to lower transaction costs. The existing networks made processing yuan payments relatively slow and bureaucratic, thus failing to put the Chinese currency on an equal footing with other global currencies. Cross-border yuan clearing required an offshore yuan clearing bank in London, Hong Kong, or Singapore, or with a bank in mainland China.

CIPS is, at first glance, little more than a platform to facilitate transactions, but its medium- to long-term consequences could be significant. It will allow banks and companies to move money around the globe on a "financial superhighway" delinked from US-centered dollar structures. Being excluded from the US-American system will thus no longer be as terrifying as it once was, reducing US leverage over perceived wrongdoers. In addition, no longer depending entirely on the SWIFT system will reduce Chinese concerns about spying, as the US National Security Agency (NSA) has targeted SWIFT to track international payments.

In 2015 a group of banks, among them HSBC, Citibank, and Standard Chartered, was selected to start implementing CIPS. While the initial stage only included onshore entities, CIPS will eventually enable offshore-to-onshore yuan payments and those in and out of China. Those who believe that current financial instability will keep the Chinese government from seeking to adjust global structures to its newfound economic power are thus likely to be mistaken. Even if China and the United States were to grow at similar speeds for the coming years, the need for reform would remain in place, and China's institutional representation is, considering its position as the world's second largest economy, still low in both the economic and security realm.

Even though CIPS will not challenge the globally dominant SWIFT system, it will enhance China's autonomy considerably and it may allow China to project its influence more easily than before, once being part of CIPS has become indispensable. For example, any country acting against Beijing's interests (e.g., still recognizing Taiwan) could be placed on the CIPS blacklist, just as US foreign policy has made use of sanctions in the past to promote its interests.

China UnionPay

An additional key element of the China-led emerging parallel order is China UnionPay (CUP), which seeks to complement existing global actors such as VISA and MasterCard. CUP is China's domestic bank card organization, the association for China's banking card industry and the only interbank network in the country, owned by around 85 banks. UnionPay cards can be used in more than 140 countries and regions around the world, making it the second-largest payment network by value of transactions processed after Visa. CUP is dominant in China: UnionPay is used by 80 percent of debit cards and accounted for 72 percent of total transaction value in 2014. In fact, there are almost as many UnionPay cards globally in circulation as Visa and MasterCard combined (4.5 billion cards since its founding in 2002), and UnionPay is projected to grow strongly in the coming years.[283] Mainland consumers dubbed the bank card company "China UP", having emerged as a new symbol of China's rising profile. Outside of mainland China, UnionPay issued 33 million cards as of the end of late 2014 and plans to "make a breakthrough" in the coming three years. In 2015, the Union-Pay chip card standard was introduced to the local banks as the standard of Thailand's banking industry. Thailand is the first overseas nation to adopt UnionPay standard as its local uniform chip card standard.[284] Global operators such as Visa and MasterCard, however, are now able to apply for licenses to clear domestic Chinese payments, so CUP may face increasing competition.

China's willingness to strengthen China UnionPay must also be seen as an attempt to gain greater autonomy from the West in the case of future confrontation. This became particularly obvious after the adoptions of Western sanctions against Russia in response to the annexation of Ukraine. If Moscow can be targeted, policy makers in Beijing reasoned, China could be next.

Indeed, in response to Western sanctions, when both Visa and MasterCard blocked the accounts of cardholders at Bank Rossiya and SMF Bank, Russia embraced China UnionPay.[285] As Russia Today (RT), a pro-government news outlet, wrote in late 2014, "Forget Visa and MasterCard. After the two American credit system payment companies froze accounts without notice in March, Russia has been looking for an alternative in China UnionPay."[286] China's UnionPay, RT further argues, would be a temporary solution for Russia to detach from the West while it prepares to launch its own payment system: the so-called NSPK (National Card Payment), even though it may take years before it can start operating.

Shanghai GFC (Global Finance Center)

In addition to the several institutions China has set up over the past years, China's State Council articulated in 2009 the goal to turn Shanghai into a global financial center (GFC) by 2020, rivaling London and New York, the world's only truly global financial centers. Financial centers concentrate enormous economic power, and being home to one is seen as crucial to complement Chinese efforts in the realm of trade expansion. Put differently, a global power cannot do without a global financial center. As Kawaii explains,

> A regional center can grow to function as a global financial center if it offers deep and liquid financial markets for global players—in addition to national and regional players; becomes a hub for global financial information; has a reservoir of highly educated and well-trained professionals (for investment banking, law, accounting, and information and communication technology); provides a conducive, responsive regulatory environment; and ensures economic freedom supported by unambiguous legal certainty.[287]

China's intent to turn Shanghai into a global hub is intimately tied to internationalizing the yuan, creating the China International Payment System (CIPS), and the establishment in 2013 of the Shanghai Pilot Free Trade Zone (FTZ), which is seen as the Chinese government's most innovative experiment. Initially the first free trade zone on the Chinese mainland, it has already led to three additional free trade zones: in Fujian, Guangdong, and Tianjin. It is in these zones (and primarily Shanghai) that the Chinese government is set to conduct liberal experiments, not only regarding trade, yuan convertibility, and interest-rate systems, but also regulatory issues concerning joint ventures in the financial sector. Indeed, full convertibility of the yuan would be a requirement for Shanghai to begin to rival the existing financial centers. Before that, any such talk seems far-fetched.

In 2014, the Shanghai Gold Exchange (SGE) was launched, a global trading platform in the city's pilot free trade zone, a move meant to challenge the dominance of New York and London in gold trade and pricing—considered to be of great strategic importance. China has recently turned into the world's leading importer of gold, and the SGE is the world's largest trading platform for physical gold. However, Shanghai does not yet rival London or New York in its capacity to influence gold pricing. It ranks fourth worldwide for global gold transactions, just ahead of Dubai. To increase Shanghai's attraction, foreign investors who are not legally established in China can now trade gold in the country. For China, a one-kilogram yuan-denominated gold index could be useful to favor its own consumers and protect them from other foreign-currency denominated indexes, which Beijing might argue are prone to manipulation, or favor "Western interests."[288] Shanghai is also seeking to establish pricing benchmarks for a number of other commodities, the most important of which is oil.

China's challenge is thus a complex one that involves not only setting up a clear regulatory framework but also attracting global talent from around the world, which requires turning Shanghai itself into an attractive city. Considering how low Chinese cities tend to rank in the global quality of life indexes (like virtually all urban centers in developing countries), the Chinese government may have to undertake profound reforms to generate the momentum necessary to make young talent prefer Shanghai over New York, Zurich, Singapore, or other financial centers around the world. To become more attractive, the government is considering lowering income tax for financial staff, particularly since income tax in Hong Kong is as low as 15 per cent. Considerable investments in education, such as the Advanced Institute of Finance at Shanghai Jiao Tong University, are meant to help enhance the city's still insufficient intellectual infrastructure. After all, banks still prefer Singapore and Hong Kong due to their larger talent pools, another area in which rich countries almost always beat poorer ones. If the Chinese government were ever to experiment with greater free speech, they should start in Shanghai, as censorship is unlikely to help bring international talent to the city. Anecdotal evidence suggests that most executives in finance from around the world would ask for substantial pay raises to accept a posting in mainland China, even though Shanghai offers a far more comfortable lifestyle than other cities on the Chinese mainland such as Beijing or Chongqing.

Shanghai's advantage is without a doubt its role as the financial hub of what will be the world's largest economy, even though a lot of financial power is still concentrated in Hong Kong and Beijing. That does not mean, of course, that Shanghai may rival the importance of London and New York in their entirety. Both cities have been central to the process of globalization over the past two centuries, and even if Shanghai were seriously to rival their financial capacity, they will remain cultural fixtures on a global scale for decades to come.

London's continued dominance is a case in point: despite the expansion of the US economy, adverse impacts of World War I, and the gradual decline of the British Empire and economic prowess, New York never overtook London as a global financial center.[289] This shows that a financial center can sustain its strength even though its economic hinterland (in this case, Great Britain) no longer plays a key role in the global economy. China's economic growth alone will therefore not be enough for Shanghai to replace existing global financial centers.

The idea of turning Shanghai into an international financial center is far from revolutionary. In the eyes of China, it is about reestablishing the city's key role, held as early as the 1920s and 1930s, when it was a metropolis with considerable international visibility. Yet today's ambition is not merely copying the past; policy makers in Beijing are interested in more than just hosting the world's most important stock exchange. Rather, they want Shanghai to be the place where the leading minds of the financial world gather to develop the ideas that will shape global finance for decades to come. Simply put, Shanghai's role as financial center would allow it, the Chinese government hopes, to become the world's leading agenda-setter in global finance. Considering that China will most likely be the world's largest economy by then, a decentralization of financial power and a more diverse, geographically evenly spread allocation of decision makers in the area is to be welcomed. After all, London and New York are far too homogeneous and similar to be able to act on behalf of a far more diverse global financial landscape.

Following reforms in Shanghai is important for another reason: it is likely to serve as a blueprint for the rest of China once the government feels safe enough to slowly release its grip on the country's financial system.

Universal Credit Rating Group

The idea of creating a BRICS-led rating agency has been discussed with some frequency over the past year, and the Russian government is said to be especially interested in pushing the project forward. Russian sous-sherpa[290] for BRICS Vadim Lukov repeatedly pointed out that experts from BRICS countries were discussing the creation of a new independent rating agency to counter a culture of supposedly geopolitically biased economic assessment by Western ratings agencies. Russia's interest in such an agency seems fairly obvious: international rating agency S&P recently downgraded the sovereign credit rating of Russia below the investment rate to BB + with a negative outlook. Of all the BRICS countries, Russia's economy is the most dependent on global commodity prices, and

Western sanctions further aggravate the country's economic outlook.

Indeed, the Russian government often accuses Western rating agencies of acting according to US political interests, saying that recent downgrades are meant to hurt Russia rather than provide an independent assessment. Evgeny Stanislavov, director of the Russian Foreign Ministry's Department of Economic Cooperation, argued that Western agencies' claims that Russia's economy is in a dire state are wrong and have matched "the logic of the consistent and well-orchestrated anti-Russian campaign."[291]

Some analysts in China echo this view. "They are all ideological criteria and have nothing to do with a central government's ability to generate revenues and its ability to repay debts. If one uses these standards to assess credit risks of the United States, one may come to the conclusion that the U.S. economy would never default, because they can repay their debts by printing more money. It is obvious that these criteria are unfair," said Guan Jianzhong, the president of Dagong, a Chinese rating agency. The only solution, according to the Russian government, is a BRICS-led "independent" rating agency.[292]

In 2013, with the support of the Russian and Chinese governments, the Universal Credit Rating Group (UCRG) was launched, but it has yet to release its first ratings. "In the beginning, the agency will assess Russian-Chinese investment projects with a view to attracting [investors from] a number of Asian countries," said Anton Siluanov, Russia's finance minister. "Gradually, based on the progress and authority of such an agency, we believe it will rise to a level where its opinions will attract other countries."[293]

There is no doubt that the geographic concentration of the "Big Three" (Moody's, Standard and Poor's, and Fitch) is highly problematic, and it is natural that China, being the world's second largest economy, seeks to build its own rating agency. After all, ratings issued by the Big Three to large-scale borrowers, such as governments and corporations, are enormously influential; they play a central role in determining how investors allocate billions of dollars. Their ratings indicate to buyers of debt how likely they are to be paid back.

The challenge will be to assure that UCRG has credibility and is seen as free of political influence. Only then will its ratings and reports be taken seriously by outside observers. Even though there is anecdotal evidence that Western governments put pressure on Western rating agencies, the newcomers face an uphill battle and must be particularly careful not to be seen as acting according to political interests. If, however, UCRG can establish international trust, the rise of a new player could indeed help spur reform of a system that failed to foresee the crisis in 2008, and which has not adjusted sufficiently since then.

While Russia and China were eager to win the backing of Brazil, India, and South Africa for a BRICS-led rating agency, the other BRICS countries have taken a more neutral stance. "A rating agency has to be fully independent from the standpoint of the governments. There is only some extent to which a rating agency can claim to be independent if it is sponsored by government," said Otaviano Canuto, then World Bank advisor and now Brazil's IMF representative, adding that the likelihood of creating such an agency by BRICS members is "very low."[294] The issue did not appear in the 2015 Ufa declaration, signed at the Seventh BRICS Summit in Russia, suggesting that neither Brazil, India, nor South Africa are fully convinced.

ASEAN+3 (APT)

In a sign of growing regional cooperation in Asia, ASEAN Plus Three (APT) is a forum that coordinates cooperation between the Association of Southeast Asian Nations (ASEAN) and China, Japan, and South Korea. Government leaders, ministers, and senior officials from the ten members of the ASEAN and the three Northeast Asian states consult on a growing range of issues. Created on an ad-hoc basis in 1996, leaders in Tokyo and Beijing soon pushed for institutionalization, and since the implementation of the Joint Statement on East Asia Cooperation in 1999 at the Manila Summit, APT finance ministers have been holding periodic consultations. While the Chiang Mai Initiative (CMI) is the grouping's most notable contribution, APT has since broadened cooperation beyond finance. Today, the grouping coordinates activities in the realm of security, economic and financial cooperation, trade, social policy, and development. For example, when the outbreak of Ebola in Western Africa created global tensions, APT leaders met in Bangkok to develop a common policy response for the region.[295] At the summit in 2014, China pledged to provide assistance worth $480 million, or 3 billion yuan, to ASEAN nations next year and help the regional bloc reduce poverty.

ASEAN+3 Macroeconomic Research Office (AMRO)

The ASEAN+3 Macroeconomic and Research Office (AMRO) started its operation in Singapore in May 2011. The office performs a key regional surveillance function of the $120 billion Chiang Mai Initiative Multilateralization (CMIM) currency swap facility. Three years later, member states (ASEAN, China, Japan, and Korea) established AMRO as an international organization. As the Bank of Thailand announced back then,

> The Agreement aims to enhance the effectiveness of the AMRO's function as an independent surveillance unit to monitor, assess and report macroeconomic stability and financial soundness of members. Indeed, the roles of identifying regional risks and vulnerabilities as well as providing timely policy recommendations have also been described.[296]

The AMRO is supposed to underpin regional financial stability together with a strengthened Chiang Mai Initiative

Multilateralization (CMIM). The AMRO frequently engages with the OECD and other existing institutions. The ASEAN+3 Finance Ministers declared in 2013,

> We appreciated the progress made by AMRO in cooperation with relevant International Financial Institutions (IFIs), such as frequent exchanges with the IMF and ADB on macroeconomic developments in the region, hosting joint seminars, and conducting joint studies.[297]

Even though it has no ambitions to globalize its activities at this stage or to seek members outside of the region, the AMRO is an institutional platform to conduct activities comparable to those of the OECD.

Trade and Investment

Just as in finance, there is a growing sinocentric institutional activism in the realm of trade and investment, described below. This will be particularly relevant considering the United States' attempts to strengthen its economic presence in China's neighborhood as part of its "pivot to Asia."

Regional Comprehensive Economic Partnership (RCEP)

After the United States' recent diplomatic disaster of trying to prevent general adherence to China's Asian Infrastructure Investment Bank (AIIB), US policy makers have been under pressure to strengthen their presence in Asia on the trade front by concluding the Trans-Pacific Partnership (TPP), a potentially historic trade agreement—if ratified by US Congress—linking the US, Japan, and ten other countries. China is likely to see its goal of reducing Washington's presence in its neighborhood severely thwarted. Furthermore, if ratified by all participating countries' legislatures, the TPP will connect the United States to the economic center of the twenty-first century, one of the fastest-growing regions of the world, and cement its relationship to Japan, its key ally. It would be the first real manifestation of Obama's pivot to Asia, which has so far consisted of mere rhetoric.

China, which is excluded from the countries negotiating the TPP, has responded by promoting the Regional Comprehensive Economic Partnership (RCEP), which excludes the United States, and which would promote rapprochement between Beijing and Tokyo. The tussle for regional influence between the United States and China has also taken hold of the debate about trade agreements. Like the TPP, the RCEP, whose negotiations were launched at the ASEAN Summit in Phnom Penh in November 2012, would connect a large chunk of the global economy, placing China and Japan at the center, and harmonizing trade-related rules, investment, and competition regimes. The RCEP includes a vast array of rules concerning investment, economic and technical cooperation, intellectual property, competition, dispute settlement, and government regulation. Notably, India, set to play a key economic role in Asia in the coming decades, is also part of the grouping.

Finalization of modalities include exchange of offers in goods, services, and investments, and disclosure of the number of products whose duties would be reduced to zero and goods that would not have any duty cut under the pact. While an agreement on RCEP was expected by the end of 2015, negotiations are likely to take more time, given the great number of interests involved. In the end, the prevailing deal will allow either Washington or Beijing to act as a regional agenda-setter, shaping the architecture of economic cooperation in the Southeast and East Asian regions, and helping to secure economic interests.

Still, in the realm of trade agreements, zero-sum thinking may not prevail. There are substantial differences between the two: the RCEP is an exercise in harmonizing and integrating existing FTAs between ASEAN and its individual partners, while the TPP is an attempt by the

United States and others to create a new, more ambitious twenty-first century trade agreement with much higher standards.

Free Trade Area of the Asia Pacific (FTAAP)

Similar to RCEP, the Free Trade Area of the Asia Pacific (FTAAP) is a Chinese-led alternative to the Trans-Pacific Partnership (TPP). Rather than actively opposing and undermining the TPP, Beijing is promoting alternatives. In addition to the countries included in the TPP, the FTAAP also includes China and Russia. APEC first formally started discussing the concept of a Free Trade Area of the Asia-Pacific (FTAAP) at a summit in 2006 in Hanoi. While the FTAAP was not a Chinese initiative, Xi Jinping decided to openly support it at the 2014 APEC summit. There were three reasons for this, according to the Brookings Institution's Mireya Solís:

> First, to make a big splash in defining the trade agenda by pursuing the most ambitious goal of all: an Asia Pacific trade grouping incorporating both China and the US. Second, to prevent the Trans Pacific Partnership (TPP) from becoming the focal point of economic integration efforts and a reaffirmation of America's leadership as a Pacific power. And third, for China to carve a much more proactive role in drafting the new rules of the economic order—from a position of equal standing with the United States. Potential entry into the TPP, after it enters into force, would not award China these advantages: China would have to abide by disciplines negotiated by others and would have to make significant concessions to ensure its accession.[298]

At the summit, the United States avoided any reference to a timeline for FTAAP conclusion, but China secured the launch of a collective strategic study on issues pertaining to FTAAP's realization. The FTAAP is thus not a direct contradiction or challenge to the US-promoted TPP, but rather an attempt to fend off being left out in a moment of agenda-setting and trade-related rule-making in the neighborhood. China's support for such an incipient scheme, however, was certainly meant to slow down and distract from negotiations for the TPP.

Conclusion

In 2009, Jacqueline Braveboy-Wagner predicted the increasing presence of cooperation among nations of the Global South. She writes that they have

> constructed an identity or a set of regional identities out of their common experiences, and that identity fosters cooperation and persists because of the persistence of hierarchy in the international system. Until that hierarchy changes, and until the international system and the states and other units that comprise that system become more inclusive, global south connectivity will be reflected in a growing number of south–south activities and institutions.[299]

And indeed, provided that China can continue its above-average growth trajectory, we will see the emergence of several new structures in the coming years. The BRICS are discussing the possibility of setting up their own credit rating agency, increased bilateral currency swaps, and mechanisms for enabling and settling BRICS cross-border trade in local currencies. The China International Payments System (CIPS) will be Beijing's equivalent to SWIFT, dramatically reducing the West's capacity to isolate wrongdoers financially. Western analysts routinely warn their Indian or Brazilian counterparts that they are about to be "trapped in a Chinese-dominated order."[300] That fails to take into account that countries such as Brazil and India remain firmly integrated in existing institutions such as the World Bank, the IMF, SWIFT, and all the other structures led or controlled by Western powers. Being part of both US- and Chinese-led institutions is likely to provide

Brasília, Delhi, and others with flexibility and room for maneuver and may help them increase their bargaining power in existing structures.

The majority of both this and the next chapter on the emerging parallel order is not forward looking, but analyzes existing structures: in several regions of the world, such as in parts of Africa, Latin America, and Central Asia, China-led structures are already at work, thus enhancing their impact (for example, in the fields of infrastructure, investment, and currency swaps). While it is difficult to imagine how the Boao Forum for Asia (described in the next chapter) will ever become more influential than the yearly World Economic Forum (WEF) in Davos, China is likely to be more successful when it comes to offering tangible benefits, such as easy credit to finance infrastructure, a proposition particularly attractive in the Global South.

This analysis did not seek to reduce the "non-West" (or the "rest") to China. As mentioned earlier, no country can represent the "rest," and many developing countries are worried about China's growing influence. Rather, this analysis largely focuses on China because it is the only non-Western power with a concrete global project—contrasting with the other BRICS countries, which harbor global ambitions but lack the diplomatic and economic clout to implement them. The analysis in this chapter also makes it clear that several institutional projects are in their early infancy and far from operational, which makes it difficult to assess their impact on international order as a whole. The BRICS Development Bank has yet to lend money to its first project, and the BRICS Contingency Reserve Agreement and the Chiang Mai Initiative Multilateralization (CMIM) are embedded within the IMF system. Closely observing the multitude of initiatives described here will be crucial to properly assess their impact.

− 5 −

Toward a Parallel Order: Security, Diplomacy, and Infrastructure

The last chapter analyzed new initiatives in the realm of finance, trade, and investment. This one will focus on the parallel order in the realms of security, diplomacy, and infrastructure, three areas that will be profoundly affected on a global scale by non-Western institutional entrepreneurship. It will be in the areas described here that the impact will be most visible to the global public eye, and activities such as the construction of the Nicaragua Canal and the Trans-Amazonian Railway, and massive Chinese investments along the "Silk Road," will undoubtedly strengthen those who argue that China is acting according to a plan to replace the United States as the world's global hegemon.[301] Rather than analyzing recent initiatives such as the BRICS grouping or the Shanghai Cooperation Organization (SCO) through the lens of a "West vs. rest" dichotomy that implies zero-sum thinking, however, it is necessary to objectively analyze each initiative's potential benefits. This perspective will allow us to appreciate not only the motivations behind each undertaking but also what the best policy response should be. Should Western countries be supportive, for instance, or should existing institutions be made more open to rising powers, to reduce the incentive to advance with the creation of the parallel order?

Early evidence suggests that many of the new initiatives may produce considerable benefits for both established powers and developing countries, even though most initiatives are incipient and it is far from clear whether all projects can be successfully implemented. For example, the New Silk Road covers an area that is home to about 70 percent of the global population, produces about 55 percent of the world's GDP, and has about 75 percent of known energy reserves. The initiative demands effective collaboration between forty governments located along both the land- and sea-based silk route.[302] This points to cooperation in many other areas, ranging from reducing trade barriers (including bureaucratic hurdles such as non-standardized clearance processes), fighting international crime, to maritime security. In the same way, the creation of the Trans-Amazonian Railroad has the potential to dramatically enhance the integration of South America into the global economy, a region that has traditionally suffered from poor infrastructure links. If implemented as planned, this will not only benefit trade ties between China and South America, but also facilitate economic links with other regions, including Europe and the United States.

Most important, perhaps, the emergence of parallel structures will provide additional platforms for cooperation (among both non-Western and between non-Western and Western powers), and spread the burden of contributing global public goods more evenly. That is not only true regarding infrastructure projects, but also regarding institutions that will help broaden the global conversation, be it during one of the countless new BRICS-related formats, or during the Boao Forum, designed to allow China to engage in global agenda-setting.

Finally, those afraid of irresponsible and unpredictable rising powers should in particular welcome and encourage the rise of the parallel order. Even though Beijing will be careful to design new institutions to its advantage, they will still force China to agree to a specific set of governance rules, which must make its behavior far more predictable than it is in the context of bilateral engagement. All these institutions will deepen China's integration into the global economy, possibly reducing the risk for conflict, and lifting all boats.

Security

Often overlooked by analysts studying non-Western powers' institutional entrepreneurship, the emerging parallel order also includes a security component.

Conference on Interaction and Confidence Building Measures in Asia (CICA)

CICA is often mentioned in the context of Chinese institutional entrepreneurship. What is often forgotten, however, is that CICA is not a new institution, nor was it invented by China. The idea was launched by Kazakhstan's President Nursultan Nazarbayev during the 1992 UN General Assembly, yet it took almost a decade (and the terrorist attacks of September 11) for CICA to convene a meeting for the first time. Since then, the grouping has met every two years. In 2014 Xi Jinping used the summit in Shanghai as a platform to articulate his broader vision, entitled "United and Harmonious Asian Countries Move Together Toward the Future." The encounter was marked by the highest attendance of heads of state and government since the institution's creation. In a direct reference to the United States' presence in the region, the Chinese president called for the creation of a "new security architecture" and argued that "Asian problems should be solved by Asian people"— a phrase that has been criticized by commentators, given its reminiscence to Japanese attempts to rule the region in the 1930s.[303] Xi's insistence that "No matter how strong China gets, it will never become a hegemon" is not yet fully convincing to all countries in the region.[304]

It is thus not entirely wrong to cite CICA in the context of China's growing institutional activism, largely because Xi Jinping has revived CICA and given it a new significance as one of Asia's main platforms for regional security affairs: a move that can be interpreted as a response to the United States' pivot to Asia. Yet beyond limiting US influence in Asia, Beijing regards CICA as a useful mechanism to convince its neighbors that China's rise will benefit the region as a whole. In this sense, it complements other regional projects such as the Asian Infrastructure Investment Bank (AIIB) and the Silk Road Fund, all of which are meant to boost regional support for Chinese leadership.

The key question will be whether smaller Asian countries would trust a security framework led by China (and, to a lesser degree, Russia) rather than the United States. CICA will hardly convince policy makers in Tokyo, Seoul, and beyond to abandon decades-old security alliances with the United States anytime soon. Japan, Indonesia, Australia, the Philippines, Myanmar, and Malaysia are not part of CICA to begin with, and it will require a long and arduous diplomatic effort by Beijing to convince them to join. Beijing's goal is certainly not to push the United States out of the region immediately. Any overtly aggressive move toward that aim would achieve the opposite. China will, however, seek to prepare the ground so that, should the United States one day no longer be able or willing to sustain its role in Asia, Beijing will be able to step in.

Several analysts have pointed out that CICA is mere symbolism, as issues such as terrorism are sufficiently covered by existing regional institutions such as the Shanghai Cooperation Organization (SCO). They overlook the subtlety of Beijing's strategy: creating a host of organizations that, in their entirety, strengthen regional socialization and slowly reduce resistance to Chinese activism among Asia's policy making elites. That partly explains why China has chosen to focus on topics such as antiterrorism and infrastructure: issues all countries in the region can easily agree on.

Shanghai Cooperation Organization (SCO)

Compared to CICA and the BRICS' National Security Advisors' meetings, the Shanghai Cooperation Organization (SCO) is the oldest and most institutionalized non-Western security grouping (even though it also discusses economic issues), despite the fact that it calls itself merely a "partnership" and not an alliance. The SCO was founded in 2001 in Shanghai by the leaders of China, Kazakhstan, Kyrgyzstan, Russia, Tajikistan, and Uzbekistan. With the exception of Uzbekistan, these countries had been members of the so-called Shanghai Five, founded in 1996 and renamed after the inclusion of Uzbekistan.

The organization has often been understood in the context of defending autocracy and limiting US influence in the region, and in 2005 the group called on Washington to set a timeline for the removal of its military bases in Central Asia. Russia's Foreign Minister Sergey Lavrov has argued that the SCO is a key element of a new "polycentric world order."[305] At the Dushanbe summit in 2000, members agreed to "oppose intervention in other countries' internal affairs on the pretexts of 'humanitarianism' and 'protecting human rights;' and support the efforts of one another in safeguarding the five countries' national independence, sovereignty, territorial integrity, and social stability."[306]

During summits, discussions usually revolve around Central Asian security-related concerns, with terrorism, separatism, and extremism regarded as the main threats to confront. Policy responses are sought in the realm of military cooperation, intelligence sharing, and counterterrorism. Regular military exercises have been held since 2003. In 2014, China hosted the SCO's largest-ever series of military drills, which included China and Russia conducting joint naval exercises in the Mediterranean.

The Shanghai Cooperation Organization is in the midst of a broad transformation; it has started dealing with economic issues, including the potential creation of an SCO development bank. Other new issues concern infrastructure, transnational border and water disputes, and cultural exchange programs. Russia has also proposed linking the Eurasian Economic Union (EEU), which consists of Armenia, Kazakhstan, Belarus, and Russia with China's Silk Road Economic Belt. All these topics will play a decisive role in the geopolitical future of Eurasia, a region that is regaining its importance as Russia partly turns its back on the West and China as it articulates its strategy to strengthen its presence in Central Asia and beyond.

In July 2015, the SCO decided to admit India and Pakistan as full members. Now, all of the key players in China's One Belt, One Road (OBOR) strategy are part of the organization, making it an ideal negotiating platform for Beijing's regional investment plans. As sanctions on Iran are being lifted, the country's accession seems only a question of time. From a geopolitical point of view, the organization's significance (though still largely symbolic) is thus seen as a potential counterweight to Western security institutions, primarily NATO. Yet contrary to what some would expect, the SCO will not rival or balance NATO frontally. Rather, it provides an alternative platform that will seek to play an increasingly important role in the agenda-setting process of geopolitical issues that affect Asia: from terrorism emanating from Afghanistan and instability in Central Asia to China's attempts to finance the region's physical integration.

Also, like so many of the institutions that may make up the parallel order, their mere existence reduces the West's capacity to diplomatically isolate countries that it believes do not play by the rules. Russia may not always get what it wants in the SCO—particularly now that India has joined the grouping—but its membership increases its legitimacy and reduces its dependence on Western partners (even though it cannot compensate for the economic losses generated by the sanctions).

The biggest winner from the SCO's expansion and growing importance, however, is Beijing. The SCO allows Chinese economic might to project itself in a more institutionalized manner and gain a platform to articulate its ambition to play a more visible role in the region. India's accession allows China to promote the Silk Road Economic Belt, China-Pakistan Economic Corridor (CPEC), Bangladesh-China-India-Myanmar (BCIM) Corridor, and Central Asia–China Gas Pipeline to policy makers in Delhi, who regard China's growing presence in the region with suspicion. The question of whether China still prioritizes SCO in this context is secondary: rather, it will provide Beijing with additional autonomy and yet another option for forum shopping.

BRICS' National Security Advisors (NSA) meeting

The BRICS grouping's origins may be economic, and the topics of its earliest meetings were global financial governance, but in May 2009, National Security Advisors (NSAs) of the BRICS met for the first time. Additional meetings followed, and now take place on a yearly basis. In Delhi in early 2013, national security advisors from Brazil, Russia, India, China, and South Africa discussed the issues of terrorism, cybersecurity, and piracy, as well as the conflicts in Syria, Libya, and Mali. While Russia and India are both experienced in combating terrorism, Brazil began to focus on the issue as it prepared for the World Cup in 2014 and the Olympics in 2016. Reflecting on the issues of cybersecurity (in the wake of the US spying revelations), a meeting in Cape Town in late 2013 agreed on the establishment of an expert working group to finalize a concrete set of proposals for adoption by the leaders' summit.[307] In addition, participants decided to strengthen cooperation on transport security, including antipiracy initiatives dealing with knowledge-sharing and capacity-building with states in piracy-affected areas.[308] Expectations that the BRICS would seek to articulate an actual security architecture over the coming years are premature and unrealistic. Rather, the meetings were seen as useful opportunities to undertake mutual consultation and identify areas of common concern.

Diplomacy

Efforts by emerging powers to enhance diplomatic ties have produced notable results over the past decade, yet they often remain misunderstood, as described below.

BRICS Leaders Summit

Since the first BRICS' Leaders Summit, the grouping has been through a notable process of institutionalization, generating ample opportunities but also global expectations, making it easier to judge the grouping's performance and capacity to address global challenges. The yearly leaders summits remain the grouping's most visible structure, and they can best be understood as a platform comparable to the G7 (or G8, prior to Russia's exclusion).

The rise of the BRICS grouping is directly related to the G7's incapacity to adapt to a new, more multipolar reality. For years, the continued centrality of the G7, which included Canada and Italy but not China and India, generated growing discontent among policy makers in Brasília, Beijing, and New Delhi. During the G8 summit in Gleneagles in 2005, therefore, Tony Blair decided to initiate a G8 + 5 "outreach" process, but failed to integrate any of the emerging powers permanently. Maria Edileuza Reis, Brazil's Sherpa at several BRICS summits, points out that at the time emerging powers were merely invited to "be informed" by the group's core, rather than to actively participate in the debates.[309] The same applied to the lack of reform among the Bretton Woods institutions. As *The*

Economist pointed out in 2006, "It is absurd that Brazil, China and India have 20 percent less clout within the fund than the Netherlands, Belgium and Italy, although the emerging economies are four times the size of the European ones, once you adjust for currency differences."[310]

The BRICS grouping has come closest to creating something similar to the G8. During a bilateral meeting in Rio de Janeiro, Russian President Dmitry Medvedev and Brazil's Luiz Inácio Lula da Silva announced that the heads of state of the BRICs countries would hold their first-ever summit in Russia in 2009. After the meeting, Brazil's President Lula argued that the financial crisis offered opportunities for emerging powers to strengthen cooperation among themselves, and their position in global affairs as a whole.[311] According to a Brazilian policy maker, "cooperation in the field of international finance would generate trust between the BRICs' governments, allowing for broader cooperation further down the road."[312] Soon after that, Brazil, India, Russia, and China's heads of state and government began to refer to themselves as "BRIC members" and agreed that they needed to strengthen "intra-BRIC" ties.[313] According to policy makers involved in the process, the frequent meetings improved government-to-government relations and helped national interests during the economic crisis.

A recent study by the University of Toronto shows that the BRICS achieved 70 percent compliance with the Fortaleza Summit Commitments made in 2014, continuing its high rate of compliance from previous summits. The authors conclude that "the BRICS countries complied well with the development commitments at the core of their agenda (with an average of +0.60 or 80 percent over all four summits)" but also point out that performance on trade issues is uneven, with an overall average of +0.10 (55 percent).[314] That shows that the final summit declarations are more than just empty statements.

While initially seen as a quirky platform of little significance, it is now taken more seriously than at any point since its transformation into a more political outfit, a process that began in 2006, when the BRICS foreign ministers met in New York for the first time. In addition to the creation of the BRICS-led New Development Bank, the BRICS grouping has made its mark in the realm of geopolitics. The most powerful example is the BRICS' declaration at the sidelines of the Nuclear Security Summit in The Hague in March 2014, when the BRICS' foreign ministers opposed restrictions on the participation of Russian President Vladimir Putin at the G-20 Summit in Australia in November 2014. This step was primarily symbolic, as Australia had no Western backing for excluding Russia. However, it effectively undermined the West's momentum attempting to isolate Russia, thus lending the BRICS grouping, for the first time, a tangible role in a global security matter (as opposed to economic issues such as IMF reform). Despite not being discussed in depth in the international media at the time, policy makers in the West rightly interpreted the move as a potentially far-reaching precedent: The BRICS' option to speak in unison and challenge the West's agenda-setting capacity was no longer a theoretical consideration, with potentially profound consequences for the West's capacity to punish perceived wrongdoers, and thus for Western-led global order as a whole. No such scenario would have been thinkable only fifteen years ago, at the perceived height of US global dominance. In that sense, the yearly BRICS grouping has generated a crucial platform for member states to engage in global agenda setting, and opine on a broad number of issues.

BRICS and IBSA working groups and other structures

The majority of assessments of the BRICS and IBSA groupings are superficial, focusing only on their capacity to align their positions regarding geopolitical matters and to reform global governance structures (what may be called growth toward the outside).[315] Whenever BRICS and IBSA leaders come together for the summits, analysts from around the world will briefly analyze the dynamics at the meeting and the summit declaration, and then offer their view on the future of the grouping.[316] Very little is known about the degree of technical intra-BRICS and intra-IBSA cooperation ("growth towards the inside"), however, which (as many diplomats from member countries pointed out during the interviews) generates a considerable part of the benefits of both groupings.[317] Since the first IBSA Summit in 2003 and the first BRICS Leaders Summit in 2009, cooperation has taken place in areas ranging from public health, trade facilitation, agriculture, statistics, cooperatives, academia, and business fora to issues of competition, the judiciary, and defense, as specified below.[318]

Merely organizing a never-ending string of meetings will not create sustainable cooperation, skeptics will argue. That is true, and the outcome of several of the gatherings may not have the desired impact. When asked to what extent the BRICS could cooperate, Roberto Jaguaribe, Brazil's Sherpa to the 2009 and 2010 BRICS Summits, enigmatically responded, "The BRICS forum is not a normative forum, not a forum for negotiations, but a forum for convergence."[319] Only time will tell how much real cooperation these meetings can generate—and several diplomats privately express doubts about whether frequent minister-level cooperation in so many areas is sustainable in the long term. Indeed, there is some evidence that the number of meetings has decreased somewhat after a peak in 2011–13. At the same time, the meetings do show that intra-BRICS cooperation is indeed taking place in many different areas. Those who criticize the BRICS concepts can no longer merely take a quick glance at the yearly leaders' summits; rather, intra-BRICS cooperation has over the past years grown far too complex to be easily dismissed.

The Seventh BRICS Summit's Ufa Declaration includes a long list of new initiatives, ranging from the creation of a platform of joint discussion for trade cooperation among BRICS countries through enhanced dialogue among the

Table 5.1 Intra-BRICS Cooperation, Main Areas

Themes	First Meeting	Frequency of Meetings
Academia	May, 2009 (BRICS Academic Forum, BRICS Think Tank Council)	Yearly Meetings
Agriculture	March 26, 2010 (BRICS Agriculture Ministers' Meeting)	Ministerial Meetings in 2010, 2012 and 2013, 2015
Business	April 15, 2010 (BRICS Business Forum, BRICS Business Council)	Yearly Meetings
Competition Forum	September 01, 2009 (BRICS International Competition Conference)	Meetings in 2009, 2011, 2013, and 2015
Cooperatives Forum	April 16, 2010 (BRICS Cooperatives' Meeting)	Yearly Meetings
Development Banks	October 12, 2010 (BRICS National Development Banks Meeting / The BRICS interbank cooperation mechanism)	Yearly Presidential Meetings
Finance and Central Banks	November 07, 2008 (BRICS Finance Ministers and Central Bank Governors' Meeting)	Yearly Ministerial Meetings
Health	July 11, 2011 (BRICS Health Ministers' First meeting)	Yearly Ministerial Meetings
Judiciary	March 12, 2010 (Exchange Program for Magistrates and Judge of BRICS countries)	Meeting in 2010
National Security	May 30, 2009 (BRICS National Security Advisors' Meeting)	Yearly Meetings
Science & Technology	September 15, 2011 (BRICS Science & Technology Senior Ministers Meeting)	Yearly Meetings
Statistics	January 21, 2011 (BRICS National Statistical Authorities' Meeting)	Yearly Meetings
Subnational government	December 03, 2011 (BRICS Friendship Cities and Local Governments Cooperation Forum)	Meetings in 2011 and 2013
Tax administration	January 18, 2013 (BRICS Heads of Revenue Meeting)	Yearly BRICS Tax Conferences
Trade	April 13, 2011 (BRICS Trade Ministers' Meeting)	Yearly Ministerial Meetings

BRICS Export Credit Agencies; stronger cooperation in the area of e-commerce; as well as a commitment to enhance existing areas of cooperation such as tax administration, energy, agriculture, science, technology, and public health: issues that are specified in more detail in the Ufa Action Plan.[320] Finally, the BRICS will explore the possibility of developing a BRICS website "as a virtual secretariat—a move that may help observers understand the scope of intra-BRICS cooperation better."

Boao Forum for Asia (BFA)

Every year in March, the Boao Forum for Asia (BFA) welcomes policy makers, business leaders, and journalists from around the world to Hainan Province. Modeled on the World Economic Forum (WEF) in Davos, the first BFA meeting took place in 2002. The annual event has since then become a key element of China's global public diplomacy strategy (it began as a joint project with other countries, but is now largely controlled by the Chinese government). Contrary to the many other Chinese initiatives that focus on finance and development, the Boao Forum for Asia falls into the soft power category of China's global strategy.

The Chinese political leadership clearly regards the event as a pillar of the country's foreign policy. The BFA's Secretary General is Long Yongtu, who negotiated China's entrance into the World Trade Organization (WTO). As in 2013, Xi Jinping gave the keynote address of the 2015 edition of the event, themed "Asia's New Future: Toward a Community of Common Destiny."[321] Among the participants have been not only political leaders from the region (more than ten heads of government and state participated in 2015) but also business leaders such as Bill Gates, George Soros, and Ratan Tata, who is a member of the BFA's board. In 2014, an additional regional BFA took place in Dubai, regarded as a strategic hub for Chinese investors.

While the BFA's official focus is to strengthen economic integration in the region (involving numerous working groups and sector-specific discussions on the sidelines of the summit), the forum's scope has recently expanded, and today helps China set the agenda of the discussions in the region. Two years ago, the BFA began discussing Asia–US relations and food security, both of great importance to China. In 2014, debates included topics such as cyberspace and the role of the United States in the Asia-Pacific region.

RT, a Russian state-funded television network, has somewhat triumphantly claimed that the BFA was on its way to rival the yearly Davos convention.[322] Yet critics are right to point out that the Boao Forum for Asia still has a long way to go before it can challenge the World Economic Forum (WEF). Contrary to the discussions in the Swiss ski resort, civil society is largely absent from the Chinese tropical island, as are discussions about human rights.

Rather than rivaling Davos, Chinese policy makers' strategy, for now, is more modest but no less astute: by hosting a vibrant regional event, it can continuously strengthen its "framing power": its capacity to frame the debate and redefine ideas and concepts in ways that serve its national interest. That may involve subtle strategies such as omitting a certain topic and promoting another, or convincing neighboring countries to use the BFA to discuss a specific issue and not other platforms that involve the United States, such as the Asia-Pacific Economic Cooperation (APEC). These details may seem insignificant at first, but they are certain to enhance China's capacity to shape discussions in its own favor in the long term, just as the United States shrewdly decides to discuss issues in forums where it possesses the greatest leverage.

For example, in 2012, the West essentially succeeded in stopping the United Nations Conference on Trade and Development (UNCTAD)—dominated by developing countries—from further analyzing the global financial crisis. As a senior US delegate declared in one of the last negotiating sessions in Doha, "We don't want UNCTAD providing intellectual competition with the IMF and the World Bank."[323] In effect, the West said, "We do not want UNCTAD to discuss any of these issues, because UNCTAD is not competent to do so. They are for the G20 and IMF."

The Boao Forum for Asia is thus a notable element of China's broader effort to engage internationally and slowly increase its autonomy on the global stage. Over the coming years, the BFA's list of participants will be a useful way to measure China's regional convening power, an important factor in a region that generally remains suspicious of Beijing's ambitions.

Infrastructure

It is perhaps in the realm of infrastructure that the emergence of a parallel order will be most visible to citizens around the world, as shown in the three examples below.

Silk Road Fund / One Road–One Belt (OBOR)

Since taking office in 2014, one of President Xi Jinping's foreign-policy priorities has been the revival of China's links to the rest of the Eurasian continent through the construction of so-called "silk roads," an allusion to the term coined in 1877 by the Prussian geographer Ferdinand von Richthofen to describe the trading routes linking China with the Mediterranean West during the Han and Tang dynasties. As Valeria Hansen, professor of Chinese history at Yale University, observes, "It is one of the few terms that people remember from history classes that does not involve hard power...and it's precisely those positive associations that the Chinese want to emphasize."[324] An additional and increasingly common shorthand for his vision is "One Belt, One Road," referred to in the Chinese

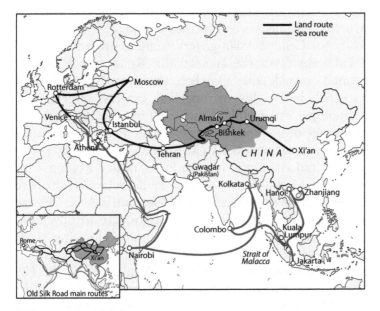

Map 5.1 The New Silk Road

media simply as "OBOR." It alludes to overland "economic belts" and "maritime roads" that reach all the way to Europe.

Xi's OBOR initiative serves a dual purpose. Domestically, he hopes that better transport links will promote growth in underdeveloped central and western regions such as Xinjiang, Gansu Province, Ningxia, Guangxi, and Yunnan Province. That would not only boost overall GDP but also reduce regional economic inequality, and thus migration into the coastal areas, a trend that may contribute to social tension. An economic boom in Xinjiang is also seen as the best way to combat the rise of Islamic extremism in the region.

From a foreign-policy perspective, the most immediate goal of the OBOR initiative is to boost China's influence in Central Asia, a resource-rich region that no longer falls into Moscow's orbit. As growing numbers of countries become dependent on Chinese transport and energy infrastructure, stronger economic ties will make it increasingly costly for Central Asian governments to oppose China.

Different from the ancient Silk Road, which mainly focused on trade, the "One Belt, One Road" project could also include the flow of financial services, information, technology, and people. China will involve its neighbors in a series of institutional setups such as the Asian Infrastructure Investment Bank (AIIB), the CICA security architecture, and corridors through Pakistan and Myanmar to the Indian Ocean that may, in the medium term, contribute to the creation of an increasingly sinocentric Asia. Chinese initiatives not only focus on infrastructure to physically connect countries involved, but also to explore free trade agreements.

China's dream of a sinocentric Asia predates Xi. The first direct train to Duisburg in Germany left Chongqing in 2011. Now, train connections are more frequent and have dramatically reduced transport times, but their economic impact will be limited to expensive goods. While trains now take a mere three weeks between China and Europe, they can only carry several hundred containers. A large ship, by contrast, can carry several thousand containers at a third of the cost. Bureaucratic hurdles at border crossings and different track standards further complicate train transports, even though China hopes to reduce such difficulties. In addition to the "economic belt," Xi Jinping therefore envisages a "maritime road" from China's Quanzhou in Fujian province to Europe, via the Malacca Strait, Kuala Lumpur, Sri Lanka, Nairobi, and Djibouti. A map of the envisioned Silk Road published by Xinhua depicts two routes: one through Kazakhstan, Kyrgyzstan, and Iran en route to Austria; and a maritime route from China to Antwerp in Belgium. While the latter is set to benefit China's eastern coastal regions, the land routes are also seen as a tool to enhance economic development in the poorer, landlocked western provinces of China.

Given how expensive and durable the construction of train and road links is, Xi's large-scale investments in the region may tie neighbors into a sinocentric Asia for decades, significantly reducing their governments' capacity or incentives to oppose China. As Kerry Brown, Director of the China Studies Centre at the University of Sydney, has recently argued, "There are obligations being created here, dependencies and commitments, that many who are included in the Silk Road idea might need to seriously consider."[325]

Western analysts often point out that China is likely to encounter strong resistance to its plan to strengthen connectivity both on land and sea. Among others, resurgent Russia and a more ambitious India are supposedly eager to block Beijing's schemes. While such a possibility indeed exists, Chinese roads and ports are more likely to be welcomed with open arms by those who rightly see them as a chance to boost economic development. Considering that China is the world's second largest economy and main trading partner of many countries around the world, anti-China sentiment is still remarkably limited. As long as China assures that others interpret OBOR as a win–win situation, China's pivot to Eurasia will cement, not undermine, China's regional leadership claims. The Fund is nothing less than the first step toward a regional system of mutually beneficial political and economic relations with China at the center.

Of course, one should not forget that lower rates of economic growth will limit China's capacity to make unprofitable investments based on political calculations. The more Chinese investments grow in politically unstable countries, the more Beijing's resolve not to get entangled in international affairs will be tested. For example, while US troops still protect a Chinese-run copper mine in Afghanistan, and Pakistani troops are stationed around large-scale projects in zones thought to be unsafe, such arrangements will one day require Chinese security components, that is, Chinese troops stationed on foreign soil. It thus may be no coincidence that a Chinese draft antiterror law legalizes posting Chinese soldiers abroad, with consent of the host nation.[326] In addition to the economic benefits, OBOR may be designed to slowly increase China's military presence in its neighborhood, as is the construction of ports that may be used for military purposes (such as in Myanmar, Pakistan, Sri Lanka, and Bangladesh): a strategy informally referred to as a "string of pearls." A key question will be how China avoids the pitfalls other great powers have faced when seeking a stronger influence in politically unstable countries, particularly in Central Asia. China's growing presence in Eurasia may increase tensions with Moscow, which may interpret Beijing's plans as an intrusion into its traditional backyard.

Implementing such a large project remains a massive challenge, and it is too early to assess its medium- to long-term consequences.

Nicaragua Canal

Construction of the so-called Grand Interoceanic Canal (usually called the Nicaragua Canal), began in early 2015. If completed, the canal would be the largest civil-engineering and construction project in the history of mankind, spanning 276 kilometers across the Central American nation.

The idea of building a canal in Nicaragua is not new. In a letter to Spain's King Carlos V, Hernán Cortés wrote, "Whoever possesses the passage between the two oceans can consider himself the owner of the world."[327] In the same way, Napoleon argued that Nicaragua could become "better than Constantinople, the necessary route of the great commerce of the world."[328] As Jon Lee Anderson writes, Cornelius Vanderbilt, a US tycoon, took a strong interest in the project:

> Soon, the United States took up the idea of a canal, and U.S. Congress began trying to decide whether to build it

in Panama or Nicaragua. In 1901, the Nicaraguan government gave the U.S. government exclusive rights to build a canal there. But before the issue went to a vote the chief of the powerful pro-Panama lobby mailed each U.S. senator a one-centavo Nicaraguan postage stamp, featuring an image of Lake Managua, luridly illuminated by an exploding volcano. Panama, which had no volcanoes in the canal zone, won by a margin of eight votes.[329]

Complete humiliation for Nicaragua would follow in 1914, when, in exchange for $3 million, Nicaragua's President Emiliano Chamorro granted the US government the exclusive right to build a Nicaraguan canal. The agreement essentially prevented Nicaragua from building a canal to compete with the Panama Canal. The treaty was only abolished in the 1970s. Since then, Nicaraguan leaders have dreamed of turning the canal into a reality, partly in the hope that it would promote development in the second-poorest country in the Western Hemisphere.

It would take the previously unknown businessman Wang Jing, with likely approval and support of the Chinese government, to revive the project. Wang's Hong Kong-listed company HKND now holds a 100-year-long concession over the canal's operation. The cost of the construction is officially estimated at forty billion dollars, even though experts believe the total cost will be closer to one hundred billion dollars. Even the feasibility studies conducted so far have cost several hundred million dollars, indicating Wang's confidence. Wang has hired the China Railroad Construction Corporation, a company that has overseen the construction of the Three Gorges Dam in China.

The project's financial viability is questionable, and its environmental consequences could be disastrous. The Nicaragua Canal could accommodate ships capable of carrying up to 25,000 containers, which may increasingly be the norm, thus successfully competing with the Panama Canal, which can only accommodate ships carrying 13,000 containers. Competition would reduce shipping prices and boost trade.

Yet China's objectives are more likely to be geopolitical. HKND is exempt from local taxes and commercial regulations, and has been granted hiring and land-expropriating powers. Along with the concession to build the canal, Wang now holds the rights to build large seaports on both coasts, new airports, railroads, and highways. He has also won contracts to build a new telecommunications network. The plan also includes a free trade zone. Notably, a recently approved reform overturned a constitutional stricture against foreign soldiers being garrisoned in Nicaragua, in theory paving the way for a Chinese military base—even though such a step seems extremely unlikely in the short or medium term, as Beijing has no interest in openly challenging the United States.

Considering that it is not officially behind the project, and that the upfront cost was relatively small, the Chinese government could still step back from the project if political or logistical problems arise. It would thus be premature to regard the Nicaragua Canal project as part of a global version of the "string of pearls", the network of Chinese military and commercial facilities in the Indian Ocean.

Yet if Wang succeeds in building the canal, the geopolitical consequences for the region would be significant. The project will employ at least fifty thousand workers, many of whom will be Chinese. At a recent OAS Summit, US Secretary of State John Kerry famously told the region's leaders that the era of the Monroe Doctrine was over. And indeed, the US government has not commented much on China's plans in Nicaragua, beyond asking for more transparency. The creation of a massive Chinese footprint in Latin America, however, would still alter regional dynamics far more than any of the previous partnerships China has set up with governments in the region.

Trans-Amazonian Railway

Compared to the Nicaragua Canal, the Trans-Pacific Railroad, set to cross South America and connect the Atlantic to the Pacific Ocean, is relatively cheap. The 5,300 kilometer rail connection, if ever built, is expected to cost $10 billion (though the cost may increase once the feasibility studies have been completed). Environmental studies from the Brazilian Institute of Environment and Renewable Natural Resources (IBAMA) won't be complete until 2017.

In addition to comparable projects at home, China is experienced with large-scale infrastructure projects abroad. In the 1970s, it financed the Tanzam Railway, which links the port of Dar es Salaam in Tanzania with the town of Kapiri Mposhi in Zambia's Central Province. At a price of $500 million, the project was completed ahead of schedule, and remains one of the largest single foreign-aid projects undertaken by China.

Yet unlike China and Tanzania, Brazil and Peru are home to one of the world's most organized civil societies, and environmental NGOs have already started voicing their concern about the project's potential negative impact on the Amazon rainforest and indigenous tribes living in the region. The Trans-Amazonian highway, built in the 1970s, accelerated the destruction of the forest as it provided illegal loggers with easy access to previously isolated regions. After all, 95 percent of deforestation in the Amazon occurs within five kilometers of a road.[330]

The second challenge is logistical: in addition to passing through dense forest, the route crosses swamps and steep mountains before reaching the Pacific coast. Finally, the border region between Peru, Bolivia, and Brazil is notorious for drug trafficking and lawlessness.

The third obstacle is Brazil's bureaucracy, which makes the implementation of complex infrastructure projects more expensive, often prolonging time to completion. Chinese investors often end up canceling projects in Brazil after realizing that bureaucratic hurdles are greater than at home in China. This is particularly so whenever several countries' governments in the region are involved.

Still, the project, much commented on by Chinese premier Li Keqiang during his visits to Brazil and Peru in May 2015, would dramatically reduce the transport cost of Brazilian soy and iron ore to China. While the demand for iron ore is slowing, China's demand for beef is set to increase in the coming years and Beijing has recently lifted a ban on Brazilian beef. For Brazil's commodity-dependent and uncompetitive economy, it would come as a boon, giving Brazilian businesses a port on the Pacific, bypassing the Panama Canal. In addition, it would provide Brazil with easier access to Peru and other markets along the Pacific coast.

The China Development Bank may finance the project, with construction done by local firms but led by the China International Water and Electric Corporation. For Beijing, using local firms is likely to help compensate for the crisis that affects many construction firms at home. From a Chinese perspective, both the Nicaragua Canal and Trans-Pacific Railroad serve a similar purpose, which may suggest that China pursues both projects as part of a hedging strategy, aware of the risks both undertakings entail.

The bad news is that the Brazilian government has traditionally cared little about the environment. Yet some analysts have argued that the route can be built by following existing roads and passing through land that has largely been cultivated already.[331] Provided that nongovernmental organizations can keep up the pressure to assure that environmental damage will be kept at a minimum, the Amazonian Railway is a tremendous opportunity to physically integrate the region and connect Brazil to the world's economic center of the twenty-first century.

Conclusion

Will China seek to oppose and overturn the existing order or will it integrate? Princeton's John Ikenberry, a prominent liberal internationalist, has often asked this question in recent years.[332] Hundreds of policy-minded scholars have followed his lead and seek to assess which way China will go as it turns into the world's leading economy, ending three centuries of Western global dominance. Ikenberry argues that China can be integrated into today's order, which he famously calls "easy to join and hard to overturn." He writes,

> Even if China and Russia do attempt to contest the basic terms of the current global order, the adventure will be daunting and self-defeating. These powers aren't just up against the United States; they would also have to contend with the most globally organized and deeply entrenched order the world has ever seen, one that is dominated by states that are liberal, capitalist, and democratic. This order is backed by a U.S.-led network of alliances, institutions, geopolitical bargains, client states, and democratic partnerships.[333]

John Mearsheimer, by contrast, predicts that China's rise will be disruptive and will show little inclination to maintain the structures set up by the United States.[334] Rising powers could create a parallel system with, as Barma, Ratner, and Weber put it, "its own distinctive set of rules, institutions, and currencies of power, rejecting key tenets of liberal internationalism and particularly any notion of global civil society justifying political or military intervention."[335]

The hope that China (and, to varying degree, the other BRICS) would integrate into Western-led order long informed US policy. Attempts to engage countries such as China or Russia shrewdly sought to increase interdependence, generate mutual wealth, and turn others into stakeholders and thus parties interested in upholding the US-led order.

Neither of the two extremes of "integration" and "confrontation" can capture China's more subtle strategy vis-à-vis international order. Evading these two extremes, the creation of several sinocentric institutions—in addition to strengthening its presence in existing structures—will allow China to pursue its own type of competitive multilateralism, choosing among flexible frameworks, depending on its national interests. China and the other BRICS countries pursue a strategy that defies the all-or-nothing choice of either rejecting the liberal international order or upholding it. A brief look at the recent Ufa Declaration, signed at the Seventh BRICS Summit, shows how committed member states are to maintaining and strengthening the UN framework and many other multilateral institutions like the WTO. Yet at the same time, emerging powers have engaged in an unprecedented wave of institutional entrepreneurship, as the creation of the New Development Bank (NDB), the BRICS' Contingent Reserve Arrangement (CRA), and China's Asian Infrastructure Investment Bank (AIIB) attest.

US policy makers have struggled to make sense of and respond to this dual strategy of both affirming existing institutions and creating alternative structures at the same time. China does not engage in any serious confrontational behavior (say, leaving the World Bank and pressuring other countries to do likewise) that would justify a swift US response. Yet, as Cynthia Roberts rightly argues, the BRICS "contest the West's pretensions to permanent stewardship of the existing system," a move that has generated confusion and ill-conceived reactions from Washington, symbolized by the decision to oppose the AIIB.[336] Washington's attempt to keep others from joining the new bank exposed that while the United States has indeed done much to build a liberal order based on rules and norms, it is deeply uncomfortable with the thought of not being in charge. The problem is that this angst alone will not be enough to rouse traditional US allies into action to contain China and other emerging powers. Europe, in particular, is not interested in helping perpetuate US global leadership at all costs if doing so affects its economic relationship

with China and others. This is particularly so because the
structures set up recently do not, in any way, undermine
the rules and norms that undergird today's order. China's
decision to create the AIIB protects it from future accusations of being an "irresponsible stakeholder" that does not
provide any global public goods. Claims that China seeks
to "demolish global order from within" amount, to many
observers, to little more than US attempts to prolong hegemony for hegemony's sake.[337]

A post-Western international architecture is in the
making, and it is undeniable that China's institutional
activism will profoundly influence both regional and global
dynamics in the coming years. Whether China-led institutions will succeed does not depend on the United States or
Europe, but on Beijing's capacity to convince its neighbors
that China's rise is good (and not dangerous) for the entire
region. While the outcome of China's bid for regional
hegemony is far from clear, the West's active opposition to
projects that could benefit the region are likely to play into
China's hands.

The United States' unwillingness to accept anything but
its own leadership or that of its allies points to a complex
transition to actual multipolarity in which other powers
such as China reduce US room for maneuver in some parts
of the world. This stance implies a deep sense of insecurity
among US policy makers that is both exaggerated and
unnecessary. The United States has no reason to fear an
intense competition of ideas with China. In fact, undermining free competition goes against the United States'
most fundamental principles. Worries that China's state-
led capitalism or authoritarianism may seem more attractive to the rest of the world are still unfounded, and there
are many signs that multipolarity could have positive consequences for global order, both politically and economically. The creation of the AIIB provides a powerful example:
its rise could force the World Bank to change its archaic
distribution of power and make the institution more effective and legitimate.

It is too early to make any specific predictions about the speed at which the China-centric institutions will gain a broad acceptance similar to Western-led institutions. Global instability outside of China's neighborhood (producing pariah regimes in need of China's support) and institutional inertia (slowing down necessary reform to provide more space for emerging powers) are likely to benefit China as they reduce the legitimacy of existing structures. Powerful examples are Russia's growing isolation from the West and the United States Congress' massive delay in ratifying the IMF's quota.

– 6 –

Post-Western World

What does the rise of the "parallel order" described in chapters 4 and 5 mean for global rules and norms? Many Western scholars believe that emerging powers will seek to undermine Western institutions and thus weaken the rules and norms that undergird them. That is based on the false understanding that the rules in place today are purely Western in nature and thus alien to emerging powers like China and India. As shown in chapter 1, this notion is the product of a Western-centric worldview that does not recognize the important role non-Western powers have played in the creation of today's global order, especially when it comes to basic pillars such as self-determination, sovereignty, and human rights. This sense of ownership explains why policy makers in Brasília, New Delhi, and Beijing are not proposing new rules. The Responsibility to Protect (R2P) is a good example. While Western commentators often believe countries like China, India, and Brazil disagree with the R2P norm, emerging powers are fully in agreement with it in principle, yet worry about the way Western powers operationalize it— as became obvious in the aftermath of the NATO-led intervention in Libya in 2011.[338]

It would therefore be wrong to assume that the new institutions—ranging from the Asian Infrastructure Investment Bank and the New Development Bank to the Conference on Interaction and Confidence Building Measures in Asia—will articulate or promote any fundamentally new norms according to which international affairs should be organized in a post-Western world. Rather, by creating new institutions and leading them, China seeks to emulate US-style leadership: rules-based but with built-in additional influence and with the right to occasionally act without asking for a "permission slip"—that is, the right to break the rules if deemed necessary by decision makers in Beijing. Other rising powers such as Brazil and India are doing the same, but on a regional level. This is symbolized by Brazil's decision to simply ignore a request by the Inter-American Commission on Human Rights (IACHR) of the Organization of American States (OAS) to halt the construction of a dam in the Amazon forest because the government had failed to properly consult with indigenous populations. This type of "regional exceptionalism" has been common for a long time, but under today's order, only the United States enjoys "global exceptionalism," symbolized by its freedom to frequently violate international law and intervene militarily in geographically distant countries since World War II without being punished by the international community.

Aside from the right to act without asking for a "permission slip" when national interest is at stake, the United States enjoys additional influence through a series of explicit or implicit agreements. China and others will seek to emulate those same privileges in the institutions they create. One very obvious advantage is location. While the United Nations, the IMF, and the World Bank headquarters are in the United States, providing the US government with easier access, the new institutions' headquarters are mostly based in China. While the United States' government can appoint the President of the World Bank, the Chinese government will play an outsized role in choosing the leadership structures of institutions like the AIIB, even though it may initially try to appear less imposing. The importance of controlling the leadership selection process cannot be underestimated. In the case of the World Bank and the IMF, it implies the ability to favor some governments over others based on strategic interests, and the United States and Europe have, over the past decades, made ample use of this privilege.

Rather than directly confronting existing institutions, then, China will continue to support them, but at the same time carve out its own institutional spaces. This will help fend off the possibility that occasional violations would lead to its expulsion. The response to the United States' intervention in Iraq is a case in point: due to its privileged institutional status, nobody at the time voiced the idea of excluding the United States from the G8. Nor did anyone propose asking MasterCard and Visa to stop dealing with US-American banks and customers. Even if someone had done so, it would have been impossible, considering that both companies are based in the United States. The United States is institutionally too central to be punished, formalizing the exceptional position to act unilaterally whenever it feels it must.

Finally, the United States has held a monopoly on the practice of competitive multilateralism, picking the institutional venue for specific problems according to its national interest. The new China-led institutions will allow Beijing to embrace that very same strategy, leading to a new form of highly competitive multilateralism, with two major powers supported by their own institutional structures, allowing each one to set up their version of "institutional imperialism."[339]

Liberalism and the Battle for Privilege

Critics point out that emerging powers have frequently questioned the foundations that underlie liberal order, expressing diverging opinions on the scope of cooperation, the location of rules, and the allocation of authority. All rising powers, according to this view, have thus voiced fundamental disagreements over substantive policies of the postwar liberal consensus. The result has been a challenge to the liberal internationalist project in substantive areas as distinct as trade, human rights, R2P, and nuclear non-proliferation. As a consequence, analysts have argued that emerging powers are "not ready for prime time"[340] or that they may become "irresponsible stakeholders" in global order.[341] Such an assessment fails to properly understand the concerns emerging powers have with so-called liberal Western order, and confuses rule-based order with Western leadership of it.

Emerging powers agree with fundamental issues such as international institutions, cooperative security, democratic community, collective problem solving, shared sovereignty, and the rule of law. They do so for an obvious reason: it was this rules-based and relatively open order that significantly contributed to their phenomenal economic rise over the past sixty years. It helped the Chinese government undertake (and take credit for) the biggest program of poverty reduction in human history. Wondering whether China or other emerging powers have an interest in undoing this international framework fails to take into consideration that they need it to remain in place for the next decades to modernize their economies and turn into rich countries.

And yet, as Amitav Acharya writes, just because rising powers have benefited from the American-dominated international order does not mean they would leave it intact and follow America's lead.[342] Indeed, emerging powers consider today's order as flawed and frequently undermined by the system's creators (to differing degrees). Brazil, South Africa, and India in particular oppose the implicit and explicit hierarchies of international institutions and the many privileges often enjoyed by great powers in international deliberations. China, while more privileged and already well integrated into many structures such as the UN Security Council, equally resents the US advantages hardwired into today's order. This is not a criticism of today's rules-based system, but rather a criticism of the hegemon's behavior in it.

It is thus skepticism about the operationalization of liberal norms, rather than the goals and values that guide them, that shapes the BRICS' relationship to today's global order. This explains why liberal internationalism continues to be, at times, interpreted by emerging powers as a form of liberal imperialism, and the power of the United States at the center of the liberal order is portrayed by them as a menace.[343]

Emerging powers consider liberal order to be imperfect due to its creator's transgressions, which frequently undermine the system. These privileges and "special rights" are symbolized by small details such as the United States' right to appoint the World Bank President, but also by the capacity to break the rules and not be punished for it, such as when the United States illegally intervened in Iraq and suffered only limited consequences. As Richard Betts points out, "Hegemons are never entirely constrained, benefiting from exceptions, escape clauses, veto rights and other mechanisms that allow the most powerful countries to use institutions as instruments of political control."[344]

This points to the decisive element of today's order, both its biggest strength and its greatest weakness: the ambiguity around how to align hierarchical principles with rules that are supposed to apply to all, irrespective of strength. In *Liberal Leviathan*, John Ikenberry summarized this contradiction by describing today's order as "hierarchical order with liberal characteristics."[345] The author attempts to explain this contradiction away by arguing that the rules do not restrain the hegemon, as it can "lead through rules," and rules can be "used as more direct instruments of political control."[346] He explicitly refers to the hegemon's exceptionalism by pointing to "escape clauses, weighted voting, opt-out agreements, and veto rights." Other countries may wonder just how that differs from an unrestrained imperial order, where the strongest operate above the law. What are rules worth if the strong can break them at will? Such a system can work in a frictionless manner in an extreme unipolarity, where the hegemon's rules are meekly embraced by the rest. Yet as soon as economic and military power deconcentrates and other powers emerge, the tension Ikenberry believes solveable through fusing US leadership to cooperation begins to mount. Liberal US scholars imply that when the end of Cold War destroyed the Second World, the "inside" order of the Western First World allegedly became the "outside" order for the rest. Such a view, however, is profoundly Western-centric and is rejected in China, India, and even in "moderate" nations like Brazil, all of whom are deeply suspicious of NATO's designs.[347]

Today, therefore, rather than questioning the intellectual precepts that undergird international order, emerging powers say they seek to create a multilateral system in which the same rules apply to all. In reality this means that, as seen in the case of the Crimean Crisis, they will increasingly seek special treatment themselves within the existing global governance regime. This will allow them to shape the agenda and its application to issues they care about, both through adjustments in the formal rules and via enhanced informal influence. Put differently, rising powers will increasingly demand exceptional treatment, which includes breaking the rules if adhering to them undermines their national interest. While China will seek "global exceptionalism," smaller emerging powers such as Brazil will be satisfied with "regional exceptionalism," that is, the capacity to break the rules whenever necessary on a regional level. Chinese researchers like to joke that China is happy with global order as it stands (and the rules and norms as they are), as long as Beijing replaces Washington; there is an element of truth in this joking remark.[348]

This is not because emerging powers have a specific interest in breaking the rules. Rather, as their economic power increases, their definition of "vital" interests grows, leading to the desire to create a regional (and later global) sphere of influence. Long-term planners in China will thus ensure that no other actor can deny them access to resources necessary for sustaining economic growth.[349]

To make those transgressions more acceptable to the international community, rising powers will provide more public goods in the realms of security and economics, thus ensuring that the system provides sufficient benefits to generate support by others. In China's case, those public goods include large-scale infrastructure projects in Central Asia (through the Silk Road Fund), Latin America, and Africa. Like the United States today, China and other emerging powers will carefully keep the balance between breaking the rules and providing public goods. Smaller rising powers such as Brazil and India provide far fewer global public goods, and their right to obtain special treatment is therefore far more limited. Still, India has turned into an important donor of development and humanitarian aid in the region, and Brazil has undertaken similar attempts in its region and in several African countries. Since 2004 Brazil has also led the UN Peacekeeping Mission MINUSTAH in Haiti and a Brazilian leads the UN Peacekeeping Mission in the Democratic Republic of the Congo.

Toward Global Competitive Multilateralism

Just as the United States intervened in Iraq outside of international law (2003), so will China (and possibly other emerging powers) break the rules if necessary, or be selective about them. This will also include using international institutions according to rising powers' needs and preferences. For example, in 2009, Western states led by the United Kingdom and the United States sidelined the United Nations General Assembly (UNGA) and assured that it would not play a key role in debating the global financial crisis and its impacts, so as to leave the subject to interstate organizations dominated by the West—which, naturally, were careful not to propose any measures that could be harmful to Western interests. At the time, Susan Rice successfully outmaneuvered those who sought to give the General Assembly (the "G192") a larger role. As a consequence, General Secretary Ban Ki Moon denied any financial assistance to the Stiglitz Commission, which had been tasked by the General Assembly to provide an independent report. Despite the Commission's competence, the United States argued that it was its "strong view...that the UN does not have the expertise or the mandate to serve as a suitable forum or provide direction."[350] The United Kingdom had diplomats pressure the Commission's members to quit. Like the West wanted, the G20 held the preliminary discussions, and the IMF (where the West is still in control) reassumed the role of sole legitimate forum for hard discussions and negotiations. In the same way, in 2012, the West almost succeeded in stopping the United Nations Conference on Trade and Development (UNCTAD) —dominated by developing countries—from further analyzing the global financial crisis. US-led competitive multilateralism has thus often been the preferred strategy. Ruth Wedgwood argues,

> The idea of competitive multilateralism avoids the stark choice of going alone or going to the United Nations. America must still support the purposes of the United Nations; it is a historic alliance, a product of World War II, and remains the only all-inclusive political organization around. America enjoys prerogatives as a permanent Security Council member that would be hard to gain again. But we do have some flexibility in how we choose to approach international cooperation.[351]

For a long time, Western powers were best positioned to play the game of competitive multilateralism to their advantage, cleverly shifting debates from one institution to the next to best achieve their objectives. The G20 is a prime example: created to avoid discussing the financial crisis in the UN General Assembly or ECOSOC, the West later sidelined the G20 and refocused on the G7 (after excluding Russia). As Steward Patrick writes, these actions "in essence resurrect[ed] the old inner sanctum of the global economy, which had been jettisoned after the global financial crisis necessitated cooperation with China."[352] Western powers regularly use the existing system for their benefit or to preserve their power, for example via the "pen-holder system," in which Britain and France control decisions in the UN Security Council that concern their former colonies.

Indeed, the West's capacity to use rules and institutions in its favor and unite in crucial periods (much more than "the rest" has been capable of) will prolong its influence in global governance. This is largely because the so-called "rest" is no cohesive unit: in fact it is so diverse that it can hardly be used as an analytical concept. Even smaller groupings such as the BRICS are incapable of aligning their interests in many cases, and this incapacity has historically been a major difficulty in articulating joint proposals.

In the BRICS' Sanya Declaration in April 2011, Brazil, Russia, India, China, and South Africa vowed that "the voice of emerging and developing countries in international affairs should be enhanced." Yet a month later, when Western powers reneged on their 2009 promise to "appoint the heads and senior leadership of the international financial institutions through an open, transparent and merit-based selection process" by quickly settling on France's Finance Minister Lagarde to replace Dominique Strauss-Kahn, emerging powers helplessly accepted the fact that Europe would once more pick the IMF's Managing Director. Emerging powers' expectations that Lagarde would step down before 2016 to make place for a non-European were illusory. The BRICS missed a chance to show that their club matters and to force the West to break with an antiquated gentlemen's agreement that only Europeans could lead the Fund, discriminating against more than 90 percent of the world's population and reducing the IMF's legitimacy.

How could the reformist zeal so visible among the emerging powers evaporate so quickly? Brazilian and Indian diplomats argued that Strauss-Kahn's departure had caught everyone by surprise, giving the BRICS little time to coordinate a joint response or even a joint candidate. But the same applies to the United States and the European Union, which speedily settled on their candidate. Given the nasty details that emerged about the IMF's sexist work culture, choosing a woman was a smart move by the Europeans, who could thus argue that Lagarde's appointment marked an important change for the Fund. The emerging powers, on the other hand, vociferously demanded a non-European to occupy the post, without first negotiating among themselves who this candidate should be. They had plenty of suitable individuals to choose from, many of whom were at least as qualified as Ms. Lagarde in international economics, if not more. After all, economists from countries such as Brazil and Turkey have precious experience in successfully managing economic crises that could help Europe's most affected countries.

When a Brazilian official sulkily admitted that "Europe is likely to keep its deep stranglehold on the position,"[353] it was an implicit admission that emerging powers had, by failing to agree on a powerful alternative to the French Finance Minister, been outmaneuvered by the West. While Europe and the United States have enough votes to push through any candidate, it would have been difficult for them to reject a viable choice that enjoyed the full support of China, India, Brazil, Russia, and South Africa. In all likelihood, many other non-European countries would have joined the BRICS. Even Australian diplomats voiced their concern about Europe's intransigence.

Finding a "BRICS-candidate" was all but impossible given the BRICS member countries' often differing opinions, strategic interests, and points of view. China, the world's second largest economy and the IMF's third largest contributor (after the United States and Japan), may see little difference between a French and a Mexican candidate. In the same way, Brazilians may feel no incentive to spend political capital in a fight for a Singaporean candidate. Brazil may even seek to undermine an Argentinean or Mexican candidate, in the same way that India may prefer a European to a Chinese Managing Director. The emerging powers' lackluster campaign for an alternative to yet another European politician as head of the IMF thus reveals that despite their visibility and attractiveness, the BRICS are not as united as they would like to think. When push comes to shove, as it did after Strauss-Kahn's fall, the alliance of the emerging powers crumbled, unable to measure up to the grand rhetoric heard so frequently at the BRICS summits.

The very same scenario occurred a year later, when Roberto Zoellick announced he would step down as World Bank President. "We will take a position together with the BRICS, making a common choice," Brazil's Minister of Finance Mantega announced, raising hopes that Okonjo-Iweala from Nigeria would win broad support among developing and emerging powers. Yet soon afterward, the Russian government declared its support for Jim Yong Kim, the US candidate, a decision that was "entirely uncoordinated with the rest of the BRICS," as one Indian diplomat commented. According to him, the Indian government had heard about the Russian decision from the media. This shows that even on a relatively simple matter (the Nigerian candidate is widely seen as better qualified) the BRICS did not have the ability to coordinate their positions. The contest of a strong African candidate against a weak US-American candidate would have provided a unique opportunity for the BRICS to show unity. As Wade rightly noted, the episode showed "how the developing countries' distrust of one another makes it easy for the Americans to split them with bilateral deals."[354] All this points to the difficulties of mounting effective balancing coalitions against the hegemon.[355]

The episodes described above make observers wonder whether the West has succeeded in transforming today's emerging powers into "useful idiots," who are so proud that they are part of the G20 that they no longer defend developing countries' interests. Seen from this perspective, the rise of the BRICS may have been a positive development for the West, now that the poor have lost powerful defendants in Brasília, Pretoria, and Delhi, who are increasingly defending big-power interests, only to see the G20 marginalized by a resurgent G7. At the same time, emerging powers should not complain: it is natural that the West will do everything to hold on to its power—after all, even China is not fully committed to permanently including Brazil and India in the UN Security Council. Western states have so far been strikingly successful in their efforts to keep control of the commanding heights. Their success owes much to specific institutional rules they put in place decades ago, long before talk of the rise of the South. Still, the South is partly to blame for not being able to unite and present more powerful ideas about why reform is necessary. Divergence among emerging powers is not limited to the IMF and the World Bank. For example, there is no consensus among the BRICS about the need to reform the UN Security Council, most notably because Russia and China are permanent members and therefore less supportive of reforming the body than Brazil, India, and South Africa.

China's institutional entrepreneurship shows that it is seeking to turn the tables and play its own game of competitive multilateralism. There is thus nothing new about forum shopping, and Western powers have excelled about having it their way on the multilateral stage for decades, as shown above.

Despite successful Western strategies to hold on to power, in the coming decades, it will most likely be emerging powers, primarily China, that may be able to use the international system according to their interests. While in fact the aspects of contemporary international order that Ikenberry calls "liberal" (institutions, rule of law, and so on) are essentially welcomed by emerging powers, they will increasingly resist the United States' hegemonic practices that so often have accompanied that order, and slowly seek to make room for their own.

Emerging powers accept global order's liberal characteristics and are likely to maintain them, but they will change the hierarchy that undergirds the system. Aside from the new institutions created by emerging powers, several existing international institutions may not look that different several decades down the line, and neither will the norms and rules they are based on. Yet while today it is the United States that can break the rules and go unpunished, this privilege will soon be China's and possibly one day that of other emerging powers. There is no evidence that they will use it any differently than the United States has over the past decades.

Still, the new wave of competitive multilateralism will seem unfamiliar to Western powers because it will involve a plethora of new institutions created by non-Western powers. Playing on China's turf will make agenda-setting far more difficult for policy makers from Washington and London. Decisive negotiations about global challenges— say, geopolitical tensions in Central Asia, or a necessary bailout for a developing country in trouble—will thus first focus on where such issues will be discussed in the first place.

Most observers will associate excessive forum shopping and excessively competitive multilateralism with an erosion of universal norms and a "race to the bottom" when it comes to global standards. It is certainly true that the multiplication of standards in some fields such as banking may make it necessary for financial institutions to operate more than one system. But there is little evidence that the growing number of development banks has negatively affected lending practices. The proliferation of institutions may even have had important positive consequences. After all, monopoly can undermine the agility and effectiveness of any institution, while competition can help generate new ideas and develop new best practices. The vast majority of observers even within the World Bank have therefore welcomed the rise of new development banks. For example, the African Union (AU) has played an important role in the discussion about peacekeeping. It will also help allow countries that are home to the majority of humanity play a more important role when it comes to dealing with global challenges. As a *Financial Times* editorial rightly argued after the Sixth BRICS Summit,

> Shifts in global economic power suggest that changes in institutional power may be logical—or even inevitable. Why should the US set the rules for the internet, when most internet traffic no longer involves Americans? Why should the dollar be the global reserve currency, when the US is no longer the unchallenged core of the global economy?[356]

More important, as pointed out above, great powers will always be careful to balance their exceptionalism with the provision of global public goods and the stability they need to protect their vital interests. Beijing is fully aware of the fact that its hard power sources can only translate into political influence when they are bound by agreed-upon rules and norms. China cannot afford to be regarded as a global rule-breaker that cares little about the rest of the world. It was this very understanding that Chinese power must be embedded in a network of rules and norms to be considered legitimate that made policy makers in Beijing create the many institutions described in the previous chapters.

While power shifts require the bargains great powers agree to with the rest of the world to be constantly rene-gotiated, they are not bad news for the future of global rules and norms.

Conclusion

As the analysis above shows, the discussion about whether rising powers will embrace or reject Western-led order is unlikely to generate satisfying answers. Since today's rules and norms are not as Western as is commonly assumed, non-Western powers will not challenge them head-on. Predictions that China will reestablish the hierarchical tributary system in place for thousands of years in Asia do not take into account that in today's world economic and military power are far too equally distributed to return to imperial structures. In addition, it overlooks China's key role in the creation of today's order, implying that today's system is somehow "unnatural" to China, and that it will intuitively overthrow it.

As Armijo and Roberts point out, "The BRICS' preferences, singly and jointly, for global governance turn on reform and evolution, not revolution. It is striking that none of the emerging (or re-emerging in the case of China and Russia) powers has displayed revolutionary aims with respect to reordering the international system."[357]

Supporting this view, an Indian diplomat argues that "[our] views [are] more non-West, than anti-West."[358] The rise of a parallel order is thus unlikely to be a threat to the rules and norms of today's order. Yet that does not mean that institutions will succeed in addressing all the dangers of power transition. While predictions of post-Western chaos lack historical or theoretical foundation and are based on a parochial Western-centric belief that only the United States and Europe can lead, great-power rivalry remains a reality. Notions that "war-driven change is removed as a historical process,"[359] as John Ikenberry argues, seem unrealistic, even though war is highly unlikely at this point. Rather, the rise of China may help temper the overly optimistic liberal rhetoric employed mainly by the United States since Woodrow Wilson. As Stephen Walt argues,

> World War I was the " war to end all wars." Then World War II was going to make the world "safe for democracy." We got the Cold War instead. When it ended, however, President George H. W. Bush talked about a "new world order" and presidential candidate Bill Clinton proclaimed that the "cynical calculus of power politics...[was] ill-suited to a new era." And smart intellectuals chimed in too, claiming that mankind had reached "the end of history" and that war was increasingly "obsolescent."... To believe that we have permanently overcome great-power rivalry is overly optimistic, potentially dangerous, and, frankly, absurd.[360]

Still, despite this caveat, the above analysis shows that there are few signs that the rise of parallel order is a harbinger of the end of liberal order. Predictions about global dissensus are motivated by Western-centrism, not an objective analysis of the dynamics that will shape global order. The rise of new multilateral institutions is an affirmation to emerging powers that the future will continue to be dominated by a solid, though often imperfect, rules-based global order.

Rather than predicting the future, this book sought to describe some of the dynamics that are likely to shape it, and underlined the importance of adapting our perspective on global affairs to truly multipolar reality.

This analysis was written at a time of crisis in the Global South. After years of stellar growth, all BRICS countries except India have plunged into economic turmoil. The Chinese economy is growing at the lowest figures in years. Russia and Brazil, which failed to diversify their economies during the commodity boom, are in the midst of a recession. Growth has also slowed in Indonesia and Turkey, the latter of which is facing a worrying turn to authoritarianism. South Africa, the fifth BRICS member, is hampered by a corrupt and incompetent government incapable of undertaking the necessary structural reforms. Nigeria, one of the few star performers of the past years, is still battling a bloody extremist insurgency in the country's north. India, the world's largest democracy and soon to be the world's largest country by population, is the only bright spot, slated to grow faster than China in the coming years.

The political effects of this development are already palpable on a global scale. Disappointing growth in the emerging world has lowered the pressure on the United States and Europe to reform international institutions and increase the representation of countries such as Brazil and India. A growing number of policy makers and commentators in the United States and Europe feel as if they have finally awoken from a decade-long nightmare. Now, thankfully, things seem to be back to the "normal" twentieth-century distribution of power. Easy money from the Federal Reserve Bank has dried up, and China is increasingly focused on boosting domestic consumption. As a consequence, emerging powers, strongly dependent on China, are suffering immensely. The "rise of the rest," which symbolized the first decade of the twenty-first century, seems to have come to an end. The world's key institutions, some believe, can maintain their Western-centric design. Such rhetoric paints the rise of the Global South as a phenomenon essentially dependent on easy Western money and Chinese imports, and emerging powers as helpless actors who happened to stumble into an unexpected and undeserved decade of growth.

Yet temporarily lower economic growth in the Global South cannot do away with the historic advances emerging powers have made, especially during the past decade, which has seen an unprecedented degree of emancipation of the Global South—including the African continent. The lull in the emerging world does not alter long-term predictions that China will overtake the US-American economy. As I have argued throughout the book, that is a largely natural phenomenon considering the demographic dominance of emerging powers. Despite current problems, India is set to become a major pillar of the world economy in the course of this century. The world economy will not return to the distribution of power after World War II.

As Zachary Karabell argues, concerning these changes,

> Sentiment may have shifted dramatically...but there is a substantial difference between that and structural collapse and crisis. Yes, emerging world economies are seeing slowing growth relative to the heightened rates of recent years, and yes, the shift to domestic demand-driven economic activity is not easy. But that is not the same as re-writing the script of the past decade and turning the achievements of many of these countries into a mirage.
>
> When it comes time to write the story of the first years of the 21st century, the global narrative will not only be the struggles of the United States to adjust to a world of diffuse power, or the rise of China and the decline of Europe. It will be the way that substantial portions of the planet emerged from agrarian poverty into the early stages of urban affluence. It will be the way the Internet and the mobile revolution anchored by the rise of China began to reshape the vast regions of sub-Saharan Africa; how India's middle classes started to redefine that country, and how millions in Latin America sloughed off decades of authoritarian incompetence and began to blossom. Never in human history have more people become more affluent more quickly than in the opening years of the 21st century.[361]

As a consequence, despite the rise of a parallel order, the fundamental need to reform global governance structures remains. For policy makers in Europe and the United States, engaging emerging powers is the only way of assuring that traditional international institutions remain functional once the traditional powers are no longer in control. The difficult process of adapting to a new reality has just begun. In the coming years and decades, far more extensive reforms—in the World Bank, the IMF, and the United Nations Security Council—will have to be implemented if these institutions are to maintain their legitimacy in the twenty-first century. After all, a mismatch between the actual distribution of power and the distribution of power within institutions is bound to lead to tension. As Carr describes in *The Twenty Years' Crisis: 1919–1939*, the Versailles system failed because of the growing gap between the order it represented and the actual distribution of power on the European continent. It is partly a consequence of this mismatch that existing institutions now have to increasingly compete with similar institutions led by rising states, which, in their entirety, can be described as an incipient parallel order.

In addition to reforming international institutions, it is necessary to adopt a post-Western view that takes diverging perspectives about global order into account. To adequately assess how global order will evolve in the coming decades, we need to go beyond the Western-centric worldview. Given how deeply ingrained our Western-centric bias is (both in the West and elsewhere), this poses a considerable challenge. There are additional obstacles. The dominant international relations literature is still produced in the United States and the United Kingdom, and ideas generated elsewhere are often either not available in English or fall short of theoretical standards necessary to appear in leading academic journals or book publishers. Few Chinese or Indian newspapers offer a global outlook similar to that of the *Financial Times*, the *New York Times*, or *The Economist*. Still, there has never been a greater need to hear from those who seek to take not only US-American but also Chinese, Indian, Brazilian, and other forms of exceptionalism and centrism into account, which do not place the same importance on Western agency in the past, present, and future.

The four key arguments around which this book is organized point to a series of implications for policy makers.

The first argument was that our Western-centric world-view leads us to underappreciate not only the role non-Western actors have played in the past and play in contemporary international politics, but also the constructive role they are likely to play in the future. This book argues that post-Western order will not necessarily be more violent than today's global order.

On a policy level, that implies assessing institutions led by non-Western actors such as the AIIB, the BRICS, and the Shanghai Cooperation Organization more objectively, asking primarily whether they succeed in providing global public goods and improving ties among their members, rather than whether they pose a threat to US hegemony. In the case of the AIIB, the United States failed to take such a pragmatic stance. Only a shortsighted zero-sum-game approach can explain the United States' decision to oppose the Chinese-led bank, which produced a diplomatic disaster. It led policy makers in Washington to seriously misjudge their capacity to convince countries around the world—Britain, Germany, Brazil, South Korea, Japan, and Australia—not to join the new institution. Perhaps most perplexing still, they decided to frame the creation of the AIIB as a diplomatic contest. Had the United States sought membership in the bank early on, or merely decided not to comment on the issue, observers around the world would not pay as much attention to the institution today, or interpret it as a watershed moment in the transition from unipolarity to multipolarity. Washington's strategy vis-à-vis the AIIB was designed on the premise that the rise of China occurs mostly in the context of inevitable tension and possible conflict. Assuming a revisionist strategy behind every move by emerging powers is misguided and parochial. The creation of the AIIB and the NDB underlines non-Western emerging powers' willingness to help fix a system that no longer satisfies existing demands. China may seek to revise Western stewardship of the system, but not necessarily the system's underlying rules and norms.

On a broader level, it means learning to see the rise of China and other emerging powers as something other than a catastrophe that symbolizes the end of the liberal cosmopolitan project. From a historical perspective, the end of Western dominance is little more than the end of an aberration that saw an extreme concentration of wealth and power in one relatively small part of the globe. It is normal that this unusual—and, one may add, unnatural—concentration of power would end eventually. Despite all the difficulties this transformation will bring, more equally distributed wealth and power across the world is a positive phenomenon that should, in principle, not be feared but welcomed.

Second, I argue that the economic rise of the rest, principally China, will allow it to enhance its military capacity and eventually its international influence and soft power. I question the commonly used argument that China will never turn into a global power because "it has no friends," as I argue that soft power is relatively easy to generate from a large hard power base. As China and other emerging powers rise economically, they will gain more friends and allies, just as the West has done in the past. The Soviet Union, of course, possessed only very limited soft power in the West, but it nonetheless generated a following around the world sizeable enough to force the West to adopt a policy entirely based on hard, not soft power: US military interventions in Central America, Indochina, and Africa showed that soft power alone was not capable of swaying global opinion, and contrary to what is often believed, the end of the Cold War was not met with celebrations in Delhi, Beijing, and Brasília, but with a hesitation and worries about the rise of unipolarity.

From a policy perspective, that means spending more time and energy to assess the way China and other rising powers are seen in developing countries. Chinese soft power may be extremely limited in Europe and the United States, but arguing that this is proof enough that China's soft power strategy has failed on a global scale would be erroneous. A more objective treatment of China's role in Africa also means questioning some of the rhetoric about the West's practices on the continent, which are often no different from those pursued by emerging powers. It also means openly recognizing the fact that China already provides a significant amount of global public goods, and encouraging that trend. Greater contributions from China, India, and others in all areas—peacekeeping, antipiracy operations, climate change, development aid, and so on—should be welcomed. Indeed, more integrated rising powers will increase the number of platforms offering intensive coordination, reducing the space for misunderstandings that could lead to suboptimal cooperation or even conflict. It means that Western policy makers should openly call on emerging powers to engage, and also offer adequate space within existing institutions to truly include rising states. Policy makers from China, India, Brazil, and other emerging powers, by comparison, must more boldly claim a protagonist role when it comes to discussion about global rules and norms.

In many ways, Brazil's initiative to launch the Responsibility While Protecting (RwP) concept—an addendum to R2P about a more transparent mechanism of monitoring humanitarian intervention—symbolized the very strategy Brasília aspires to pursue: turn into a bridge-builder, mediator, and consensus seeker through thought leadership. RwP, despite its flaws, was an innovative and constructive proposal to bridge the gap between an overly trigger-happy NATO and excessively resistant China and Russia. Academics in Brazil and abroad lauded the initiative. It was the Rousseff administration's finest multilateral initiative.[362]

And yet, a year after its launch in November 2011, diplomats in New York privately confessed to be disappointed with what some have called Brazil's "enigmatic retreat." RwP continued to be mentioned during debates, yet there was no longer the sense that Brazil prioritized the matter. Much more would have been possible. R2P only prospered because of a small group's tireless efforts to promote the topic. In the same way, RwP was unlikely to have a lasting impact on the debate without a powerful and credible sponsor like Brazil. No matter whether Brazil disengaged passively or actively, the move hurt Brazil's national interest: future attempts to act as an agenda-setter may receive a more hesitant reception because of a general uncertainty about Brazil's willingness to follow up and withstand the initial (and normal) criticism. On the other hand, the RwP initiative may have been useful to provide a glimpse of what Brazil is capable of on a global scale. Despite Brazil's limited hard power, it temporarily exercised international leadership in a debate that is likely to shape international affairs for decades to come.[363]

The third key argument of the book is that, rather than directly confronting existing institutions, rising powers (primarily China) are quietly building a so-called parallel order that will initially complement today's international institutions. This order is already in the making, including institutions such as the BRICS-led New Development Bank and the Asian Infrastructure Investment Bank (to complement the World Bank), Universal Credit Rating Group (to complement Moody's and S&P), China UnionPay (to complement MasterCard and Visa), and the BRICS (to complement the G7). These structures do not emerge because China and others have new ideas about how to address global challenges; rather, they create them to project their power, like Western actors have done before them.

The policy implications for all sides are clear. Both emerging powers and established actors will do well to fully embrace, rather than criticize or try to isolate, these new institutions. Their emergence is natural and inevitable (and has been accelerated by the resistance to reforming existing institutions), and opposing them will weaken the West. Great Britain adopted such a far-sighted and pragmatic stance, and it became the first major Western government to apply for membership in the AIIB. Washington should follow Britain's lead. Ceasing efforts to better integrate China and others into existing institutions, as a response to China's institutional entrepreneurship, would be a grave mistake, unnecessarily limiting the number of platforms where Chinese and Western policy makers will manage asymmetric bipolarity in the coming decades. Support for Great Britain's stance vis-à-vis the AIIB should not be misunderstood as a call for keeping quiet on issues China seeks to avoid, such as human rights. On the contrary, together with countries like South Korea, Germany, and Australia, it should explicitly insist that the AIIB's governance rules include clear human rights standards.

Fourth, as part of a hedging strategy, emerging powers— led by China—will continue to invest in existing institutions and embrace most elements of today's "liberal hierarchical order," but they will seek to change the hierarchy in the system to obtain "hegemonic privileges" so far only enjoyed by the United States. The creation of several China-centric institutions will allow China to embrace its own type of competitive multilateralism, picking and choosing among flexible frameworks, in accordance with its national interests—thus slowly institutionalizing its own exceptionalism and enhancing its policy autonomy by becoming increasingly immune to Western threats of exclusion.

This last point is likely to be most painful for Western foreign-policy makers, and it indeed poses an important challenge to their previously held room for maneuver, frequently used to their advantage by exerting pressure on smaller states behind the scenes or by choosing the platform that would most likely allow the West to have its way. It would therefore be wrong to accuse non-Western rising states of seeking to use the multilateral system to their advantage. After all, the West has done so for many decades.

The West has benefited enormously from being able to design a common project in several areas, symbolized by organizations like NATO, the G7, the EU, and the OECD. While disagreements exist, they cannot be compared to the disputes that still exist between India and China, China and Japan, or India and Pakistan. In the same way, groupings such as the BRICS, IBSA, or the G77 have historically had great difficulty articulating a common project, and there is little prospect that this will change fundamentally in the coming years. That will allow the West to play an outsized role for many years to come.

From a Chinese perspective, the plan to create separate institutions is both shrewd and fully understandable. The new scenario will reduce Western powers' ability to skew the game to their advantage. In the future, China will be able to pick and choose its preferred platform more easily, as Western powers have done in the past.

The classic Western-centric historical account, this analysis has shown, is one-sided and generates an understanding of global order that will be unhelpful as we seek to understand and make sense of contemporary trends. It vastly overemphasizes the West's role in global history, oversimplifies the sources of the West's rise, and thus generates a false notion that the ongoing process of multipolarization is a key rupture that will inevitably lead to fundamental changes.

Throughout history, the great powers have always sought to institutionalize and solidify their temporary superior power in international norms, making international social mobility more difficult.[364] Adopting an exceptionalist discourse, the major justification is always that maintaining hegemony is crucial to preserve stability: a line of argument currently embraced in Western capitals. Yet fears about a post-Western order are misguided partly because the past and present system are far less Western than is generally assumed. Non-Western powers have made important contributions to the creation of global rules and norms, often before Western actors did, and countries such as China and India are increasingly willing and able to take the lead in providing global public goods. Although the transition to genuine multipolarity—not only economically but also militarily and with regard to agenda-setting capacity—will be disconcerting to many, post-Western multipolarity will be, in the end, far more democratic than any previous order. It will open possibilities for greater levels of open dialogue and the spread of knowledge, and enable ways to address more effectively the key global challenges in the twenty-first century.

Notes

Introduction

1 While used frequently in the media, politics, and academia, the concept of the West remains abstract and often misunderstood. It is not static but in motion, continuously adapting to new realities, and imagined in new ways by different groups—both Western and non-Western—with different interests. While agreeing with Lazarus that "there is a tendency to fetishize the West as the super-agent of domination in the modern world," I consider it indispensable to use this term, "widely, but with enough reflection," as Morozov proposes. The West contains differentiation and hierarchies, its borders are porous, and the concept's ownership is not limited to those who claim to be part of it. The objective is thus not to offer a precise definition, which would inevitably turn the West into something one-dimensional, but rather to embrace the term's contested nature. See Neil Lazarus, "Spectres haunting: Postcommunism and postcolonialism," *Journal of Postcolonial Writing* 48: no. 2 (March 2012), 122, http://www.tandfonline.com/doi/abs/10.1080/174498 55.2012.658243, and Viatcheslav Morozov, *Russia's Postcolonial Identity: A Subaltern Empire in a Eurocentric World* (London: Palgrave Macmillan, 2015), 24.

2 John M. Hobson, *The Eurocentric Conception of World Politics: Western International Theory* (Cambridge: Cambridge University Press, 2012), 1. A historic example is, among others, Karl Marx, who wrote within a profoundly Western-centric framework, and believed the East had no prospects for progressive self-development. Yet a Western-centric bias remains visible in most contemporary analysis of international affairs as well.

3 See, for example, Edward W. Said, *Orientalism* (New York: Vintage Books, 1979); Mark Mazower, *No Enchanted Palace: The End of Empire and the Ideological Origins of the United Nations* (Princeton: Princeton University Press, 2013); John Darwin, *After Tamerlane: The Rise and Fall of Global Empires, 1400–2000* (New York: Penguin Books, 2008) and Edward Keene, *Beyond the Anarchical Society: Grotius, Colonialism and Order in World Politics* (Cambridge: Cambridge University Press, 2002).

4 Starting in the 1960s and 1970s there has been a massive wave of postcolonial scholarship that explicitly seeks to challenge Western-centrism. This critique focuses on the dominant International Relations scholars and pundits who dominate the field, not historians or anthropologists, who are far less Western-centric.

5 Marcos Tourinho, "Beyond expansion: Political contestation in the global international society (1815–1960)" (PhD diss., Graduate Institute of International and Development Studies of Geneva, 2015), 24.

6 Henry Kissinger, *World Order: Reflections on the Character of Nations and the Course of History* (New York: Penguin Press, 2014), 277.

7 There is a vivid debate about the degree to which coercion and attraction played a role in the rise of the so-called post-World War II order. Western scholars such as Geir Lundestad, "Empire by invitation? The United States and Western Europe, 1945–1952," *Journal of Peace Research* 23, no. 3 (1986): 163–277, http://jpr.sagepub.com/content/23/3/263; Mark A. Stoler, *Allies and Adversaries: The Joint Chiefs of Staff, the Grand Alliance, and U.S. Strategy in World War II* (Chapel Hill: The University of North Carolina Press, 2003) or Frank Costigliola, *Roosevelt's Lost Alliances: How Personal Politics Helped Start the Cold War*

(Princeton: Princeton University Press, 2013) tend to emphasize the inherent attraction of the liberal system, while non-Western scholars like Ayse Zarakol, *After Defeat: How the East Learned to Live with the West* (Cambridge: Cambridge University Press, 2011) regard coercive elements as more decisive. Realist scholars like Nuno Monteiro (Nuno Monteiro, "Monteiro on Ikenberry, 'Power, Order, and Change in World Politics,' " *H-Diplo*, September, 2015, https://networks.h-net.org/node/28443/reviews/ 85222/monteiro-ikenberry-power-order-and-change-world -politics) argue that the distinction between rule and domination, and coercion and legitimacy, is blurred and often lacks clear evidence.

8 The arguments have been made by, among others, Janet L. Abu-Lughod, *Before European Hegemony: The World System A.D. 1250–1350* (Oxford: Oxford University Press, 1991) and J. M. Blaut, *The Colonizer's Model of the World* (New York: The Guilford Press, 1993).

9 This argument is made by Beate Jahn, *Liberal Internationalism: Theory, History, Practice* (London: Palgrave Macmillan, 2013). As Odd A. Westad, *The Global Cold War: Third World Interventions and the Making of Our Times* (Cambridge: Cambridge University Press, 2007) shows, the end of the Cold War was not marked by liberal pro-Western forces, but far more by the rise of political Islam.

10 Graham Allison, "The Thucydides trap: Are the U.S. and China headed for war?" *The Atlantic*, September 24, 2015, http://www.theatlantic.com/international/archive/2015/09/ united-states-china-war-thucydides-trap/406756/.

11 When *LIFE* magazine created a list of the 100 most important people and events of the millennium for its September 1997 issue, it commented, "Westerners have done a disproportionate amount of the global moving and shaking. All but 17 [of the 100] are of European extraction. ... This reflects not the biases of LIFE's editors and expert advisers but the sociopolitical realities of the past thousand years." Excerpt of *LIFE* magazine, September 1997, 135, quoted by Andre Gunder Frank, in *ReOrient: Global Economy in the Asian Age* (Berkeley: University of California Press, 1998), 12.

12 Tourinho, "Beyond expansion," 9.

13 These arguments have been made by, among others, Amartya Sen, *Identity and Violence: The Illusion of Destiny* (New York: W. W. Norton & Company, 2007), and Jack Goody, *The Theft of History* (Cambridge: Cambridge University Press, 2007).

14 Robbie Shilliam, *International Relations and Non-Western Thought: Imperialism, Colonialism and Investigations of Global Modernity* (New York: Routledge, 2011). A notable example is how, with the exception of thinkers like Amitav Acharya, Kanti Bajpai, or Raja Mohan, in the discipline of international relations there has long been a lack of deep, critical engagement with Nehru's political thought, even though he developed crucial ideas regarding nonalignment, the anticolonial movement, and nonproliferation.

15 Michael Mastanduno, "Order and change in world politics: the financial crisis and the breakdown of the US–China grand bargain" in *Power, Order and Change in World Politics*, ed. G. John Ikenberry (Cambridge: Cambridge University Press, 2014), 183.

16 This idea has been articulated by several scholars before, but particularly elegantly by Ayse Zarakol, *After Defeat: How the East Learned to Live with the West* (Cambridge: Cambridge University Press, 2011).

17 Richard Betts, for example, writes about a "titanic struggle over which ideology would be the model for organizing societies around the globe—fascism, communism, or Western liberal democracy," implying that the former two were not of Western origin. "Conflict or cooperation? Three visions revisited," *Foreign Affairs* (November/December 2010), https://www.foreignaffairs.com/reviews/review-essay/conflict-or-cooperation.

18 John Mearsheimer, "Can China Rise Peacefully?" *The National Interest*, October 24, 2015.

19 Randall L. Schweller, *Maxwell's Demon and the Golden Apple* (Baltimore: Johns Hopkins University Press, 2014), 67.

20 See, for example, Henry Kissinger, *On China* (New York: Penguin Books, 2012), Harald Müller and Carsten Rauch, "Make converts, not war: Power change, conflict constellation, and the chance to avoid another 1914" in *Lessons from World War I for the Rise of Asia*, ed. Andreas

Herberg-Rothe (London: Lessons from World War I for the Rise of Asia, 2015) and Daniel W. Drezner, *The System Worked: How the World Stopped Another Great Depression* (Oxford: Oxford University Press, 2014).

21 "The APEC summit and the Pacific Rim Bridge over troubled water," *The Economist*, November 15, 2014, http://www.economist.com/news/leaders/21632452-weeks-summit-beijing-helped-great-power-rivalry-still-threatens-pacific-bridge.

22 Mastanduno, "Order and change in world politics: the financial crisis and the breakdown of the US–China grand bargain," 183.

23 Anders Fogh Rasmussen, during panel debate at the London Conference at Chatham House, June 1–2, 2015.

24 "Losing the Middle East: Why America must not abandon the region," *The Economist*, June 6, 2015, cover, http://www.economist.com/printedition/covers/2015-06-04/ap-e-eu-la-me-na-uk.

25 Several of those perspectives consider non-Western actors to have been crucial in shaping global history and in creating and maintaining today's order, thus evaluating the current global shift of power differently from the Western narrative. For example, sinocentric perspectives point out that the rise of the West during the past centuries was made possible partly through the appropriation of Chinese ideas and technologies, and through military domination. It was not, as is often suggested in the West, inevitable, and China's recovery will soon end Western economic superiority, returning to what China considers "normal." Rather than considering these perspectives as closer to the truth or more adequate, they will merely be described to obtain a more complete picture. In addition to a broad literature review, this analysis will be based on primary research conducted over the past years, and during 2015, in China, India, Russia, Brazil, among others.

26 I recognize that "the rise of the rest" is an analytically very limiting concept, and I will early on explain that I merely use it as an initial shorthand, explaining the broad diversity in the "rest"—and, most important, that concepts such as the "rest" or "non-West" are all part of a Western-centric worldview that this book seeks to question.

27 See David Shambaugh, *China Goes Global: The Partial Power* (New York: Oxford University Press, 2013).

28 A somewhat similar idea was first articulated by Naazneen Barma et al., "A world without the West? Empirical patterns and theoretical implications," *Chinese Journal of International Politics* 2, no. 4 (2009): 525–44, http://cjip.oxfordjournals.org/content/2/4/525.extract, and by Moritz Rudolf et al., "Chinas Schatten-Außenpolitik: Parallelstrukturen fordern die internationale Ordnung heraus," *China Monitor* 18 (September 23, 2014), http://www.merics.org/fileadmin/templates/download/china-monitor/China_Monitor_No_18.pdf.

29 Cemil Aydin, *The Politics of Anti-Westernism in Asia: Visions of World Order in Pan-Islamic and Pan-Asian Thought* (New York: Columbia University Press, 2007), 75.

30 Viatcheslav Morozov, *Russia's Postcolonial Identity: A Subaltern Empire in a Eurocentric World* (London: Palgrave Macmillan, 2015), 33.

31 Ivo Daalder and James Stavridis, "NATO's victory in Libya: The right way to run an intervention," *Foreign Affairs* (March/April 2012), https://www.foreignaffairs.com/articles/libya/2012-02-02/natos-victory-libya.

32 Oliver Stuenkel and Marcos Tourinho, "Regulating intervention: Brazil and the responsibility to protect," *Conflict, Security & Development* 14, no. 4 (2014): 379–402, http://www.tandfonline.com/doi/abs/10.1080/14678802.2014.930593?journalCode=ccsd20.

33 Oliver Stuenkel, "The BRICS and the future of R2P: Was Syria or Libya the exception?" *Global Responsibility to Protect* 6, no. 1 (2014): 3–28, http://booksandjournals.brillonline.com/content/journals/10.1163/1875984x-00601002.

34 Matias Spektor, "How to read Brazil's stance on Iran," *Council on Foreign Relations* (March 4, 2010), http://www.cfr.org/brazil/read-brazils-stance-iran/p21576.

35 Charles Kupchan, *No One's World: The West, the Rising Rest, and the Coming Global Turn* (New York: Oxford University Press, 2013).

36 Kupchan, *No One's World*.

37 Hedley Bull and Adam Watson, *The Expansion of International Society* (London: Oxford University Press, 1985).

38 The BRICS are in fundamental agreement about the principles that undergird R2P. Their support for R2P's pillars I and II is absolute, therefore sponsoring the idea that states have the primary responsibility to protect their populations from genocide, war crimes, ethnic cleansing, and crimes against humanity, and that the international community must have a role in assisting States to do so. As for pillar III, the BRICS at times diverge from Western countries, not regarding the existence of the norm that prescribes the international community's responsibility to take "timely and decisive action" to prevent and halt the crimes abovementioned, in case the State is "manifestly" failing to protect its populations, but about when and how to apply this norm. See Oliver Stuenkel, "The BRICS and the Future of R2P," 3–28.

39 Isaac T. Sampson, "The Responsibility to Protect and ECOWAS mechanisms on peace and security: Assessing their convergence and divergence on intervention," *Journal of Conflict and Security Law* 16, no. 3 (2011), http://jcsl.oxfordjournals.org/content/16/3/507.abstract.

40 Sampson, "The Responsibility to Protect and ECOWAS," 2.

41 Rahul Rao, *Third World Protest: Between Home and the World* (New York: Oxford University Press, 2010), 43.

42 Ryan Pickerell, "China: Projecting power through peacekeeping," *The Diplomat*, October 15, 2015, http://thediplomat.com/2015/10/china-projecting-power-through-peacekeeping/.

43 See, for example, Jonathan Fenby, *Will China Dominate the 21ˢᵗ Century?* (Cambridge: Polity Press, 2014).

44 Aaron Friedberg, *A Contest for Supremacy: China, America, and the Struggle for Mastery in Asia* (New York: W. W. Norton & Co., 2011), 176.

45 Friedberg, *A Contest for Supremacy*, 158.

46 "Not just straw men: The biggest emerging economies are rebounding, even without recovery in the West," *The Economist* (June 18, 2009), http://www.economist.com/node/13871969.

47 Samir Saran and Vivan Sharan, "Banking on BRICS to deliver," *The Hindu*, March 27, 2012, http://www.thehindu.com/opinion/lead/article3248200.ece.

48 Eman El-Shenawi, "The BRIC. The BRICS. The who?" *Al Arabia News*, June 13, 2011, http://english.alarabiya.net/articles/2011/06/13/153140.html.

49 Philip Stephens, "A story of Brics without mortar," *Financial Times*, November 24, 2011, http://www.ft.com/intl/cms/s/0/352e96e8-15f2-11e1-a691-00144feabdc0.html.

50 For a complete analysis of the history of the BRICS grouping, see Oliver Stuenkel, *The BRICS and the Future of Global Order* (New York: Lexington Books, 2015).

51 Rebecca Liao, "Out of the Bretton Woods: How the AIIB is Different," *Foreign Affairs* (July 27, 2015), https://www.foreignaffairs.com/articles/asia/2015-07-27/out-bretton-woods?cid=soc-tw-rdr.

52 Nazneen Barma, Ely Ratner and Steve Weber, "A World Without the West," *The National Interest*, July/August, 2007. The authors identify a "third way" between alignment and confrontation, yet their scenario contains many elements of confrontation, as it is hardly possible to simply "ignore" the Western-dominated system without causing considerable friction.

53 G. John Ikenberry, *Liberal Leviathan: The Origins, Crisis, and Transformation of the American World Order* (Princeton: Princeton University Press, 2011), Preface, xiv.

54 Hale et al., *Gridlock*, 31.

55 G. John Ikenberry et al., *The Crisis of American Foreign Policy: Wilsonianism in the Twenty-First Century* (Princeton: Princeton University Press, 2009), 14.

56 Mark Mazower, *Governing the World: The History of an Idea, 1815 to Present* (New York: Penguin Books, 2013).

57 Jean L. Cohen, "Reply to Scheuerman's review of *Globalization and Sovereignty*," *Global Constitutionalization* 3, no. 1 (2014): 126.

58 Rao, *Third World Protest*, 22.

59 Thomas Carothers and Saskia Brechenmacher, "Closing Space: Democracy and Human Rights Support Under Fire," *Carnegie Endowment for International Peace* (2014). It must also be pointed out, though, that today's emerging powers such as Brazil and India are no less concerned about human rights abuses and the erosion of democracy than the United States, yet they go about dealing with these

challenges on their own terms, and under different premises than foreign-policy makers in Washington, D.C.

60 Charles Kupchan. "Unpacking hegemony: the social foundations of hierarchical order," in *Power, Order and Change in World Politics*, ed. G. John Ikenberry (Cambridge: Cambridge University Press, 2014), 39.

61 Andrew Hurrell, "Can the study of global order be de-centred?" (working paper, Institut für Politikwissenschaft, Universität Hamburg, Hamburg, 2015), 12, http://www .primo-itn.eu/PRIMO/wp-content/uploads/2015/07/ WorkingPaper-2_Andrew-Hurrell.pdf.

62 Hurrell, "Can the study of global order be de-centred?" 23.

63 Both Islamic and Chinese civilizations' worldviews were equally self-centered: Those who are not within the umma of believers blessed with the emperor's masterly rule were either infidel or barbarians, yet hardly able to become full members.

64 Moisés Naím, *The End of Power: From Boardrooms to Battlefields and Churches to States, Why Being in Charge Isn't What It Used to Be* (New York: Basic Books, 2013), 52.

65 Kupchan, *No One's World*, 145.

66 Schweller, *Maxwell's Demon and the Golden Apple*, 132.

67 Martin Jacques, *When China Rules the World: The End of the Western World and the Birth of a New Global Order* (New York: Penguin Press, 2009), 11–12.

Chapter 1

68 Hedley Bull and Adam Watson, eds. *The Expansion of International Society* (Oxford: Clarendon Press, 1984), 1. See also: Adam Watson, *The Evolution of International Society: A Comparative Historical Analysis* (London: Routledge, 1992).

69 Kupchan, *No One's World*, 65.

70 Hugh Trevor-Roper, *The Rise of Christian Europe* (London: Thames & Hudson, 1965), 1.

71 Daniel Deudney and G. John Ikenberry, "Democratic internationalism: An American grand strategy for a post-exceptionalist era," *Council on Foreign Relations* (working paper, International Institutions and Global Governance

Program, Council on Foreign Relations, New York, 201),
http://www.cfr.org/grand-strategy/democratic-internation-
alism-american-grand-strategy-post-exceptionalist-era/
p29417.

72 Robert Kagan, *The Return of History and the End of
Dreams* (New York: Alfred A. Knopf, 2008).

73 An older example is Gombrich's *A Little History of the
World*, published in 1923, which includes only a cursory
analysis of non-Western history.

74 For one of the best analyses on this subject, see Sen, *Identity and Violence*, 2007.

75 Ayse Zarakol, *After Defeat: How the East Learned to Live
with the West*, (Cambridge: Cambridge University Press,
2011), 54. As Zarakol explains, "Even today it is difficult to
separate these concepts. At the very least, Europe is still seen
as totally and naturally 'modern', where as in other places,
Westerners look for 'authentic' experiences untouched by
modernity (...). Media coverage of non-Western areas
almost invariably focuses on un-'modern' aspects of life,
which are at best described as cute, quaint, exotic, and at
worst as scary, unsafe, and unpredictable."

76 Darwin, *After Tamerlane*, 499.

77 "Statue of Liberty inspired by Arab woman", *AFP News*,
December 2, 2015, http://www.afp.com/en/news/statue-
liberty-inspired-arab-woman-researchers-say.

78 Janet L. Abu-Lughod, *Before European Hegemony: The
World System A.D. 1250–1350* (Oxford: Oxford University Press, 1989), 10.

79 William Dalrymple, "The Great & Beautiful Lost King-
doms," *The New York Review of Books*, May 21, 2015,
http://www.nybooks.com/articles/archives/2015/may/21/
great-and-beautiful-lost-kingdoms/.

80 Dawkins, *After Tamerlane*, 38.

81 Ian Brownlie, "The expansion of international society: The
consequences for international law," in *The Expansion of
International Society*, ed. Hedley Bull and Adam Watson
(London: Oxford University Press, 1985), 360.

82 Robin Law, *Ouidah: The Social History of a West African
Slaving 'Port' 1727–1892* (Athens: Ohio University Press,
2004), 37.

83 Darwin, *After Tamerlane*, 492.

84 Amartya Sen, "India: The stormy revival of an international university," *The New York Review of Books* (August 15, 2015).

85 Paul Bairoch, "Geographical structure and trade balance of European foreign trade from 1800 to 1970," *Journal of European Economic History* 3, no. 3 (1974), in Andre Gunder Frank, *ReOrient: Global Economy in the Asian Age* (Berkeley: University of California Press, 1998), 12.

86 R. Bin Wong, *China Transformed: Historical Change and the Limits of European Experience* (Ithaca and London: Cornell University Press, 2000), in Martin Jacques, *When China Rules the World: The End of the Western World and the Birth of a New Global Order* (New York: Penguin Press, 2009).

87 Jacques, *When China Rules the World*, 31.

88 Suzuki et al., *International Orders in the Early Modern World* (London: Routledge, 2013), 24.

89 Jacques, *When China Rules the World*, 36.

90 Angus Maddison, *Contours of the World Economy, 1–2030 AD* (Oxford: Oxford University Press, 2007).

91 Tourinho, "Beyond expansion," 69.

92 Frank, *ReOrient*, 166.

93 Jack Goody, *The Theft of History* (Cambridge: Cambridge University Press, 2007), 6.

94 Samuel P. Huntington, "The West: Unique, not universal," *Foreign Affairs* 75, no. 6 (November/December 1996), 32.

95 Sen, *Identity and Violence*, 50.

96 Darwin, *After Tamerlane*.

97 Charles Kupchan, "Unpacking hegemony: The social foundations of hierarchical order" in *Power, Order and Change in World Politics*, ed. John Ikenberry (Cambridge: Cambridge University Press, 2014), 45.

98 Jacques, *When China Rules the World*, 50.

99 Blaut, *The Colonizer's Model of the World*, 181.

100 Suzuki et al., *International Orders in the Early Modern World*, 170.

101 Darwin, *After Tamerlane*, 26.

102 Jacques, *When China Rules the World*, 35.

103 Hobson, *The Eastern Origins of Western Civilisation*, 10.

104 Edward Gibbon, *The History of the Decline and Fall of the Roman Empire*, vol. 3 (Philadelphia: B. F. French, 1830), 399, in David Levering Lewis, *God's Crucible: Islam and the Making of Europe, 570–1215* (New York: W. W. Norton & Co., 2008), 171.

105 Levering, *God's Crucible: Islam and the Making of Europe*, 172.

106 Frank, *ReOrient*, 16.

107 Peter Katzenstein, ed. *Sinicization and the Rise of China: Civilizational Processes Beyond East and West* (London: Routledge, 2013), 8.

108 Pankaj Mishra, *From the Ruins of Empire: The Intellectuals Who Remade Asia* (New York: Farrar, Straus and Giroux, 2012), 64.

109 Hobson, *The Eastern Origins of Western Civilisation*, 29.

110 Frank, *ReOrient*, 11.

111 Anna M. Davies, "Nineteenth-century linguistics" in *History of Linguistics*, vol. 4, ed. Giulio Lepsehy (London: Longman, 1998), referenced by Robbie Shilliam, *International Relations and Non-Western Thought: Imperialism, Colonialism and Investigations of Global Modernity* (New York: Routledge, 2011), 2.

112 James Mill, *The History of British India*, vol. 1 (London: Baldwin, Cradock, and Joy, 1817), 225–6, in Sen, *Identity and Violence*, 87.

113 T. B. Macaulay, "Indian education: Minute of the 2nd February, 1835," in *Macaulay, Prose and Poetry*, ed. G. M. Young (Cambridge, Mass: Harvard University Press, 1952), 722, in Sen, *Identity and Violence*, 128.

114 Jacques, *When China Rules the World*, 36.

115 Goody, *The Theft of History*, 287.

116 Uday S. Mehta, *Liberalism and Empire: A Study in Nineteenth-Century British Liberal Thought* (Chicago: University of Chicago Press, 1999).

117 Robert A. Dahl, *Democracy, Liberty, Equality* (Oxford: Oxford University Press, 1988), 208.

118 Sen, *Identity and Violence*, 85.

119 John M. Hobson, *The Eurocentric Conception of World Politics: Western International Theory* (Cambridge: Cambridge University Press, 2012), 6.

120 Sen, *Identity and Violence*, 92.

121 Karl Marx, *The Future Results of British Rule in India*. Available at: https://marxists.anu.edu.au/archive/marx/works/1853/07/22.htm. All that is particularly noteworthy considering how important Marx is to China's Communist Party's ideology today, and how essential the German thinker is in current efforts to "protect" Chinese universities from Western influence. Earlier this year, for example, a commentary in the People's Daily, the party's principal mouthpiece, quoted the party chief of Renmin University in Beijing as saying that Marxist thinking must "enter textbooks, enter classrooms and enter brains."

122 Ibid.

123 Pankaj Mishra, *Temptations of the West: How to Be Modern in India, Pakistan, Tibet, and Beyond* (New York: Farrar, Staus & Giroux, 2006).

124 Zarakol, *After Defeat*, 55.

125 Blaut, *The Colonizer's Model of the World*, 5.

126 Darwin, *After Tamerlane*, 496.

127 Jared M. Diamond, *Guns, Germs, and Steel: The Fates of Human Societies* (New York: W. W. Norton & Co., 1997).

128 Ian Morris, *Why the West Rules—for Now: The Patterns of History, and What They Reveal About the Future* (New York: Farrar, Straus and Giroux, 2010).

129 Tourinho, "Beyond expansion," 161.

130 Mark Mazower, *Governing the World: The History of an Idea, 1815 to Present* (New York: Penguin Books, 2013), 169 in Tourinho, "Beyond expansion," 161.

131 Shashi Tharoor, "This House Believes Britain Owes Reparations to her Former Colonies" (speech, Oxford Union Debate, May 28, 2015).

132 Tourinho, "Beyond expansion," 265.

133 Vijay Prashad, *The Darker Nations: A People's History of the Third World* (New York: The New Press, 2007), 145.

134 Tourinho, "Beyond expansion", 259.

135 Ibid., 159.

136 Ch'ien to King George III, Peking, 1792, University of California, History Department, http://www.history.ucsb.edu/faculty/marcuse/classes/2c/texts/1792QianlongLetterGeorgeIII.htm.

137 Tourinho, "Beyond expansion," 139.

Chapter 2

138 Sen, *Identity and Violence*, 12.
139 Joseph S. Nye, Jr., *Is the American Century Over?* (Cambridge: Polity Press, 2015).
140 Nuno P. Monteiro, *Theory of Unipolar Politics* (Cambridge: Cambridge University Press, 2014), 11.
141 Simon Reich and Richard Lebow, *Good-bye Hegemony! Power and Influence in the Global System* (Princeton: Princeton University Press, 2014), back cover.
142 There is a broad and to this day unresolved debate about how to measure power in international affairs. Most indices of overall national power rely primarily on measures like GDP, but are sometimes supplemented with demographic and military measures. One interesting concept has been developed by the Correlates of War Project (Susumu Suzuki, Volker Krause and J. David Singer, "The Correlates of War Project: A bibliographic history of the scientific study of war and peace, 1964–2000," *Conflict Management and Peace Science* 19, no. 2 (2002): 69–107). As Baldwin writes, "The difficulty with all such measures, however, is that they treat power as a property rather than a relation. The escape through redefining power to be a property, though seductive, warps the very essence of what interests us." (David A. Baldwin, "Power and International Relations" in *Handbook of International Relations*, ed. Walter Carlsnaes, Thomas Risse and Beth A. Simmons (London: SAGE Publications, 2002), 243). While recognizing the existing difficulty, the first part of this chapter will take GDP (size of the economy) as a proxy for power, and the second part will discuss how economic power affects military power. Chapter 3 will discuss how economic power affects soft power. Ultimately, this approach embraces the classic definition of power as the capacity to get what one wants by convincing or coercing others to do something that they would not otherwise do (Baldwin, "Power and international relations").
143 Famously, a few months before the revolution, the CIA's highest-ranking analyst testified to Congress that the shah of Iran would remain in power. Robert Jervis, *Why*

Intelligence Fails: Lessons from the Iranian Revolution and the Iraq War (Ithaca: Cornell University Press, 2010), 15.

144 M. Ayhan Kose and Eswar S. Prasad, *Emerging Markets: Resilience and Growth Amid Global Turmoil* (Washington: The Brookings Institution, 2010), 2.

145 The "middle-income trap" describes a frequently observed situation where a country that attains a certain income gets stuck at that level.

146 Eric X. Li, "A tale of two political systems" (speech, TED Global, June 215), https://www.ted.com/speakers/eric_x_li.

147 Yukon Huang, "China's brightened prospects," *Financial Times*, December 13, 2013, http://carnegieendowment. org/2013/12/13/china-s-brightened-prospects.

148 Arvind Subramanian, "The inevitable superpower," *Foreign Affairs* (September/October 2011), https://www .foreignaffairs.com/articles/china/2011-08-19/inevitable -superpower.

149 David Shambaugh, "The coming Chinese crackup," *The Wall Street Journal*, March 6, 2015, http://www.wsj.com/ articles/the-coming-chinese-crack-up-1425659198.

150 Robert A. Rohde and Richard A. Muller, "Air pollution in China: Mapping of concentrations and sources," *Berkeley Earth* (July 2015), http://berkeleyearth.org/wp-content/ uploads/2015/08/China-Air-Quality-Paper-July-2015 .pdf.

151 John Mathews and Hao Tan, "China's green-energy revolution," *Project Syndicate*, May 8, 2015, http://www.project -syndicate.org/commentary/china-green-energy-revolution -by-john-a–mathews-and-hao-tan-2015-05.

152 Mark Clifford, "Chinese coal cuts," *Project Syndicate*, April 2, 2015, http://www.project-syndicate.org/commentary/ china-reducing-carbon-emissions-by-mark-l-clifford -2015-04.

153 Adair Turner, "China's balancing act," *Project Syndicate*, October 8, 2014, http://www.project-syndicate.org/ commentary/china-s-risky-rebalancing-by-adair-turner -2014-10.

154 Turner, "China's balancing act."

155 Gordon Orr and Erik Roth, "China's innovation engine picks up speed," *McKinsey Quarterly*, January 2013.

156 Daniel A. Bell, *The China Model: Political Meritocracy and the Limits of Democracy* (Princeton: Princeton University Press, 2015), 9.

157 Bell, *The China Model*, 13.

158 Francis Fukuyama, *Political Order and Political Decay: From the Industrial Revolution to the Globalization of Democracy* (New York: Farrar, Straus and Giroux, 2014), 524.

159 Gordon G. Chang, *The Coming Collapse of China* (New York: Random House, 2001), front face.

160 Li Fan, "Grassroots democracy in China," *Project Syndicate*, December 10, 2001, http://www.project-syndicate. org/commentary/grassroots-democracy-in-china.

161 Shambaugh, "The coming Chinese crackup."

162 David Shambaugh, *China's Communist Party: Atrophy and Adaptation* (Berkeley: University of California Press, 2008), 176.

163 Margaret MacMillan, *The Rhyme of History: Lessons of the Great War* (Washington, D.C.: The Brookings Institution, 2013), Kindle edition, 12.

164 Jahangir Aziz and Steven Dunaway, "China's rebalancing act," *Finance and Development* 44, no. 3 (September 2007), http://www.imf.org/external/pubs/ft/fandd/2007/09/ aziz.htm.

165 Stephen S. Roach, "China's complexity problem," *Project Syndicate*, August 25, 2015, http://www.project-syndicate. org/commentary/china-complexity-problem-by-stephen-s– roach-2015-08. The World Bank predicts that "over the coming two decades, the increase in the urban population will be the equivalent of more than one Tokyo or Buenos Aires each year as the share of urban residents in the total population climbs from about one-half to near two-thirds in 2030." "China 2030: Building a modern, harmonious, and creative society," *World Bank* 9, http://www.world-bank.org/content/dam/Worldbank/document/China-2030-complete.pdf. See also "Urban population (percentage of total)," *World Bank*, http://data.worldbank.org/indicator/ SP.URB.TOTL.IN.ZS/countries?display=default.

166 Justin Y. Lin, "How fast will China grow?" *Project Syndicate*, January 29, 2015, http://www.project-syndicate.org/

commentary/china-2015-five-year-plan-by-justin-yifu-lin
-2015-01.

167 United Nations Department of Economic and Social Affairs,
Population Division, "World population prospects: The
2015 revision—DVD edition" (2015).

168 Friedberg, *A Contest for Supremacy*, 124.

169 Gideon Rachman, "The future still belongs to emerging
markets," *Financial Times*, February 3, 2014, http://www.
ft.com/intl/cms/s/0/e77a70cc-8a9b-11e3-9465-00144fe
ab7de.html.

170 The Congressional Budget Office's long-term growth fore-
cast for the US is 2.2 percent per year. "The budget and
economic outlook: 2015 to 2025," *Congress of The United
States Congressional Budget Office*, January 2015, https://
www.cbo.gov/sites/default/files/114th-congress-2015
-2016/reports/49892-Outlook2015.pdf.

171 Jeffrey Frankel, "China is still number two," *Project Syndicate*, May 5, 2014, http://www.project-syndicate.org/
commentary/jeffrey-frankel-pours-cold-water-on-the
-claim-that-the-us-economy-has-been-surpassed.

172 Chris Giles, "For every economic growth laggard, there
is a gazelle," *Financial Times*, October 8, 2015, http://
www.ft.com/intl/cms/s/0/190a48e0-5216-11e5-b029
-b9d50a74fd14.html#axzz3odGmrv4m.

173 Stephen G. Brooks and William C. Wohlforth, *World Out
of Balance: International Relations and the Challenge of
American Primacy* (Princeton: Princeton University Press,
2008), 34.

174 Gideon Rachman, "Is America's new declinism for real?"
Financial Times, November 24, 2008, http://www.ft.com/
intl/cms/s/0/ddbc80d0-ba43-11dd-92c9-0000779fd18c.
html#axzz3odGmrv4m.

175 Christopher Layne. "This time it's real: The end of unipolarity and the Pax Americana," *International Studies Quarterly* 56 (2012): 203–13.

176 Allison, "The Thucydides trap."

177 Graham Allison and Robert Blackwill, *Lee Kuan Yew: The
Master's Insights on China, the United States and the World*
(Cambridge: The MIT Press, 2013), 42.

178 Brooks and Wohlforth, *World Out of Balance*, 28.

179 Mearsheimer, "Can China rise peacefully?"

180 Kupchan, "Unpacking hegemony," 27.

181 This does not mean that ideologies, nationalism, and identities will cease to matter in international affairs. What I do believe, however, is that the classic Cold War dynamics, where great powers actively sought to influence internal domestic politics in many smaller countries in an ideological stand-off, are less likely in a future Sino–US bipolar order.

182 Allison and Blackwill, *Lee Kuan Yew*, 38.

183 Monteiro, *Theory of Unipolar Politics*, 19.

184 In the same way, Asian policy makers have often pointed out that US rhetoric toward China is condescending. As Lee Kuan Yew argued, "The State Department draws up its report on China's human rights like a headmaster drawing up a pupil's annual report for the parents. This may make Americans feel good and make Chinese look small, but East Asians are uneasy over its long-term consequences." Allison and Blackwill, *Lee Kuan Yew*, 44.

185 Megha Rajagopalan, "Under Xi, China's defense budget seen defying economic slowdown," *Reuters*, February 16, 2015, http://www.reuters.com/article/2015/02/16/us-china-defence-idUSKBN0LK1U520150216.

186 Nuno Monteiro, review of *Power, Order and Change*, ed. G. John Ikenberry, *H-Diplo* (September 2015), https://networks.h-net.org/node/28443/reviews/85222/monteiro-ikenberry-power-order-and-change-world-politics.

187 "Chinese lending to LAC in 2014: Key findings" (February 27, 2015), http://chinaandlatinamerica.com/2015/02/27/chinese-lending-to-lac-in-2014-key-findings/.

188 Charles Kenny, "America's No. 2! And that's great news." *The Washington Post*, January 17, 2014. Adapted from the author's book: Charles Kenny,*The Upside of Down: Why the Rise of the Rest Is Good for the West* (New York: Basic Books, 2013).

189 Monteiro, *Theory of Unipolar Politics*, 26.

190 See, for example, Jeremi Suri, *Liberty's Surest Guardian* (New York: Simon and Schuster, 2011).

191 Mearsheimer, "Can China rise peacefully?"

192 Christopher Layne, "The end of Pax Americana: How Western decline became inevitable," *The Atlantic*, April 26, 2012, http://www.theatlantic.com/international/archive/

2012/04/the-end-of-pax-americana-how-western-decline -became-inevitable/256388/.

193 The question of whether we describe order in the coming decades as bipolar or multipolar largely depends on how quickly powers such as India and Brazil will develop. While I believe these countries will play a more important role in the course of the twenty-first century, I expect China to be the only emerging power to play a great power role in the next decades.

194 Monteiro, *Theory of Unipolar Politics*, 5.

195 Reich and Lebow, *Good-Bye Hegemony!*, 171.

196 Amitav Acharya, *The End of American World Order* (Cambridge: Polity Press, 2014), 31.

197 Frans-Paul van der Putten, "Defence and security," in *Brussels–Beijing: Changing the Game?* ed. Nicola Casarini (Paris: European Union Institute for Security Studies, 2013), 57.

198 Acharya, *The End of American World Order*, 105.

199 Kissinger, *World Order*, 226.

200 Mastanduno, "Order and change in world politics," 165.

201 Mearsheimer, "Can China rise peacefully?"

202 Friedberg, *A Contest for Supremacy*, 41.

Chapter 3

203 Layne, "This time it's real."

204 Joseph S. Nye, *Bound to Lead: The Changing Nature of American Power* (New York: Basic Books, 1990).

205 Shambaugh, for example, argues that China will never be a global power due to its lack of soft power. Shambaugh, *China Goes Global*.

206 Kent Harrington, "How China is winning Southeast Asia," *Project Syndicate*, August 5, 2015, http://www.project -syndicate.org/commentary/how-china-is-winning-southeast-asia-by-kent-harrington-2015-08.

207 Michael Hirsh, "The Clinton legacy: How will history judge the soft-power Secretary of State?" *Foreign Affairs* (May/June 2013), https://www.foreignaffairs.com/articles/united-states/2013-04-03/clinton-legacy. Shashi Tharoor, "Why nations should pursue soft power" (Lecture, TED

India, November 2009), http://www.ted.com/talks/shashi_tharoor/transcript?language=en.

208 See, for example, a study conducted by Ernst and Young, "Rapid-growth markets soft power index—Spring 2012" (2012), http://emergingmarkets.ey.com/wp-content/uploads/downloads/2012/05/TBF-606-Emerging-markets-soft-power-index-2012_LR.pdf or Victoria Berry (ed.), *Country Brand Index 2012–13* (London: Future Brand, 2013), http://www.futurebrand.com/images/uploads/studies/cbi/CBI_2012-Final.pdf

209 Celso Amorim, "Hardening Brazil's soft power," *Project Syndicate*, July 16, 2013, http://www.project-syndicate.org/commentary/a-more-robust-defense-policy-for-brazil-by-celso-amorim.

210 Matt Robinson, "In fight for influence, Russia can play good cop too," *Reuters*, November 30, 2014, http://www.reuters.com/article/2014/11/30/us-europe-russia-influence-insight-idUSKCN0JE07I20141130.

211 Ibid.

212 Joseph S. Nye, *Soft Power: The Means To Success in World Politics* (New York: Public Affairs, 2004), 2.

213 Todd Hall, "An unclear attraction: A critical examination of soft power as an analytical category," *The Chinese Journal of International Politics* 3, no. 2 (2010): 189–211.

214 Christopher Layne, "The unbearable lightness of soft power," in *Soft Power and US Foreign Policy: Theoretical, Historical and Contemporary Perspectives*, ed. I. Parmar and M. Cox (New York: Routledge, 2010), 51–82.

215 The best book on this episode is Eriz Manela, *The Wilsonian Moment: Self-Determination and the International Origins of Anticolonial Nationalism* (Oxford: Oxford University Press, 2007).

216 Boris Bruk, "Attract and rule? Lessons of soft power from BRICS countries," *Institute of Morden Russia* (April 18, 2013), http://imrussia.org/en/analysis/politics/439-attract-and-rule-lessons-of-soft-power-from-brics.

217 Yu-Shan Wu and Chris Alden, "BRICS' public diplomacy and the nuances of soft power," *South African Institute of International Affairs* (January 16, 2014), http://www.saiia.org.za/opinion-analysis/brics-public-diplomacy-and-the-nuances-of-soft-power.

218 Simon Romero, "Murder of Brazilian journalist furthers alarming trend," *The New York Times*, August 7, 2015, http://www.nytimes.com/2015/08/08/world/americas/murder-of-brazilian-journalist-furthers-alarming-trend.html?_r=0.

219 While Brazil is generally seen in a positive light all over the world, its image in South America is mixed and has reached low points in the past years. For example, the Bolivian public has at times been very critical of resource exploitation by Brazilian companies. See, for example, Joana Neitsch, "Liderança Hesitante," *Gazeta do Povo*, June 25, 2011, http://www.gazetadopovo.com.br/mundo/lideranca-hesitante-5hdmlvht0b4ziuv3yr1y51pam.

220 Trefor Moss, "Soft power? China has plenty," *The Diplomat*, June 4, 2013, http://thediplomat.com/2013/06/soft-power-china-has-plenty/.

221 Moss, "Soft power? China has plenty."

222 Joseph S. Nye, "China's soft power deficit," *The Wall Street Journal*, May 8, 2012, http://online.wsj.com/article/SB10001424052702304451104577389923098678842.html.

223 Many other examples show that the concept fails to withstand more rigorous scrutiny. How to think about cultural products that generate ire and rejection abroad? Do movies like Rogen and Goldberg's *The Interview*, which ridicules Kim Jong-Un, reduce US soft power in North Korea?

224 Christina Stolte, *Brazil's Africa Strategy: Role Conception and the Drive for International Status* (New York: Palgrave Macmillan, 2015), 25.

225 Li Yan, "Guest post: China's culture power," *Financial Times*, November 9, 2011, http://blogs.ft.com/beyond-brics/2011/11/09/guest-post-chinas-culture-power/; and David Pilling, "China needs more than a five-year charm offensive," *Financial Times*, November 9, 2011, http://www.ft.com/intl/cms/s/0/12ff0d6e-0abc-11e1-b9f6-00144feabdc0.html#axzz3nnYOiAi8.

226 Andrew Jacobs, "Pursuing soft power, China puts stamp on Africa's news," *The New York Times*, August 16, 2012, http://www.nytimes.com/2012/08/17/world/africa/chinas-news-media-make-inroads-in-africa.html.

227 Willy Lam, "Chinese state media goes global," *Asia Times*, January 30, 2009, in Michael Pillsbury, *The Hundred-Year*

Marathon: China's Secret Strategy to Replace America as the Global Superpower (New York: Henry Holt, 2015).

228 Jacobs, "Pursuing soft power."

229 Joseph S. Nye, "Putin's rules of attraction," *Project Syndicate*, December 12, 2014, http://www.project-syndicate.org/commentary/putin-soft-power-declining-by-joseph-s-nye-2014-12.

230 Zachary Keck, "Destined to fail: China's soft power push," *The Diplomat*, January 7, 2013, http://thediplomat.com/2013/01/destined-to-fail-chinas-soft-power-offensive/.

231 Pilling, "China needs more than a five-year charm offensive."

232 Reich and Lebow, *Good-bye Hegemony!*, 37.

233 Tomila Lankina and Kinga Niemczyk, "What Putin gets about soft power," *The Washington Post*, April 15, 2014, http://www.washingtonpost.com/blogs/monkey-cage/wp/2014/04/15/what-putin-gets-about-soft-power/.

234 Hall, "An unclear attraction."

235 Joshua Kurlantzick, *Charm Offensive: How China's Soft Power is Transforming the World* (New Haven: Yale University Press, 2007).

236 Jonathan Mirsky, "Pope Francis's China problem," *The New York Review of Books*, December 15, 2014, http://www.nybooks.com/blogs/nyrblog/2014/dec/15/pope-francis-china-dalai-lama/.

237 Shogo Suzuki, "Chinese soft power, insecurity studies, myopia and fantasy," *Third World Quarterly* 30, no. 4 (2009): 781.

238 Lucy J. Corkin, "China's rising soft power: The role of rhetoric in construction of China-Africa relations," *Revista Brasileira de Política Internacional* 57 (2014), http://www.scielo.br/scielo.php?pid=S0034-73292014000300049&script=sci_arttext.

239 Christina Stolte, *Brazil in Africa: Just Another BRICS Country Seeking Resources?* (briefing paper, The Royal Institute of International Affairs, London, November 1, 2012), 3, https://www.chathamhouse.org/publications/papers/view/186957.

240 Kenneth King, *China's Aid & Soft Power in Africa: The Case of Education and Training* (Woodbridge: James Currey, 2013).

241 Moss, "Soft power? China has plenty."

242 Joseph S. Nye, "What China and Russia don't get about soft power," *Foreign Policy* (April 29, 2013), http://foreignpolicy.com/2013/04/29/what-china-and-russia-dont-get-about-soft-power/.

243 Edward Wong, "Indonesians seek words to attract China's favor," *The New York Times*, May 1, 2010, http://www.nytimes.com/2010/05/02/world/asia/02chinindo.html.

244 Jiang Xueqin, "How China kills creativity," *The Diplomat*, July 2, 2011, http://thediplomat.com/2011/07/how-china-kills-creativity/.

245 Regina Abrami, William Kirby, and Warren McFarlan, "Why China can't innovate," *Harvard Business Review* (March 2014), https://hbr.org/2014/03/why-china-cant-innovate.

246 Jacques, *When China Rules the World*, 112.

247 Francis Fukuyama, interview by Emanuel Pastreich, *The Diplomat*, October 15, 2015, http://thediplomat.com/2015/10/interview-francis-fukuyama/.

248 Morozov, *Russia's Postcolonial Identity*, 119.

249 Li Yan, "Guest post: China's cultural power," *Financial Times*, November 9, 2011, http://blogs.ft.com/beyond-brics/2011/11/09/guest-post-chinas-culture-power/.

250 Jie Zong and Jeanne Batalova, "Frequently requested statistics on immigrants and immigration in the United States," *Migration Policy Institute Journal* (February 26, 2015), http://www.migrationpolicy.org/article/frequently-requested-statistics-immigrants-and-immigration-united-states.

251 Su Changhe, "Soft power," in *The Oxford Handbook of Modern Diplomacy*, ed. Andrew Cooper, Jorge Heine, and Ramesh Thakur (Oxford: Oxford University Press, 2012), 550.

Chapter 4

252 Asia Development Bank, *Infrastructure for a Seamless Asia* (2009), http://adb.org/sites/default/files/pub/2009/2009.08.31.book.infrastructure.seamless.asia.pdf.

253 Michael Strutchbury and Greg Earl, "Keating slams China bank snub," *The Australian Financial Review*,

October 30, 2014, http://www.afr.com/p/special_reports/
opportunityasia/keating_slams_china_bank_snub_ifYIwI
Rcid6jz8ysVqpMjP.

254 Zheng Wang, "Three steps to dealing with the 'new'
China," *The Diplomat*, December 31, 2014, http://
thediplomat.com/2014/12/three-steps-to-dealing-with-the
-new-china/.

255 Amitav Acharya, "No need to fear the AIIB," *The Straits
Times*, June 19, 2015, http://www.straitstimes.com/opinion/
no-need-to-fear-the-aiib.

256 Wildau, "New BRICS bank in Shanghai to challenge major
institutions."

257 David Malone, Raja Mohan, and Srinath Raghavan eds.,
The Oxford Handbook of Indian Foreign Policy (Oxford:
Oxford University Press, 2015), 533.

258 Benn Steil, "The Brics bank is a feeble strike against dollar
hegemony," *Financial Times*, October 1, 2014, http://
www.ft.com/intl/cms/s/0/3c84425c-48a9-11e4-9d04
-00144feab7de.html#axzz3Ub2APXHk.

259 Radhika Desai, "The Brics are building a challenge to
western economic supremacy," *The Guardian*, April 2,
2013, http://www.guardian.co.uk/commentisfree/2013/apr/
02/brics-challenge-western-supremacy.

260 Rasna Warah, "Africa rises as BRICS countries set up a
different development aid model," *Daily Nation*, April
28, 2013, http://www.nation.co.ke/oped/Opinion/-/440808/
1760878/-/k2cwt4z/-/index.html.

261 David Smith, "Brics eye infrastructure funding through
new development bank," *The Guardian*, March 28, 2013,
http://www.guardian.co.uk/global-development/2013/mar/
28/brics-countries-infrastructure-spending-development
-bank.

262 Henry Mance, "Global shift: A bank of and for the Brics
is in the air," *Financial Times*, September 23, 2012, http://
www.ft.com/intl/cms/s/0/63400496-024f-11e2-8cf8
-00144feabdc0.html#axzz2TV0h9qg4.

263 Paul Ladd, "Between a rock and a hard place," *Poverty
in Focus* 20 (2010): 5, http://www.ipc-undp.org/pub/IPC
PovertyInFocus20.pdf.

264 Kevin Gray and Craig N. Murphy, "Introduction: Rising
powers and the future of global governance," *Third World*

Quarterly 34, no. 2 (2013): 183–93, http://www.tandfonline.com/doi/abs/10.1080/01436597.2013.775778.

265 Matt Quingley, "Achievements lauded as BRICS Summit ends," *The BRICS Post*, March 27, 2013, http://thebricspost.com/achievements-lauded-as-brics-summit-ends/#.VgAnE99Vikp.

266 Steil, "The Brics bank is a feeble strike against dollar hegemony."

267 The ASEAN members are Brunei Darussalam, Cambodia, Indonesia, Laos, Malaysia, Myanmar, the Philippines, Singapore, Thailand and Vietnam. The group of China, Japan, and South Korea, along with the 10 members of the ASEAN, is known as 'ASEAN+3'. In September 1997 already, at the start of the last global financial crisis, the Japanese Ministry of Finance proposed the creation of an Asian Monetary Fund. Although this particular proposal was rejected, the idea of a common regional fund on which East Asian governments might draw in times of financial turmoil survived. In C. Randall Henning, "The future of the Chiang Mai Initiative: An Asian Monetary Fund?" (policy brief, Peterson Institute for International Economics, Washington, DC, February, 2009), http://jfedcmi.piie.com/publications/pb/pb09-5.pdf.

268 The Chiang Mai Initiative (CMI) has two components: (1) an expanded ASEAN Swap Arrangement encompassing the ten ASEAN countries; and (2) a network of Bilateral Swap Arrangements and repurchase arrangements basically encompassing the thirteen ASEAN+3 countries. These two aspects make it by far the most advanced component of East Asian financial regionalism.

269 Mark Landler, "Healthy Countries to Receive I.M.F. Loans," *The New York Times*, October 29, 2008, http://www.nytimes.com/2008/10/30/business/worldbusiness/30global.html.

270 Desai, "The Brics are building a challenge to western economic supremacy."

271 Yung Park and Yunjong Wang, "The Chiang Mai Initiative and Beyond," *The World Economy* 28, no. 1 (2005): 94.

272 Mashiro Kawai, "From the Chiang Mai Initiative to an Asian Monetary Fund," in "The Future Global Reserve System-an Asian Perspective," ed. Jeffrey D. Sachs et al.,

Asian Development Bank Institute, June, 2010, http://aric .adb.org/grs/report.php?p=Kawai%205.

273 William W. Grimes, "The Asian Monetary Fund reborn? Implications of Chiang Mai Initiative multilateralization," *Asia Policy* 11, no. 1 (2011): 79–104, http://muse.jhu.edu/ login?auth=0&type=summary&url=/journals/asia_policy/ v011/11.grimes.html.

274 Park and Wang, "The Chiang Mai Initiative and beyond", 91.

275 Hu Jintao, "Q&A with Hu Jintao," *The Wall Street Journal*, January 18, 2011, http://www.wsj.com/articles/SB1000142 4052748703551604576085514147521334.

276 Christopher Layne, "This time it's real," 56.

277 Fion Li, "China extends yuan clearing network, RQFII program to Chile," *Bloomberg Business*, May 26, 2015, http://www.bloomberg.com/news/articles/2015-05-26/ china-extends-yuan-clearing-network-rqfii-program-to -chile.

278 "Rich but rash," *The Economist*, January 29, 2015, http:// www.economist.com/news/finance-and-economics/ 21641259-challenge-world-bank-and-imf-china-will-have -imitate-them-rich.

279 Injoo Sohn, "Five political challenges in China's monetary ambitions," *Brookings*, March 2015, http:// www.brookings.edu/research/opinions/2015/03/09-china -monetary-ambition-sohn.

280 Mallaby and Wethington, "The future of the yuan."

281 Sohn, "Five political challenges in China's monetary ambitions."

282 Barry Eichengreen, "China the responsible stakeholder," *Project Syndicate*, June 10, 2015, http://www.project -syndicate.org/commentary/china-silk-road-aiib-policy -initiatives-by-barry-eichengreen-2015-06#KVxYHWQk OEoLcifT.99.

283 Clifford Coonan, "Irish a kind, simple and helpful people, China's UnionPay advises travelers," *The Irish Times*, July 28, 2015, http://www.irishtimes.com/business/ personal-finance/irish-a-kind-simple-and-helpful-people -china-s-unionpay-advises-travellers-1.2298752.

284 "Thailand becomes the first stop of UnionPay Chip Card Standard that is 'going global'," *PR Newswire*, August 19,

2015, http://www.prnewswire.com/news-releases/thailand
-becomes-the-first-stop-of-unionpay-chip-card-standard
-that-is-going-global-300130541.html.

285 "Visa, Mastercard block US-sanctioned Russian Banks,"
RT, March 21, 2014, http://rt.com/business/visa-master-
card-russia-sanctions-285/.

286 "Russia launches China UnionPay credit card," *RT*, August
15, 2014, http://www.rt.com/business/180696-china-russia
-union-pay/.

287 Soogil Young et al., *Competition among Financial Centres
in Asia-Pacific: Prospects, Benefits, Risks and Policy Challenges* (Singapore: ISEAS, 2009), 180.

288 Raphael Balenieri, "China clamours to set global gold
prices," *Al Jazeera*, July 2, 2015, http://www.aljazeera.com/
indepth/features/2015/06/china-clamours-set-global-gold
-prices-150629082056754.html.

289 Dariusz Wojcik, "The dark side of NY-LON: Financial
centres and the global financial crisis" (working paper,
Oxford University, Oxford, 2011), http://economics.ouls.
ox.ac.uk/15278/1/geog11-12.pdf.

290 "Sherpas" are the diplomats chosen by governments to
assist heads of state during specific summits and to conduct
the negotiations ahead of the encounter. The term was
originally used for bearers for mountain climbers in
Nepal.

291 "Russia mulls founding of independent credit rating
system," *Shanghai Daily*, February 25, 2015, http://www
.shanghaidaily.com/article/article_xinhua.aspx?id=269795.

292 Atul Aneja, "Talks on over a BRICS rating agency," *The
Hindu*, April 5, 2015, http://www.thehindu.com/todays
-paper/tp-international/talks-on-over-a-brics-rating
-agency/article7069202.ece.

293 Kathrin Hille, "Russia and China plan own rating agency
to rival western players," *Financial Times*, June 3, 2014,
http://www.ft.com/intl/cms/s/0/03ae1bb8-eb2c-11e3
-9c8b-00144feabdc0.html?siteedition=uk#axzz3j0LT7I00.

294 "Likelihood of creating BRICS rating agency 'very low'—
World Bank advisor," *Sputnik*, May 19, 2015, http://
sputniknews.com/business/20150519/1022297068.html.

295 Prashanth Parameswaran, "ASEAN, partners strengthen
regional commitment to tackling Ebola," *The Diplomat*,

December 19, 2014, http://thediplomat.com/2014/12/asean -partners-strengthen-regional-commitment-to-tackling -ebola/.

296 Bank of Thailand, "The signing ceremony for the Agreement Establishing the ASEAN+3 Macroeconomic Research Office (AMRO Agreement)," press release, October 14, 2014, https://www.bot.or.th/Thai/PressandSpeeches/Press/ News2557/n4657e.pdf.

297 ASEAN+3 Finance Ministers and Central Bank Governors, "The Joint Statement of the 18th ASEAN+3 Finance Ministers and Central Bank Governors' Meeting in Baku," May 3, 2015, http://www.asean.org/news/asean-statement -communiques/item/the-joint-statement-of-the-18th -asean3-finance-ministers-and-central-bank-governors -meeting-3-may-2015-baku-azerbaijan-2.

298 Mireya Solís, "China flexes its muscles at APEC with the revival of FTAAP," *East Asia Forum*, November 23, 2014, http://www.eastasiaforum.org/2014/11/23/china-flexes-its -muscles-at-apec-with-the-revival-of-ftaap/.

299 Jacqueline Braveboy-Wagner, *Institutions of the Global South* (New York: Routledge, 2009), 216.

300 Roberts, "Are the BRICS building a non-Western concert of powers?"

Chapter 5

301 See, for example, Pillsbury, *The Hundred-Year Marathon*.

302 Wolfgang Lehmacher and Victor Padilla-Taylor, "Hurdles ahead along 'New Silk Road'," *Financial Times*, September 17, 2015, http://blogs.ft.com/beyond-brics/2015/09/17/ hurdles-ahead-along-the-new-silk-road/.

303 "China focus: China's Xi proposes security concept for Asia," *Xianhuanet*, May 21, 2014, http://news.xinhuanet. com/english/china/2014-05/21/c_133351210.htm. Also see: Minxin Pei, "Why China should drop its slogan 'Asia for Asians'," *The Straits Times*, December 5, 2014, http://www .straitstimes.com/opinion/why-china-should-drop-its -slogan-of-asia-for-asians.

304 Shannon Tiezzi, "The Maoist origins of Xi's security vision," *The Diplomat*, June 30, 2014, http://thediplomat. com/2014/07/the-maoist-origins-of-xis-security-vision/.

305 "Russia, China to seek polycentric world—Lavrov," *Sputnik*, April 15, 2014, http://sputniknews.com/voiceofrussia/news/ 2014_04_15/Russia-China-to-seek-polycentric-world -Lavrov-7696/.
306 Bates Gill, "Shanghai Five: An attempt to counter U.S. influence in Asia?" *Brookings*, May 4, 2001, http://www .brookings.edu/research/opinions/2001/05/04china-gill.
307 "BRICS announce joint cybersecurity group," *The BRICS Post*, December 7, 2013, http://thebricspost.com/brics -announce-joint-cyber-group/#.U5Smsi9hsXx.
308 "BRICS officials meet on national security," *China Daily USA*, December 6, 2013, http://usa.chinadaily.com.cn/ world/2013-12/06/content_17158710.htm.
309 Maria Edileuza Fontenele Reis, "BRICS: surgimento e evolução," in *O Brasil, os BRICS e a agenda internacional* (Brasília: Fundação Alexandre de Gusmão, 2012), 34.
310 "Reality check at the IMF," *The Economist*, April 20, 2006, http://www.economist.com/node/6826176.
311 "Crise econômica pode fortalecer países do Bric, afirma Lula," *Agência Brasil*, November 26, 2008, http://econo- mia.uol.com.br/ultnot/2008/11/26/ult4294u1943.jhtm.
312 Brazilian diplomat, interviewed by the author, Brasília, April 2013.
313 Luiz Inácio Lula da Silva, "Building on the B in BRIC," *The Economist*, November 19, 2008, http://www.economist .com/node/12494572.
314 BRICS Research Group, "2014 BRICS Fortaleza Summit Compliance Report," *BRICS Information Centre*, July 6, 2015, http://www.brics.utoronto.ca/compliance/2014-for- taleza-compliance.pdf.
315 Philip Stephens, "A story of Brics without mortar," *Finan- cial Times*, November 24, 2011, http://www.ft.com/intl/ cms/s/0/352e96e8-15f2-11e1-a691-00144feabdc0.html #axzz3mSoX6oB6.
316 BRICS Summits occur yearly, while no IBSA Summit has taken place since 2011. However, the IBSA grouping's foreign ministers meet yearly on the sidelines of the UN General Assembly.
317 Interviews conducted by the author with diplomats from BRICS countries, Brasília, New Delhi, Beijing, Moscow, Pretoria, 2012 and 2013.

318 Indian Ministry of External Affairs, "BRICS [Brazil, Russia, India, China and South Africa]," April 2013, http://www.mea.gov.in/Portal/ForeignRelation/BRICS_for_XP_April_2013.pdf.

319 Ambassador Roberto Jaguaribe, "Conversa sobre IBAS e BRIC" (press conference at the Brazilian Ministry of Foreign Affairs), April 8, 2010, https://www.youtube.com/watch?v=yWaU4jj6XYc.

320 "Ufa Action Plan," *BRICS Information Centre*, July 9, 2015, http://www.brics.utoronto.ca/docs/150709-ufa-action-plan-en.html.

321 Xi Jinping, "Towards a community of common destiny and a new future for Asia," (keynote speech, BOAO Annual Conference, 2015), http://english.boaoforum.org/hynew/19353.jhtml.

322 "Boao Forum: Chinese convention rivals Davos," *RT*, April 6, 2013, http://rt.com/news/boao-forum-asia-davos-429/.

323 John F. Sammis, "Statement by John F. Sammis, Alternate Head of Delegation, on the adoption of the outcome at the United Nations Conference on the World Financial and Economic Crisis and Its Impact on Development," *United States Mission to the United Nations*, June 26, 2009, http://usun.state.gov/remarks/4335.

324 Charles Clover and Lucy Hornby, "China's Great Game: Road to a new empire," *Financial Times*, October 12, 2015, http://www.ft.com/intl/cms/s/2/6e098274-587a-11e5-a28b-.50226830d644.html?ftcamp=social/free_to_read/chinagreatgame/twitter/awareness/editorial&segid=0100320#axzz3oLVvuVtn.

325 Kerry Brown, "The New Silk Road: China reclaims its crown," *The Diplomat*, November 18, 2014, http://thediplomat.com/2014/11/the-new-silk-road-china-reclaims-its-crown/.

326 Clover and Hornby, "China's Great Game."

327 Jon L. Anderson, "The Comandante's Canal," *The New Yorker*, March 10, 2014, http://www.newyorker.com/magazine/2014/03/10/the-comandantes-canal.

328 Ibid.

329 Ibid.

330 Christopher P. Barber et al., "Roads, deforestation, and the mitigating effect of protected areas in the Amazon,"

Biological Conservation 177 (September 2014): 203–9, http://www.sciencedirect.com/science/article/pii/S0006320 71400264X.

331 Jake Bicknell, "China's Trans-Amazonian railway might be the lesser of two evils," *The Conversation*, June 19, 2015, http://theconversation.com/chinas-trans-amazonian -railway-might-be-the-lesser-of-two-evils-43075.

332 Ikenberry, *Liberal Leviathan*, 343.

333 G. John Ikenberry, "The illusion of geopolitics: The endur- ing power of the liberal order," *Foreign Affairs* (May/June 2014), https://www.foreignaffairs.com/articles/china/2014 -04-17/illusion-geopolitics.

334 Mearshheimer, "China's unpeaceful rise."

335 Nikolas K. Gvosdev, "World without the West watch," *The National Interest*, November 21, 2007, http:// nationalinterest.org/commentary/rapid-reaction-world -without-the-west-watch-1879.

336 Cynthia Roberts, "Are the BRICS building a non-Western concert of powers?" *The National Interest*, July 8, 2015, http://nationalinterest.org/feature/are-the-brics-building -non-western-concert-powers-13280?page=show.

337 Sean Mirski, "The false promise of Chinese integration into the liberal international order," *The National Interest*, December 3, 2014, http://nationalinterest.org/feature/the -false-promise-chinese-integration-the-liberal-11776?

Chapter 6

338 Stuenkel and Tourinho, "Regulating intervention."

339 Richard K. Betts, "Institutional imperialism," *The Natio- nal Interest*, May/June, 2011, http://nationalinterest.org/ bookreview/institutional-imperialism-5176.

340 Jorge G. Castañeda, "Not ready for prime time," *Foreign Affairs* (September/October 2010), https://www.foreignaffairs .com/articles/south-africa/2010-09-01/not-ready-prime -time.

341 Stewart Patrick, "Irresponsible stakeholders?" *Foreign Affairs* (November/December 2010), https://www.foreignaffairs .com/articles/south-africa/2010-11-01/irresponsible -stakeholders.

342 Acharya, *The End of American World Order*, 50.

343 Matthew Taylor and Oliver Stuenkel, "Brazil on the global stage: Origins and consequences of Brazil's challenge to the global liberal order," in *Brazil on the Global Stage* (New York: Palgrave Macmillan, 2015), 1–16.

344 Richard K. Betts, "Institutional imperialism," *The National Interest*, May/June 2011, http://nationalinterest.org/bookreview/institutional-imperialism-5176; Randall L. Schweller, "The problem of international order revisited: A review essay," *International Security* 26, no. 1 (2011): 161–86, http://www.mitpressjournals.org/doi/abs/10.1162/016228801753212886#.VhUJmflViko.

345 Ikenberry, *Liberal Leviathan*, 7.

346 Betts, "Institutional imperialism."

347 Ibid.

348 Yun Sun, "China's 3 desires: More influence, more respect, and more space," *The National Interest*, September 21, 2015, http://nationalinterest.org/blog/the-buzz/chinas-3-desires-more-influence-more-respect-more-space-13893.

349 Stephen M. Walt, "The end of the American era," *The National Interest*, November/December, 2011, http://nationalinterest.org/article/the-end-the-american-era-6037.

350 John F. Sammis, "Statement by John F. Sammis, Alternate Head of Delegation, on the adoption of the outcome at the United Nations Conference on the World Financial and Economic Crisis and Its Impact on Development," *United States Mission to the United Nations*, June 26, 2009, http://usun.state.gov/remarks/4335.

351 Ruth Wedgwood, "Give the United Nations a little competition," *The New York Times*, December 5, 2005, http://www.nytimes.com/2005/12/05/opinion/give-the-united-nations-a-little-competition.html?_r=2.

352 Stewart M. Patrick, "Present at the Creation, Beijing-style," *The Internationalist*, March 20, 2015, http://blogs.cfr.org/patrick/2015/03/20/present-at-the-creation-beijing-style/.

353 Moisés Naím, "In the IMF succession battle, a stench of colonialism," *The Washington Post*, May 20, 2011, https://www.washingtonpost.com/opinions/in-the-imf-succession-battle-a-stench-of-colonialism/2011/05/19/AF5e6n7G_story.html.

354 Robert Wade, "The art of power maintenance," *Challenge* 56, no. 1 (2014): 29.

355 Brooks and Wohlforth, *World Out of Balance*, 37.

356 "The world calls time on western rules," *Financial Times*, August 1, 2014, http://www.ft.com/intl/cms/s/0/9205153a -196f-11e4-8730-00144feabdc0.html#axzz3mOoa2FFg.

357 Leslie Armijo and Cynthia Roberts, "The emerging powers and global governance: Why the BRICS matter," in *Handbook of Emerging Economies*, ed. Robert E. Looney (New York: Routledge, 2014), 524.

358 Indrani Bagchi, "BRICS summit: Member nations criticize the West for financial mismanagement," *The Times of India*, March 30, 2012, http://timesofindia.indiatimes.com/ india/BRICS-summit-Member-nations-criticizes-the-West- for-financial-mismanagement/articleshow/12462502.cms.

359 Ikenberry, *Liberal Leviathan*, 130.

360 Stephen M. Walt, "The U.N. Security Council. What's up with that," *Foreign Policy* (April 7, 2015), https:// foreignpolicy.com/2015/04/07/the-u-n-security-council -whats-up-with-that/?wp_login_redirect=0.

361 Zachary Karabell, "Our imperial disdain for the emerging world," *Reuters*, August 23, 2013, http://blogs.reuters. com/edgy-optimist/2013/08/23/our-imperial-disdain-for- the-emerging-world/.

362 Gareth Evans, "Responsibility While Protecting," *Project Syndicate*, January 27, 2012, http://www.project-syndicate. org/commentary/responsibility-while-protecting.

363 Oliver Stuenkel, Marcos Tourinho, and Sarah Brockmeier, "'Responsibility While Protecting': Reforming R2P Implementation," *Global Society* 30, no. 1 (2016), http://www .tandfonline.com/doi/full/10.1080/13600826.2015.10944 52#.Vmr3JUorIdU.

364 Tourinho, "Beyond expansion," 282.

Index